DATE DUE

PRINTED IN U.S.A.

FIRST EDITION

Macmillan Publishing Company
866 Third Avenue, New York, N.Y. 10022
Collier Macmillan Canada, Inc.

Library of Congress Cataloging-in-Publication Data
Brumbaugh, James E.
    Upholstering.

Includes index.
    1. Upholstery. I. Title.
TT198.B74 1983   684.1′2   82-17781
ISBN 0-672-23372-X

Macmillan books are available at special discounts for bulk purchases
for sales promotions, premiums, fund-raising, or educational use. For
details, contact:
        Special Sales Director
        Macmillan Publishing Company
        866 Third Avenue
        New York, N.Y. 10022

10 9 8 7 6 5 4 3 2 1

Printed in the United States of America

AUDEL®

UPHOLSTERING

by James E. Brumbaugh

Macmillan Publishing Company
New York

Collier Macmillan Publishers
London

Foreword

This book is designed to provide the layman and apprentice with the technical and practical information necessary for an understanding of the basic principles of upholstering. The author recognizes that there are a number of equally effective methods of upholstering furniture. However, it would have been extremely difficult to have included all of these methods in the limited scope of an introductory work. To have done so would have resulted in a book of encyclopedic proportions.

The author would like to take this opportunity to thank those individuals and manufacturers whose advice and contribution of time proved so valuable in the writing of this book.

JAMES E. BRUMBAUGH

Contents

CHAPTER 1

Furniture Styles

Every book should establish its limits at the outset. That is the intent of this chapter. Except for brief comments for the purpose of establishing a frame of reference, this is not a history of furniture styles. This chapter is concerned with style for its form rather than its historical origin.

After close examination, a person will find that the wood finish and the method of frame construction of a particular chair does not differ in great detail from that of a buffet, settee, or table by the same designer. The finish that appears on the exposed wood of a chair's arms and legs is usually also found on the wood surfaces of companion pieces of furniture. Cabinetmakers have a tendency to favor certain woods and finishes over others. An individual will probably find himself doing the same, whether he collects antique furniture, buys new, or builds his own. It is simply a matter of personal taste.

Both old and new wood finishes are discussed in a chapter within this book.

Wood frame construction, upholstering methods, types of fabrics, and other specifics of upholstering and furniture construction is presented in later chapters. This chapter is solely concerned with the various forms of furniture styles, and concentrates upon the two types of furniture most frequently upholstered: the chair and the sofa (or couch).

BACKGROUND

The chair, as a furniture form, has been with us far longer than most people realize. Chairs equalling the design excellence of the best examples of eighteenth and nineteenth century furniture have been recovered from the tombs of ancient Egypt. Apparently this early Egyptian furniture was also covered with several different fabrics which may qualify it as the earliest example of upholstered furniture. Stone carvings depict chairs used by Assyrians, Greeks, and Romans; chairs which do not differ in great detail from modern ones. Renaissance paintings show chairs of that period in the background, and the similarity in form with modern furniture is striking. As can be seen, the form of the chair has remained basically the same down through the centuries: a seat, a back (with or without arms), four legs (there have been a few examples of three-legged chairs), and sometimes stretchers such as the rods used as horizontal braces between the legs (Fig. 1).

Historically, the chair appears to have been the immediate offshoot of the stool and the forerunner of a number of familiar furniture forms.

At one time the occupant of a chair with arms was instantly recognized as the most important person in the room. Those of

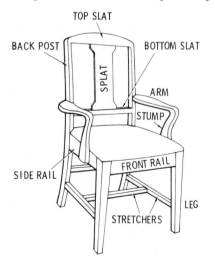

Fig. 1. Typical chair parts.

lesser rank were relegated to side chairs or benches. This distinction has been forgotten over the years, but we still retain these two basic categories of chair forms—the armchair and the side chair. Either type may be found with or without upholstery, but it is the armchair whose design culminates in the stuffed easy chair of modern times (Fig. 2).

It was already mentioned that in early times people of higher rank were granted the privilege of sitting in armchairs while their social inferiors were relegated to side chairs or benches. The bench, of course, permitted more than one person to be seated at the same time, making it even less exclusive than the armless side chair. The bench developed along the same lines as the stool (the predecessor of the chair) adding both arms and a high wood back. This all-wood piece of furniture was called a *settle* (Fig. 3A), a word which can be traced back to the Gothic language. The *settee* (the word is a corruption of settle) is a more recent development of this form and can be found completely upholstered (Fig. 3D), partially upholstered (Fig. 3C or Fig. 3E), or without any upholstery at all (Fig. 3B). There are modern settees constructed so that they can be converted into beds.

The word *couch* comes to English from the French language, and is probably derived from the French verb *coucher* (to lay down, put to bed). In any event, this piece of furniture is used for both sitting and lying down. The psychiatrist's couch is armless and usually has an upholstered headrest at one end. Couches designed primarily for sitting, on the other hand, have both arms and backs. Most couches are upholstered.

Sofa is used synonymously for couch, but generally refers to those types of couches used for sitting. This word comes to English from the Arabic *suffah*, "a long bench." The *sofa bed* is a variety that can be converted to a bed usually by lowering a hinged back to a horizontal position. The *studio couch* is a variation of this style in which a single bed frame slides out from beneath the couch itself.

Davenport is also used synonymously for either couch or sofa. It is said to be the name of a Boston furniture maker who specialized in upholstered sofas (couches). They were of such excellent quality that it became fashionable to refer to them as "davenports," a name still in use today. See Fig. 4 for the evolution of the modern sofa.

Another word used to describe this type of furniture is *divan*. It appears to have come to English from the Persian and Turkish languages, although the word "divan" is used today by the French.

Finally, one should mention the *lounge*. Although the pronunciation of the word is suspiciously French, its origin is unknown. It provides for both the sitting and lying-down functions of the couch. One side has an upholstered arm, but the opposite side is open. The back is stepped (that is, the half of the back closest to the upholstered arm is higher than the other half).

COGSWELL   TUB   LAWSON

FANBACK   CHARLES OF LONDON   SHELL

COCKFIGHT   OPEN ARM PULL-UP   CORNER

Fig. 2. Examples of

Thus, the early bench developed into several forms and an even greater number of names. Because of the confusion caused by the overlapping of terms, the word *"sofa"* will be used in this text to mean an upholstered piece of furniture designed to seat two or more people. It is felt the word *"sofa"* can be accepted as a loose synonym for couch, davenport, and divan. The settee is a distinct development of the bench that is separate from that of the sofa. In some respects a settee can be regarded as a very elegant bench (Fig. 5).

Wood has always predominated as the favorite building material for chairs or sofas, although others (from stone to steel) have been used. Some woods were more popular with certain cabinetmakers than others. For example, Thomas Chippendale (eighteenth century English cabinetmaker) seemed to prefer mahogany. George

WING   CLUB   BANK OF ENGLAND

FIRESIDE   BARREL   CLOSED ARM OCCASIONAL

Courtesy Seng Co.

upholstered chair styles.

13

Hepplewhite, on the other hand, although a contemporary and countryman of Chippendale, favored satinwood. Sometimes a period itself will be characterized by a preference for a certain type of wood. Oak dominated English furniture down to the seventeenth century. Later cabinetmakers became broader in their selection of

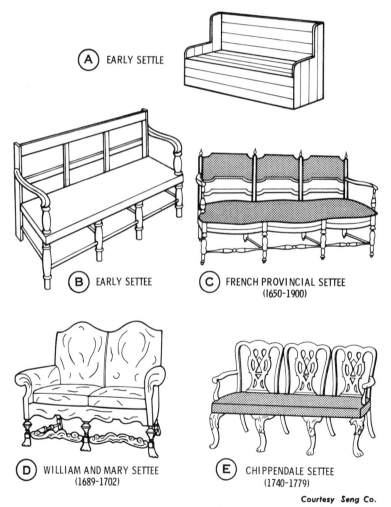

Ⓐ EARLY SETTLE

Ⓑ EARLY SETTEE

Ⓒ FRENCH PROVINCIAL SETTEE
(1650-1900)

Ⓓ WILLIAM AND MARY SETTEE
(1689-1702)

Ⓔ CHIPPENDALE SETTEE
(1740-1779)

Courtesy Seng Co.

Fig. 3. The early settle and the development of the settee.

CHIPPENDALE DIVAN
(1740-1779)

ENGLISH REGENCY SOFA
(1793-1830)

SHERATON SOFA
(1780-1806)

DUNCAN PHYFE SOFA
(1790-1830)

VICTORIAN SOFA
(1830-1890)

MEDITERRANEAN SOFA
(CURRENT)

EARLY AMERICAN (COLONIAL)
SOFA (CURRENT)

MODERN SOFA

Courtesy Seng Co.

Fig. 4. Evolution of the modern sofa.

materials. Duncan Phyfe, an American cabinetmaker who flourished from the 1790's to the early nineteenth century, worked equally well in both mahogany and black walnut.

Upholstering is essentially the process of covering the chair or sofa with certain fabrics to enhance its comfort and beauty. The upholstering can be total or it can cover certain portions of the frame allowing the arms or legs (or other areas) to remain exposed to view.

Upholstered chairs can be classified according to what is placed under the fabric. That is, whether or not the chair is of spring or nonspring construction. The latter category includes various types of padding (moss, hair, foam, etc.) not supported by springs. The padding is supported by either webbing or a piece of wood (usually

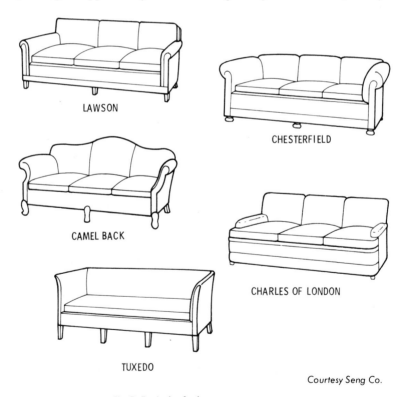

LAWSON

CHESTERFIELD

CAMEL BACK

CHARLES OF LONDON

TUXEDO

Courtesy Seng Co.

Fig. 5. Typical sofa shapes.

plywood) which covers the frame opening. The former is more comfortable; the latter stronger. Spring construction is of two types: (1) spring-supported seats with padded backs, or (2) springs in both the seat and the back. The latter is generally referred to as *overstuffed* furniture and will usually have two sets of springs in the seat. The lower set is the base and is always permanently set in position. The top layer can also be permanent or it can consist of a removable cushion with springs.

A more detailed discussion of the various aspects of upholstering is found in later chapters. The remainder of this chapter will examine the variety of forms that can usually be found in furniture styles.

As previously mentioned, the chair form has remained basically unchanged down through the centuries. By this is meant that almost all chairs have had the usual four legs, a seat, and a back. Sometimes arms were added. Because the preceding items can be combined in a myriad of forms, each will be considered in detail. With some modifications, these forms hold true for sofas (and related styles) as well.

LEGS, FEET, AND STRETCHERS

The seventeenth century marked a turning point in English furniture construction of such great magnitude that it can be regarded as a revolution. Some historians point to the restoration of the Stuart kings as the impetus for this revolution in English furniture. The exiled royal family returned with tastes for furniture styles that showed strong French and Dutch influences. Whether or not the restoration of the Stuarts was the major contributing factor to this rapid rate of change can be argued, but the fact of the change itself can be neither denied nor ignored. The heavy oak furniture gave way to lighter forms using a variety of woods. Veneering and marquetry became increasingly more intricate and complex in pattern. The upholstering of chairs and other furniture became more and more common during this period. These revolutionary changes of the seventeenth century laid the foundation for the great century of furniture design and construction that was to follow.

The eighteenth century is frequently regarded as the "golden age" of furniture design. It is during this period that such famous styles as *Queen Anne* (1702-1715), *Early Georgian* (1714-1754), *Chippendale* (1740-1779), *Adam Brothers* (1760-1798), *Hepplewhite* (1770-1786), and *Sheraton* (1780-1806) established themselves as names of excellence in the furniture world. A visit to any

Table 1. Chronological Table of Period Styles.

TIME	ENGLAND	FRANCE	AMERICA	OTHER COUNTRIES
Early Styles	Gothic (1100-1500)	Gothic (1100-1500)		Gothic (1100-1500) in Spain, Germany, Italy, etc.
Sixteenth Century	Renaissance Tudor (1509-1558) Elizabethan (1558-1603)	Renaissance (1500-1610)		Early Renaissance (1500-1600) in Italy, Spain, Holland, Germany.
Seventeenth Century	Jacobean (1603-1649) Commonwealth (1649-1660) Carolean (1660-1688) William & Mary (1689-1702)	Louis XIII (1610-1643) Louis XIV (1643-1715) Early French Provincial (1650-1800)	Early Colonial (1620-1700)	Late Renaissance (1600-1700) in Italy, Spain, Holland, Germany.
Eighteenth Century	Queen Anne (1702-1715) Early Georgian (1714-1754) Late Georgian (1754-1795) including: (Chippendale, 1740-1779) (Hepplewhite, 1770-1786) (Sheraton, 1780-1806) (Adam Bros., 1760-1792)	French Regency (1715-1723) Louis XV (1723-1774) Louis XVI (1774-1793) Directoire (1795-1804) Early French Provincial (1650-1800)	Late Colonial (1700-1790) (copies of English, French and Dutch styles) Duncan Phyfe (1790-1830)	European furniture of this time greatly influenced by French, Dutch, English craftsmen.

Nine-teenth Century	English Regency (1793-1830) Victorians (1830-1890) Eastlake (1879-1895)	French Empire (1804-1815) Late French Provincial (1800-1900)	Federal (1795-1830) (also Duncan Phyfe) Victorian (1830-1900)	Biedermeier (1800-1850) in Germany
Twentieth Century	Arts & Crafts (1900-1920) Modern Utility (1939-1947)	L'Art Nouveau (1890-1905) Arte Moderne (1926) Modern	Mission (1895-1910) Modern	Swedish Modern in Sweden. Modern in other countries.

quality furniture store today will provide the individual with numerous examples of faithful reproductions of these styles. Table 1 indicates the relative chronological position of each of the above-mentioned furniture styles with respect to one another and to other periods not mentioned here.

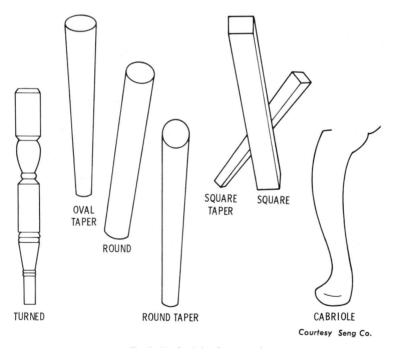

OVAL TAPER

SQUARE TAPER   SQUARE

ROUND

TURNED   ROUND TAPER   CABRIOLE

Courtesy Seng Co.

Fig. 6. Five basic leg forms.

As mentioned previously, the basic structure of the chair has remained fundamentally unchanged. Apparently furniture styles reached some sort of high point in the eighteenth century. Many furniture experts regard this period as having produced the world's finest furniture. There may be some merit to this view. How else can one explain the fact that so many of today's furniture manufacturers attempt to imitate these styles? Usual attempts at creating new styles have proven to be relatively short-lived.

The five categories of leg forms are: (1) the square leg, (2) the round leg (and the oval variant), (3) the turned leg, (4) the cabriole leg, and (5) the tapered leg (Fig. 6).

The square leg is the easiest to construct. The width dimensions at the bottom are identical to those at the top. The sides are straight and identically proportioned. The round leg is somewhat more difficult to construct. The easiest method is to round the edges on a lathe. Hand tools can also be used to produce the round legs, but it is a much longer process and requires more care in making certain that the dimensions match on all four legs. A variant of the round leg is the oval leg. Both the round and the oval leg taper toward the foot-end as a general rule. There are examples of round (or oval) legs with tapering at both ends, or without any tapering at all. The sides of the tapered leg slant inward, gradually decreasing in width toward the foot. Tapered legs may have either two (a wedge shape) or four sides slanted. The tapered leg form is often regarded as simply a variant of the square or round leg forms rather than a separate category of its own. Turned legs range in design from the very simple to the very complex, depending upon the taste of the individual cabinetmaker. Some go to such extremes that the leg appears to be nothing more than a series of balls, ovals, and rectangular shapes piled one upon the other. The cabriole leg forms a curve away from the frame of the chair. This is not only the most difficult leg form to construct, but it also requires a knowledge of the correct wood (both in strength and durability) to select for it.

The surfaces of legs may be plain or decorated. Decorations are either surface applications or carvings. A carving may be one of three categories: (1) complex design, (2) reeding, or (3) fluting. A complex design can include leaves, fruits, scrolls, geometric patterns, small animal heads, or other items of a pictorial nature. Reeding is a process which produces convex lines formed by cutting away the wood between them. Fluting results in the opposite. That is, concave depressions running the length of the leg.

Until the seventeenth century, the chair (or sofa) leg was a straight-up-and-down affair whose design had to fit within the limiting factor of the strength of the wood. Thus, the most revolutionary change in leg design at this time was the introduction of the short, thick, curved (or cabriole) leg from Holland. It first appeared in *William and Mary* (1689-1702) furniture in England along with a distinctive serpentine stretcher. These stretchers were x-shaped, flat, and usually adorned with carvings. The cabriole leg ended in a simple pad foot, although a variety of other foot styles were also used (pear, bun, club, animal hoof).

This revolution in leg design resulted from the use of walnut in place of oak (the *William and Mary* period is sometimes referred to as "The Age of Walnut"). Walnut is much easier than oak to work with hand tools.

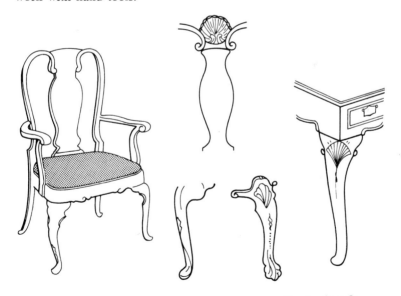

Courtesy Seng Co.

Fig. 7 Examples of Queen Anne style.

21

The cabinetmakers turned to mahogany at the beginning of the eighteenth century. This strong, easily carved wood produced the simple, flowing lines of the *Queen Anne* (1702-1715) period in English furniture (Fig. 7). Mahogany possessed not only great strength, but it was even easier to work with hand tools than walnut. Although both walnut and mahogany were used in *Queen Anne* furniture, this period of design has been referred to as "The Age of Mahogany."

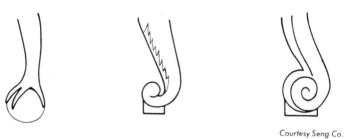

Courtesy Seng Co.

Fig. 8. Chippendale leg styles.

The short, thick cabriole leg of the *William and Mary* period became longer and more graceful in *Queen Anne* chairs. This was undoubtedly due to the greater strength of mahogany. In later periods (particularly in *Chippendale* furniture) the cabriole leg was heavily decorated with scroll carvings. Whereas *Queen Anne* usually completed the leg with the addition of a simple, unadorned pad foot, Thomas Chippendale seemed to prefer the highly ornate ball-and-claw, leaf carved, or scrolled foot (Fig. 8).

Modern imitators of the cabriole leg show a preference for the earlier simplicity of the *Queen Anne* style. The cabriole leg also serves to distinguish between American and English Windsor chairs. Whereas the American Windsors have straight turned legs slightly sloped from the perpendicular, the English Windsors have cabriole legs with a club foot.

In American examples of the *Chippendale* period, the front legs are highly decorated cabriole pieces which generally end in a ball-and-claw foot. However, the back legs are left plain.

The fluted-column leg was introduced by Robert Adam in the second half of the eighteenth century and it reflects the heavy

Courtesy Seng Co.

Fig. 9. Examples of Adam Brothers style.

influence of neo-classical culture. The lines are distinctly Roman or Greek. The leg terminated in a square foot. The *Adam Brothers* (1760-1792) period was also noted for tapered legs that were either round or square (Fig. 9).

At about the same time, George Hepplewhite also introduced a straight, tapered leg. He used either a spade foot or he would finish the leg with a brass cup (a very common practice today which may be regarded as having originated with Hepplewhite). Hepplewhite used the fluted leg in chair and sofa construction alike (Fig. 10).

Courtesy Seng Co.

Fig. 10. Examples of Hepplewhite style.

Thomas Sheraton, an English cabinetmaker who produced from 1780 to 1806, introduced a graceful leg style which was straight but slightly rounded, showing the strong influence of both the Adam brothers and George Hepplewhite. Sheraton's chair legs frequently terminated in collared or spade feet. Unfortunately, many of Sheraton's later designs became almost grotesque with overworked ornamentation (Fig. 11).

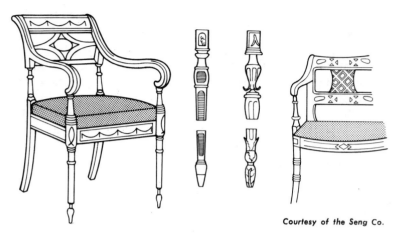

Fig. 11. Examples of Sheraton style.

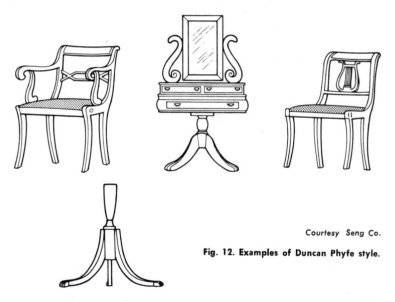

Fig. 12. Examples of Duncan Phyfe style.

The chair legs of Duncan Phyfe also show the strong influence of his eighteenth century predecessors (especially the Classical style), but he introduced distinctive, bold curves in the legs (Fig. 12).

There is one leg that is found exclusively on modern furniture. This is a round, tapered leg that screws into a plate attached to the corner of the frame. It does not have the strength of a leg that forms an integral part of the chair frame. These legs are usually made from maple or walnut, and are sold in lengths ranging from 4 inches to 29 inches.

A final word should be added here concerning stretchers. It was mentioned previously that the seventeenth century witnessed a revolution in furniture construction and design. This period of great change that produced so many new construction methods also resulted in the obsolescence of the stretcher. New methods of gluing and joinery made the stretcher no longer necessary as a leg reinforcement. One of the last examples of a functional stretcher was that used in *American Colonial* (1620-1790) furniture. The stretcher itself was constructed from kiln-dried wood; the legs were cut from green wood. No glues were used. As the green wood of the legs seasoned, they contracted around the stretcher for a tight fit. The stretchers used since the seventeenth century have become increasingly more decorative and nonfunctional in use.

ARMS

The arms of chairs (and sofas) can take a great number of forms. For example, they can be fully upholstered, partially upholstered, or not upholstered at all.

The arms may also be full or set back. A full arm extends all the way to the front edge of the seat. A set-back arm begins at a

SET-BACK

FULL

Courtesy Seng Co.

Fig. 13. Full and set-back arm styles.

point somewhat further back from the front edge. It depends entirely upon the style and the preference of the designer. Generally, the height of the arm will extend approximately from the top of the seat to the average person's elbow (Fig 13).

Another distinction may be made by the manner the arm attaches to the back. Not only may it be a full or set-back arm, it can also be either an independent piece attached to the back (at a point lower than the back top rail) or it may be a continuation of the back top rail itself. These can also be full or set-back arms (Fig. 14).

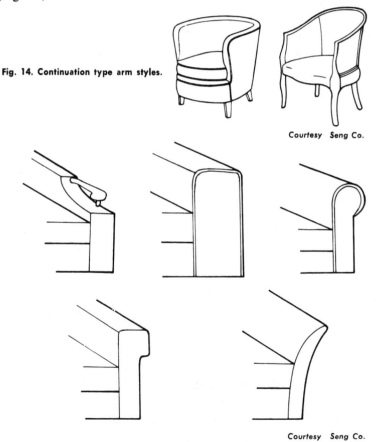

Fig. 14. Continuation type arm styles.

Courtesy Seng Co.

Courtesy Seng Co.

Fig. 15. Types of upholstered arms.

27

The design of the arm itself has an extensive list of possibilities. For example, the upholstered arm is produced with a simple square edge, a round edge, a knife edge, or a scroll edge (Fig. 15). The all-wood arm offers an equally great number of forms extending from the simple square type to the more complicated serpentine, concave, and curved varieties. Those with padded arm rests represent an intermediate style between upholstered and all-wood types (Fig. 16).

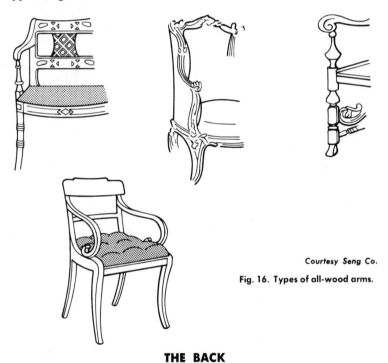

Courtesy Seng Co.

Fig. 16. Types of all-wood arms.

THE BACK

The back can be all-wood, caned, partially upholstered, or completely upholstered. The all-wood back takes a variety of forms including the solid back (plain or carved), the slat back (i.e. thin, sometimes narrow, lengths of wood), the splat back (a single piece of wood connecting the back of the seat to the top of the back rail), and the spindle back (rounded spokes set in a vertical pattern across the back).

During the *Jacobean* (1603-1649) period in English furniture, the chair back still retained a form which had remained unchanged in England for centuries. It served as a culmination of basically English influences. The back of the chair rose straight up from the seat, generally as a continuation of the back legs. These backs were either solid carved pieces or caned. The back retained its extra height during the *William and Mary* period but it was either carved or upholstered.

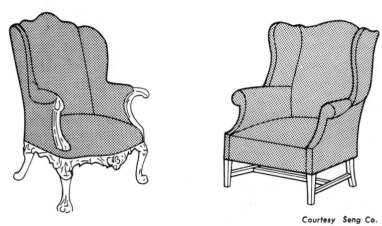

Courtesy Seng Co.

Fig. 17. Examples of wing-back styles.

The high backs and extended "wings" were originally designed to protect the individual from the cold drafts that frequently swept the poorly heated rooms. With the improvement in heating, these became nonfunctional designs, although they retained their popularity with furniture buyers (Fig. 17). It is in *William and Mary* furniture that one finds the extensive introduction of upholstered styles.

There are some very fine examples of sixteenth and seventeenth century chairs with carved backs. The patterns were intricate and frequently supplemented with inlays. Solid backs in use today are normally plain and are frequently found in auditoriums or theaters.

The slat-back chair is found most commonly in the ladder-back style. Thomas Chippendale introduced a distinctive ladder-back with pierced slats. However, the ladder-back is generally far simpler

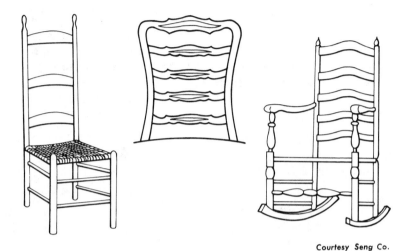

Courtesy Seng Co.

Fig. 18. Slat-back chairs.

in design than Chippendale's example. The *Shaker* (1776-1859) slat-back, for example, is the last word in simplicity. The slats are arranged in either a curved pattern or a straight pattern parallel to the edge of the seat (Fig. 18).

It is in the use of the splat that one finds the greatest variety of designs. The splat is a thin piece of wood connecting the back of

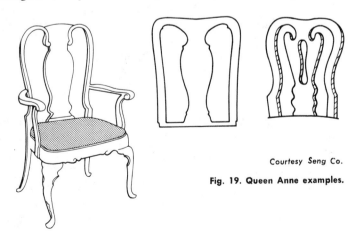

Courtesy Seng Co.

Fig. 19. Queen Anne examples.

30

the seat rail with the top rail of the back. Unlike the slat, it is wide enough to be produced in a variety of shapes.

The *Queen Anne* (1702-1715) period is characterized by a solid, plain splat in either a fiddle or vase shape (Fig 19). George Hepplewhite introduced a distinctive shield-back. He is also noted for many fine examples of the hoop shield, heart, and rectangular-back styles (Fig. 20). Thomas Sheraton's backs were basically square or rectangular, and adorned with finely carved urns, lyres, shields, or interlaced, open rectangles (Fig. 21). Under the Adam Brothers, one finds examples of open backs with a single horizontal

Courtesy Seng Co.

Fig. 20. Hepplewhite examples.

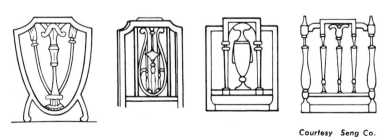

Courtesy Seng Co.

Fig. 21. Sheraton examples.

31

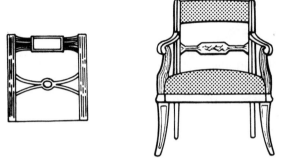

Fig. 22. Adam Brothers examples.

Courtesy Seng Co.

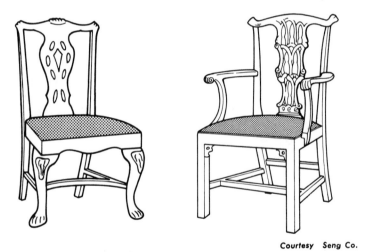

Courtesy Seng Co.

Fig. 23. Chippendale examples.

ribbon band or a crisscross effect (Fig. 22). Thomas Chippendale introduced the popular pierced fiddle-back (Fig. 23) while Duncan Phyfe chair backs are known for their distinctive lyre pattern. *Chinese Chippendale* (1750-1800) provides many excellent examples of a highly intricate lattice-back style (Fig. 24).

The banister back is a form of the splat. However, its appearance would suggest that it could be better classified as a spindle back.

Fig. 24. Chinese Chippendale examples.

Courtesy Seng Co.

Fig. 25. Banister-back American
Colonial example.

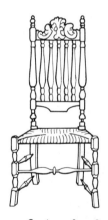

Courtesy   Seng Co.

The vertical members of a banister back are sometimes turned, sometimes flat. An excellent example of the banister back is shown in the example of an *American Colonial* (1620-1790) chair in (Fig. 25).

The spindle back is most commonly represented by the Windsor chair (Fig. 26). The spindles usually taper at both ends, leaving a bulge in the middle (although the area with the greatest diameter can also be toward the bottom of the spindle). The back rail of

Fig. 26. Windsor examples.

Courtesy Seng Co.

the Windsor chairs, which held the spindles in place (this is particularly true of the hoop style), was formed from green wood, bent to shape, and inserted in the holes in the seat frame. When the wood dried, the fit became very tight. Spindle backs were originally constructed so that the spindles were arranged in a straight pattern. Later a variety of forms became common among which one finds the hoop back and the fan back.

Upholstered backs may have either spring construction or non-spring (padded) construction. The shape of the padded back (shield, heart, square, circle, etc.) is outlined by forming a burlap roll around the edges and beneath the surface material. Exposed wood then surrounds the padded portion (Fig. 27). The upholstery may also be drawn completely around the entire back of the chair ex-

Courtesy Seng Co.

Fig. 27. Examples of upholstered backs.

tending down either to the top of the seat frame or ending several inches above the bottom edge of the frame. The latter is quite commonly found in modern dining room chairs (Fig. 28).

The classification of upholstered chairs according to their internal construction (spring versus padded) has already been discussed. The upholstered backs can also be classified according to the style in which the fabric is applied. These styles are: (1) plain, (2) piped or channel back, and (3) tufted back. In Fig. 2 the "fireside," "barrel," and "cockfight" styles are examples of tufted backs; whereas the "shell" style depicts a piped or channel back.

The plain back may have a removable cushion or the back may be one solid piece. The piped or channel back chair consists of vertical columns of stuffing that have been sewn to a base fabric

35

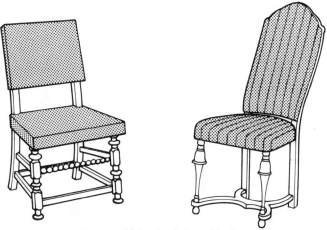

Fig. 28. Additional upholstered backs.

and covered with muslin and an upholstery fabric. Piping can be found in a straight-back, a curved-back, a shell-back, or a fan-back design.

Rush weaving and caning (particularly the latter) were far more common at one time than they are today. Before the introduction of upholstery on a large scale, the caned back was quite common. Today it is a specialty item.

SEATS

Chairs seats can be divided into four basic categories: (1) wood seats, (2) cane seats, (3) webbed seats, and (4) upholstered seats. Upholstered seats can be divided into slip seats, spring construction, and no spring construction or padded.

The wood seats are found primarily in Windsor chairs, dining-room and kitchen chairs, and modern imitations of colonial furniture. They are usually constructed from a solid piece of wood. The center portion of the wood seat is scraped or scooped out to accommodate the contours of the body and thereby provide greater comfort. This operation was at one time accomplished with a Hand Seat Saddler. Today, a machine performs this function.

Hand-woven caned and rush seats were far more popular than upholstered furniture prior to the seventeenth century. Although

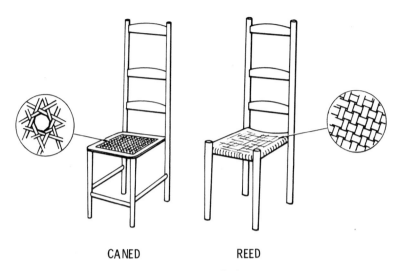

CANED   REED

Fig. 29. Caned and rush chair seats.

upholstered furniture now predominates, caned seats are still produced. These are primarily side chairs or dining-room furniture (Fig. 29).

Webbed seats are those that have multicolored, decorative webbing. The webbing is made from plastic and is exposed to view. This form is of very recent origin and is primarily found in patio or yard furniture.

Slip seats are upholstered seats that can be removed from the chair and slipped back in. They are held in place with screws or metal fasteners. Slip seats are usually found in kitchen or dining-room chairs. (Fig. 30).

The nonspring or padded construction in upholstered chairs is similar to the slip seat except that the seat is permanently attached. These are most commonly found in dining-room chairs and side chairs. The upholstery may cover the entire frame or expose various portions of the wood.

Seats supported by springs are found in the Lawson-type chair as well as other examples of overstuffed furniture. (Fig. 2).

Just as backs may have removable cushions, the same style can be found in upholstered seats. Removable upholstered seat

37

Fig. 30. Typical slip seat.

cushions may be either padded or spring-filled. The shape of the cushion may be circular, square, or T-shaped with the last two predominating. The application of upholstery fabric is either in a tufted or plain pattern.

This has been a very brief examination of the historical development of a variety of furniture forms. No attempt has been made to produce an exhaustive study of the history of furniture. This subject is covered in a number of very excellent volumes readily available to the interested reader. The purpose of this chapter is to provide an introduction not only to a variety of terms that will be encountered in following chapters, but also to make the reader aware of the problem of classifying furniture forms. The forms that one points to as characteristic of a certain period or a certain cabinetmaker all too often prove to be shared by others. Furniture styles overlap. The dates given for furniture periods are the approximate dating of their greatest popularity.

CHAPTER 2

Tools and Equipment

Certain tools and equipment have been designed for upholstering and the construction (or repair) of furniture frames. These tools are made to fulfill specific needs. There are other types of tools and equipment that are also useful in upholstering and wood working. The purpose of this chapter is to examine the use of these tools and equipment with respect to their application to this type of work.

UPHOLSTERING HAMMERS

The *magnetic upholstering hammer* is used for numerous tacking operations in upholstering. In view of this, it should not be heavy in weight and it should not possess a broad head. The hammer used by professional upholsterers has a weight ranging between 6 and 9 ounces with an 11 to 12 inch handle (the best quality wood handles are made of hickory) and a 5½ inch curved head (Fig. 1).

The surface of the hammer used for tacking has a diameter of approximately ½ inch. The opposite end is smaller ($\frac{5}{16}$ inch diameter), usually split, and magnetized. This smaller end is used to hold and start the small tacks. Trying to work without this convenient tool can be quite frustrating.

Upholsterers also use a specifically designed double-edged *ripping* hammer for removing old fabric. It is slightly heavier (about a 10 ounce weight) than the hammer used for tacking operations. It has a 5 inch head with a $1-\frac{3}{16}$ inch bit. Staple guns (manual

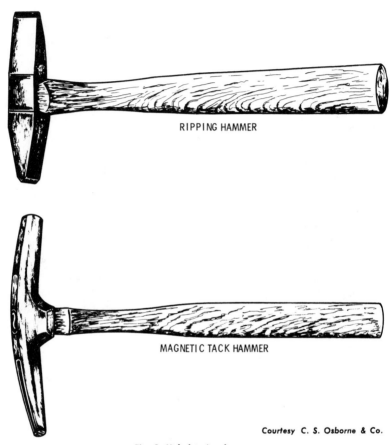

RIPPING HAMMER

MAGNETIC TACK HAMMER

Courtesy C. S. Osborne & Co.

Fig. 1. Upholstering hammers.

and automatic) are also gaining popularity for certain tacking operations, both temporary and permanent. The automatic types, air and electrically operated, are for high-volume usage (Fig. 2).

UPHOLSTERING SHEARS

Upholstering shears must be strong enough to cut heavy or coarse materials. Consequently, it is advisable to purchase shears with a 10 to 12 inch length (which provides a cutting edge of about

AIR OPERATED

MANUALLY OPERATED

Courtesy Fastener Corp.

Courtesy Fastener Corp.

Fig. 2. Typical stapling guns.

7 inches). Shears with a bent handle are more suitable, because they will not raise and distort the fabric during cutting (Fig. 3).

WEBBING STRETCHERS

The *webbing stretcher* is a hard block of wood shaped so that it can be grasped in the center by the upholsterer (Fig. 4).

The end which rests against the frame is usually padded with rubber. This prevents damage to the wood surface and also assists in preventing slippage when the webbing is pulled taut. The other end of the webbing stretcher has steel points for piercing the webbing (Fig. 5).

There are also steel webbing stretchers for use when steel webbing, or bands, form a part of the construction (Fig. 6).

PLIERS USED IN UPHOLSTERING

Webbing pliers (Fig. 7) are designed to grasp the material between wide, grooved jaws. There is a protrusion beneath the jaw to give greater pulling pressure. It is advised to use some protection, such as a wooden block, to protect the wood surface of frame.

41

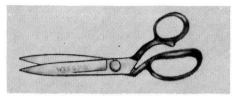

INLAID BLAIDS - ENAMELED HANDLES
POLISHED BLADES

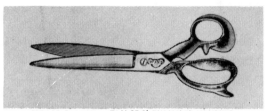

INLAID BLADES - TAILORS' ENAMELED HANDLES

(RAISED BLADE)

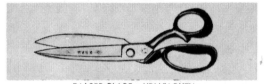

RAISED BLADE - HEAVY DUTY
INLAID BLADES - ENAMELED HANDLES

Courtesy C. S. Osborne & Co.

Fig. 3. Upholstering shears.

Webbing pliers are less desirable than webbing stretchers because they are more limited in use. They are most suitable for working with shorter lengths of webbing, for pre-stretching webbing that has become loose, and for stretching leather.

There are a number of other pliers created for specific operations in upholstering. The *spring clip plier* (Fig. 8) is specifically designed for setting spring or edge wire clips. The purpose of the *hog ring plier* (Fig. 8) is to set the standard hog ring clips (upholstery fasteners resembling hog rings). Nail pliers (Fig. 8) are available for the purpose of removing tacks and upholstery nails.

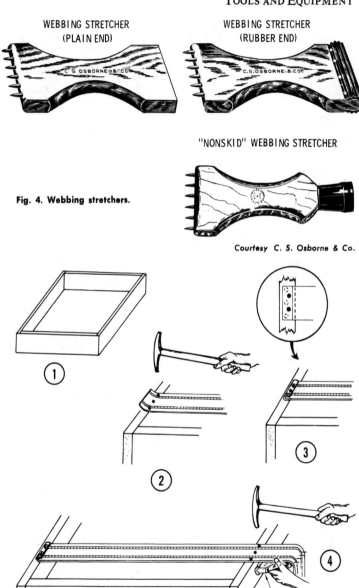

WEBBING STRETCHER
(PLAIN END)

WEBBING STRETCHER
(RUBBER END)

"NONSKID" WEBBING STRETCHER

Fig. 4. Webbing stretchers.

Courtesy C. S. Osborne & Co.

WEBBING STRETCHER

Fig. 5. Use of webbing stretcher.

43

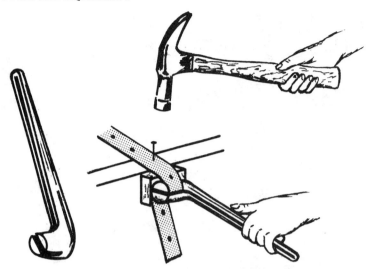

Fig. 6. Using the steel webbing stretcher.

Courtesy C. S. Osborne & Co.

Fig. 7. Webbing (or leather) stretcher pliers.

THE RIPPING TOOL AND CLAW TOOL

Two tools which perform similar functions are the *ripping tool* and *claw tool* (Fig. 9). Both are used to remove tacks when replacing old covers. The major distinction is that the claw tool has a notch for gripping the tack whereas the ripping tool does not. The beginner often prefers the claw tool because the notched blade grips the tack better. As experience improves this will prove to be a disadvantage, because the tacks have a tendency to stick in the notch, reducing the efficiency of the removal operation. Most upholsterers prefer the ripping tool.

44

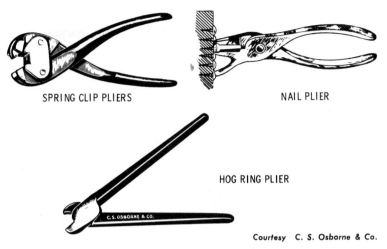

SPRING CLIP PLIERS   NAIL PLIER

HOG RING PLIER

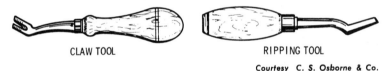

Courtesy C. S. Osborne & Co.

Fig. 8. Hog ring, spring clip, and nail removal pliers.

CLAW TOOL   RIPPING TOOL

Courtesy C. S. Osborne & Co.

Fig. 9. Claw and ripping tools.

Fig. 10. Rubber mallet.

A combination tool has been designed in an attempt to incorporate both the ripping and tack pulling functions in a single tool.

MALLETS

A *rubber mallet* of either 16 or 32 ounces is recommended for driving the ripping tool (or claw tool) when stripping fabric from the frame (Fig. 10).

Mallets of rolled rawhide are also available. Both rubber and rolled rawhide are used to avoid scarring the wood surface.

SINGLE ROUND POINT

Light

Size	4	5	6	8	10	12	14	16	18	20 in.
Gauge	15	14	14	14	13	13	13	12	12	12

Heavy

Size	6	8	10	12	14	16	18	20 inches
Gauge	13	13	12	12	12	11	11	11

DOUBLE ROUND POINT

Extra Light

Size	10	12	14	16 inches
Gauge	14	14	14	14

Light

Size	6	8	10	12	14	16	18	20 inches
Gauge	14	14	13	13	13	12	12	12

Heavy

Size	6	8	10	12	14	16	18	20 inches
Gauge	13	13	12	12	12	11	11	11

SINGLE 3 SQUARE POINT

Light

Size	6	8	10	12	14	16	18 inches
Gauge	14	14	13	13	13	12	12

Heavy

Size	6	8	10	12	14	16	18 inches
Gauge	13	13	12	12	12	11	11

Courtesy C. S. Osborne & Co.

Fig. 11. Straight needles.

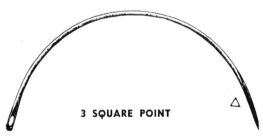

ROUND POINT

Cord, Extra Light

	2	2½									inches over all
Size	2	2½									
Gauge	23	23									

Cord, Light

Size	2	2½									inches over all
Gauge	19	19									

Extra Light

Size	2	2½	3	3½	4						inches over all
Gauge	21	20	19	18	18						

Light

Size	2	2½	3	3½	4	5	6	7	8		inches over all
Gauge	19	18	18	17	17	16	15	15	15		

Heavy

Size	2	2½	3	3½	4	5	6	7	8	10	inches over all
Gauge	17	17	16	16	15	14	14	14	13	13	

3 SQUARE POINT

Extra Light

Size	2	2½	3	3½	4						inches over all
Gauge	21	20	19	18	18						

Light

Size	2	2½	3	3½	4	5	6	7	8		inches over all
Gauge	19	18	18	17	17	16	15	15	15		

Heavy

Size	2	2½	3	3½	4	5	6	7	8	10	inches over all
Gauge	17	17	16	16	15	14	14	14	13	13	

Courtesy C. S. Osborne & Co.

Fig. 12. Curved needles.

UPHOLSTERING NEEDLES

Upholsterers must use several types of needles, each designed for a specific function in the trade. The three basic types are the straight needle, the curved needle, and the packing needle.

Straight needles (Fig. 11) range in length from 4 to 20 inches, and are either single or double pointed. The double pointed needles are preferable as they can be pushed back through the material without the need of reversing them.

Curved needles (Fig. 12) can be purchased in 2 to 10 inch lengths (this is a circumference measurement), and in extra light, light, and heavy grades. The lightweight curved needle is used for the thinner cover fabrics. The advantage of the curved needle is that it does not require the upholsterer to reach behind his work and push it through each time as would be the case with a straight needle. These are manufactured with round or triangular points.

Packing needles (Fig. 13) are used for sewing that requires a heavier needle than the heaviest gauge straight or curved needles. These needles are characterized by a thickening of the shaft near the point. They range in length from 3 to 10 inches, and can be purchased in either a bent or straight shaft style.

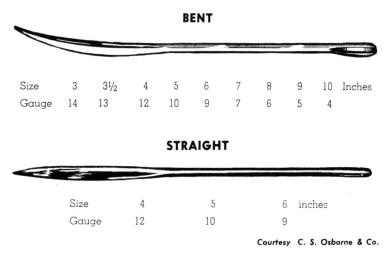

BENT

Size	3	3½	4	5	6	7	8	9	10	Inches
Gauge	14	13	12	10	9	7	6	5	4	

STRAIGHT

Size	4	5	6	inches
Gauge	12	10	9	

Courtesy C. S. Osborne & Co.

Fig. 13. Packing (pack) needles.

Tufting tools are available to simplify the tufting process. One type eliminates the use of twine (Fig. 14). A pronged tufting button is inserted into a hollow needle. The needle pierces the material and is then removed. A special washer is put on the prongs which in turn are then bent to secure the button. *Tufting needles,* used with twine, are also available for the tufting process. See Chapter 13 for detailed tufting instructions and alternate methods.

STUFFING REGULATORS

Stuffing regulators (Fig. 15) are similar in appearance to needles, but are constructed of a heavier gauge steel. They range in length from 6 to 12 inches. Stuffing regulators are only used for working on the interior of the furniture because their large size would leave unsightly puncture holes on the cover fabric. Stuffing regulators are used to remove irregularities in the stuffing materials (a process which is best performed beneath a sub-layer muslin cover).

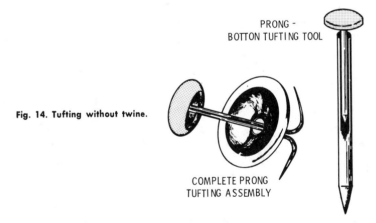

PRONG -
BOTTON TUFTING TOOL

Fig. 14. Tufting without twine.

COMPLETE PRONG
TUFTING ASSEMBLY

Courtesy Handy Button Machine Co.

STUFFING ROD

A *stuffing rod* (or *stuffing iron*) is a length of steel (usually about a foot and a half long) used for pushing stuffing back into difficult-to-reach corners. One end has a tooth edge for gripping the stuffing (Fig. 16).

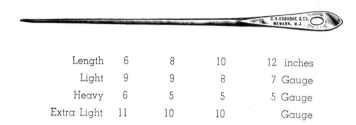

Length	6	8	10	12 inches
Light	9	9	8	7 Gauge
Heavy	6	5	5	5 Gauge
Extra Light	11	10	10	Gauge

Courtesy C. S. Osborne & Co.

Fig. 15. Stuffing regulator.

Fig. 16. Stuffing iron.

UPHOLSTERERS' PIN (SKEWER)

The *upholsterers' pin* (or *skewer*) is a short length of steel wire used for positioning the stuffing before tacking or sewing. They are generally about 3 to 4 inches in length. One end is pointed while the other contains a loop for grasping (Fig. 17).

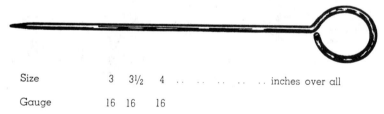

Size	3	3½	4	.. .. inches over all
Gauge	16	16	16	

Courtesy C. S. Osborne & Co.

Fig. 17. Upholsterers' pin.

CUSHION IRON

Cushion irons (Fig. 18) are used in pairs to compress the cushion to make it easier to apply the final cover. Before the cover is put on, the cushion irons are placed over opposite sides of the cushion

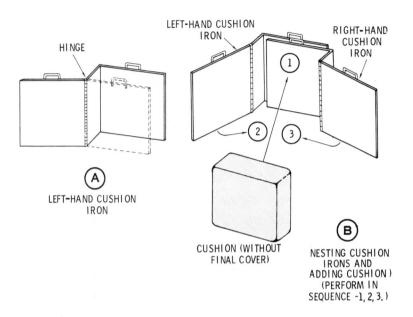

Fig. 18. Cushion irons and their use.

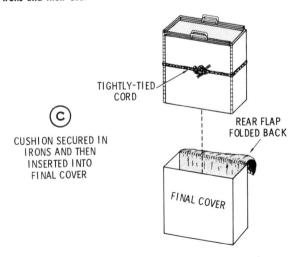

stuffing and are pulled tightly together with a piece of cord. Once the cushion covering has been put on the cushion, the cushion irons are removed. Cushion irons take the place of the expensive cushion-filling machines found in professional upholstery shops. Cushion irons can be purchased (as shown in Fig. 18) or can be constructed from corrugated cardboard (Fig. 19).

SEWING MACHINE

In addition to the tools mentioned, there are several pieces of equipment that make the upholsterer's task easier. First and fore-

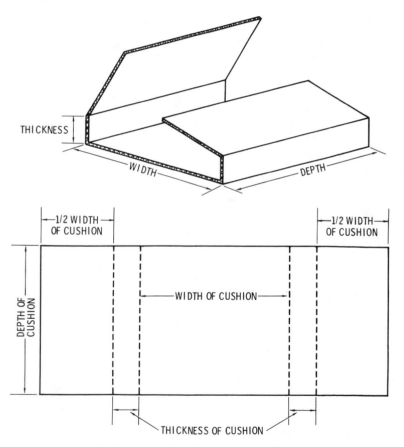

THICKNESS

WIDTH

DEPTH

1/2 WIDTH OF CUSHION

1/2 WIDTH OF CUSHION

DEPTH OF CUSHION

WIDTH OF CUSHION

THICKNESS OF CUSHION

Fig. 19. Construction of a homemade stuffing box.

most among these is the sewing machine. Needless to say, a portable machine would be too light for many types of the heavier fabrics. The most desirable machine would be a heavy duty one.

TRESTLES

Trestles are essentially benches with padded tops and are used to raise the piece of furniture to a height that will be most comfortable for those working on it. They closely resemble the carpenter's horse. The trestles are normally used in pairs.

CUTTING TABLE

A *cutting table* is very useful for laying out and cutting the fabric. These tables can be inexpensively constructed from ¾ inch plywood and 2 × 4's.

BUTTON COVERING MACHINES

Some pieces of equipment are suitable only if the upholstering is done on a production or semi-production basis. This is true, for

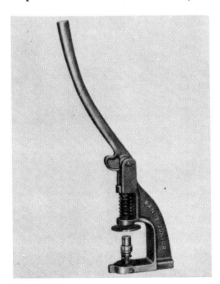

Fig. 20. Button covering machine (manual).

Courtesy Handy Button Machine Co.

example, of the *button covering machines* (Fig. 20). These machines are manufactured in both hand-operated and power-operated (electric and air) models.

In addition to the tools mentioned, many types of saws, planes, drills, etc., usually employed in woodworking, are essential in the construction and repair of furniture. It is not the intent of this book to review the application of all the woodworking tools, but to highlight those tools designed more specifically for upholstery work.

Excellent work can be performed with a small percentage of the available tools. However, depending upon the volume of work, it would be the decision of the individual as to whether or not it would be advantageous to acquire certain tools.

CHAPTER 3

Stripping

It is during the stripping away of the old fabric and stuffing that the beginner can learn much to his own benefit. He should carefully note the layers of construction as they are removed, since the re-upholstering process will be essentially the same except in reverse order.

Two tools used in the stripping process were described in the second chapter. These were the ripping tool and the claw tool. It is advised that the ripping tool be used, because its chisel-like head does not have a slot in which tacks can stick (this is often the case with the claw tool).

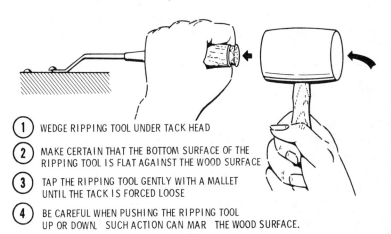

1. WEDGE RIPPING TOOL UNDER TACK HEAD

2. MAKE CERTAIN THAT THE BOTTOM SURFACE OF THE RIPPING TOOL IS FLAT AGAINST THE WOOD SURFACE

3. TAP THE RIPPING TOOL GENTLY WITH A MALLET UNTIL THE TACK IS FORCED LOOSE

4. BE CAREFUL WHEN PUSHING THE RIPPING TOOL UP OR DOWN. SUCH ACTION CAN MAR THE WOOD SURFACE.

Fig. 1. Using a stripping tool.

The ripping tool (and a mallet for the more stubborn tacks) is used to remove the tacks attaching the upholstery materials to the wood frame. The chisel-like blade of the ripping tool is inserted under the tack head and the handle is pressed down (Fig. 1).

Great care should be taken to protect the wood surface as you work. This is particularly true of those surfaces that will be exposed to view (arms, legs, lower seat rails, etc.).

Be particularly careful not to split the wood. Striking movements should be in line with the grain of the frame wood (Fig. 2).

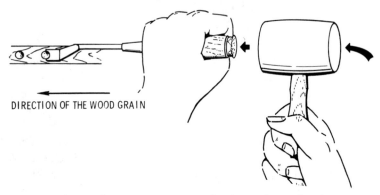

DIRECTION OF THE WOOD GRAIN

Fig. 2. Striking movement in same direction as the wood grain.

The motion of removing the tacks should be away from the body (never toward) since this gives greater stability and control.

MEASUREMENTS

Before you begin stripping, it might be wise to decide *when* and *how* you are going to measure the furniture piece for the new cover. If you are constructing a new piece of furniture from the frame up, take your measurements for the outer upholstery fabric (the final cover) after the muslin cover has been attached. The planning and cutting of the muslin cover will have provided you with rough patterns for the more expensive outer fabric. You must be careful to provide a fabric allowance for handling, tucking in around the edges, overlaps, seam construction, and corner pleats (this is explained more fully in Chapter 9 (Pattern Layout).

The reupholstering of a used piece of furniture presents a slightly different approach. If it is not necessary to replace anything other than the outer fabric, then this old fabric can be used as a pattern for cutting the new material. Remove the old fabric as carefully as you can. Press the individual pieces with an iron so that they will lie flat.

If you find it necessary to replace the webbing or the springs (or both), the fabric can still be used as a pattern but you should do so with some caution since extensive repairs may alter the shape of the chair. In addition, the seat may have pushed higher or the cushions may be fuller than they were originally. After the muslin cover has been sewn into place, take the old pieces of fabric and temporarily pin them onto the muslin. (If you do not intend to use a muslin cover, pin them to the padding or simply hold them across the area to be covered.) This should give you an indication of how close these old fabric pieces now come to matching the measurements of the repaired piece of furniture. It may be necessary to add or subtract an inch here or there, and this is the time to make that decision. It can be quite expensive to discover extra material is needed *after* you have cut the fabric.

Sometimes it is desirable to alter the frame. This is usually for purposes of modernizing older furniture. Should this be the case, then the old fabric is of little use as a pattern since the measurements of the frame will have changed. It is recommended that the measurements for the outer fabric be taken after the muslin cover or final padding is attached.

THE STRIPPING PROCESS

The remainder of this chapter concentrates on a general description of the stripping process. The steps in the stripping process (from outer fabric to frame) parallel those of construction, but in reverse order. Since there are variations in construction, some differences may be encountered in the procedures discussed. Sometimes two layers of stuffing will be used, at other times only one. In some cases the stuffing will be sewed down, in others it will not (see Chapter 13, Channels and Tufts, for more on this). Whatever the variations, the important thing to do is to note the order in which the particular piece of furniture was constructed. It is suggested that a notebook, complete with detailed sketches, be kept during the stripping operation.

It may not be necessary to completely strip the piece of furniture. The intent of stripping is to remove only the damaged portions of the upholstery. In most re-upholstery shops, every attempt is made to salvage as much of the piece of furniture as possible. If the webbing is good, then use it. This holds true for the cotton padding, springs, burlap, and anything else still in usable condition.

This chapter describes a complete stripping process. That is, every aspect of the stripping process is considered down to the bare wood frame. It is rare that such a situation would be encountered by the upholsterer. It is presented here simply for the sake of instruction.

SPRING CONSTRUCTION

There are two principal categories of furniture that use springs. One type uses coil (or sagless) springs in both the seat (usually two layers of springs) and the back. This generally referred to as the *overstuffed* chair or sofa. The second type of furniture found in spring construction substitutes a padded back for the springs. This is known as *tight spring* construction.

A brief outline of the steps involved in stripping an *overstuffed* chair is given in Fig. 3. Although these outlined steps refer specifically to the chair in the illustration, most upholstered chairs and sofas will have a similar *upholstery* construction. That is, the sequence of the layers of materials (from outer upholstery cover to the frame) will be largely similar.

The following is a more detailed examination of the steps involved in the stripping away of these various layers of material from an upholstered piece of furniture. Although this is the description of the stripping of a specific piece of furniture, each numbered step represents a different stage in the stripping process and can be applied to any number of different types of upholstered furniture. The piece of furniture selected to illustrate the stripping process is an upholstered chair with a removable T-cushion (Fig. 4.) The cushion, seat, and back are of coil spring con-

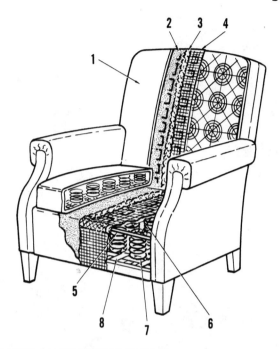

1 — FINAL COVER . SEAMS HIDDEN BY WELTS.
REMOVE THE WELTS, CUT THE THREAD HOLDING THE SEAMS TOGETHER, AND REMOVE THE FINAL COVER MATERIAL. REMOVE THE CAMBRIC FROM THE BOTTOM.

2 — LAYER OF COTTON. REMOVE THE LAYER OF COTTON.

3 — STUFFING. THE STUFFING IS SEWN TO THE BURLAP LAYER BELOW. CUT THE THREAD AND REMOVE THE STUFFING.

4 — BURLAP. THE BURLAP IS SOMETIMES SEWN TO THE SPRING LAYER BELOW; CUT THE TWINE AND REMOVE THE BURLAP.

5 — SPRING EDGE WIRE. EITHER SEWN OR CLIPPED TO THE SPRINGS. CLIPS MUST BE REMOVED WITH PLIERS.

6 — SPRING TYING. CUT THE TWINE.

7 — SPRINGS FASTENED TO WEBBING. THIS IS EITHER FASTENED WITH TWINE (SEWN TO THE WEBBING OR A BURLAP BASE) OR WITH SPECIAL METAL CLIPS.

8 — WEBBING. REMOVE THE TACKS AND WEBBING.

Courtesy   Seng   Co.

Fig. 3. A brief outline of steps involved in stripping an overstuffed chair.

Fig. 4. Chair ready for stripping.

Courtesy Kwik-Bed Sofa Corp.

Courtesy Kwik-Bed Sofa Corp.

Courtesy Kwik-Bed Sofa Corp.

Fig. 5. Removing the cambric dust cover.

Courtesy Kwik-Bed Sofa Corp.

struction. Note that the top of the left arm has been badly worn and torn. The chair will be stripped to determine the extent of damage and wear. Those portions of the construction still in a usable condition will not be removed. In the case of this particular chair, it will be found that the springs and burlap are in excellent condition. However, the removal of everything down to the bare wood frame will be discussed.

1. Remove the cushion, turn the chair or sofa upside down on a padded bench or pair of padded trestles (or on a pad placed on the floor), and remove the cambric dust cover from the bottom (Fig. 5). This dust cover will probably be tacked in place with No. 8 upholstery tacks. Staples are also frequently used. Use the ripping tool (or claw tool) in the same direction as the grain (this will mean along the length of the frame board). If a mallet is necessary, tap the ripping tool as gently as possible. Splitting or marring the frame must be avoided. The operator in the figure is using an air-operated ripping tool, commonly used in commercial operations.

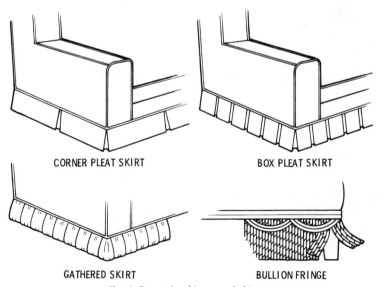

CORNER PLEAT SKIRT   BOX PLEAT SKIRT

GATHERED SKIRT   BULLION FRINGE

Fig. 6. Decorative fringes and skirts.

61

Some chairs may have a decorative fringe or skirt (flounce) around the bottom (Fig. 6). Usually this has been added after the dust cover was tacked into position. If this is the case, then it should be removed before the dust cover. These skirts are commonly attached by blind tacking them to the frame. Decorative borders lighter in weight (such as gimp) may be glued to the bottom edge of the chair (Fig. 7).

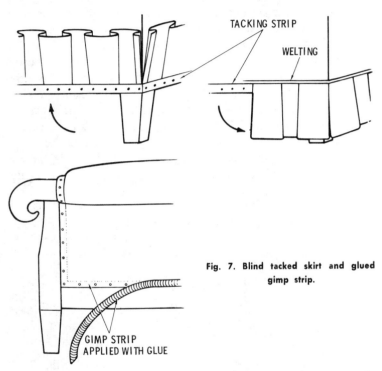

Fig. 7. Blind tacked skirt and glued gimp strip.

2. Remove the outside back and loosen the outside arm panels (Fig. 8). The back will probably have been blind tacked. That is, the tacks were driven through a cardboard tacking strip and the upholstery fabric was folded over them to conceal the tacks from view. Blind tacking may also have been used on the outside arm panels. Sometimes in blind tacking, the seams are sewed to draw them closer together (although this is not normally the case). Take a razor blade

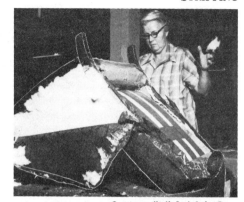

Fig. 8. Removing outside back and loosening outside arm panels.

Courtesy Kwik-Bed Sofa Corp.

Fig. 9. Removing tacks from inside arms and front seat.

Courtesy Kwik-Bed Sofa Corp.

Fig. 10. Removing inside back.

Courtesy Kwik-Bed Sofa Corp.

63

or a knife and carefully cut the thread holding such seams together. It will probably be necessary to cut the seam threads across the top and down both sides of the back.

3. Turn the chair right side up and completely remove the outside arm panels. Remove the tacks (or staples) from the top of the *inside* arm and the bottom of the front seat (Fig. 9).
4. Remove the inside back cover. Note that the inside back cover is one piece that extends around the sides and top of the back (Fig. 10).
5. Remove the inside arm covers and the seat cover (Fig. 11). Note that on this particular chair there was no muslin cover

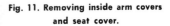
Fig. 11. Removing inside arm covers and seat cover.

Courtesy Kwik-Bed Sofa Corp.

Courtesy Kwik-Bed Sofa Corp.

Fig. 12. Examining the webbing.

Courtesy Kwik-Bed Sofa Corp.

Fig. 13. Removing the webbing.

Courtesy Kwik-Bed Sofa Corp.
Fig. 14. Examining the bottom burlap layer.

between the upholstery cover and the layer of cotton padding. At this point, you should examine the cotton padding to determine if any of it is re-usable. Remove all the padding and lay the re-usable portions to one side.

6. Turn the chair upside down on a pair of padded trestles and examine the webbing (Fig. 12). On this particular chair, you will note that one piece of webbing is torn. Although the rest of the webbing shows no damage, it was considered old enough to merit replacement. Remove all the webbing (Fig. 13).

7. The burlap to which the bottoms of the seat coil springs are sewed is now exposed (Fig. 14). An examination of this layer of construction reveals no damage or decay. By turning the chair right side up and examining the rest of the burlap, we find a similar condition (Fig. 15). All the springs are securely tied, and appear to be in excellent condition. It is not necessary to proceed any further in stripping this chair. This particular chair will be used in later chapters to illustrate the process of re-upholstering.

8. Sometimes front arm panels are constructed separately on a wood base cut to shape and nailed or glued into position (Fig. 16). Another method is to pad the front of the arm.

Courtesy Kwik-Bed Sofa Corp.

Fig. 15. Examining the remaining burlap.

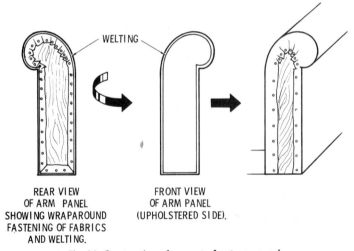

WELTING

REAR VIEW
OF ARM PANEL
SHOWING WRAPAROUND
FASTENING OF FABRICS
AND WELTING.

FRONT VIEW
OF ARM PANEL
(UPHOLSTERED SIDE).

Fig. 16. Construction of separate front arm panels.

In this case, burlap is tacked to the frame surface. A roll edge is sewed or tacked around the edge of the frame and stuffing is tacked into place. If you wish, you may cover this with muslin before covering it with the upholstery cover (Fig. 17). Note that the chair illustrated in Fig. 4 represents still another variation. Here, the front of the arm is an extension of the frame. Because it is exposed to view, it has been given several coats of a varnish finish.

The following is a detailed examination of the steps involved in the stripping away of the remaining layers of material from an upholstered piece of furniture. Although this is not a description of the chair used in the previous illustrations, each numbered step represents a different stage in the stripping process and can be applied to any number of different types of upholstered furniture.

9. *THE MUSLIN COVER.* Some upholsterers will place a layer of muslin underneath the upholstery cover. This is optional and you will probably note that the chair used in Fig. 4 did not have a muslin cover. Using muslin has several advantages that you should be aware of. The cotton (or stuffing) can be regulated by shoving the regulator through the cheap, muslin cover rather than the more expensive upholstery. Although many upholsterers will push the regulator through the upholstery fabric, it takes some experience not to leave holes or distort the weave.

The muslin cover is measured, cut, and sewed into position in the same manner as the upholstery cover. Note: sometimes a layer of cotton padding is placed between the outer

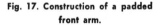

Fig. 17. Construction of a padded front arm.

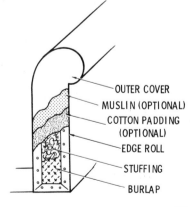

OUTER COVER
MUSLIN (OPTIONAL)
COTTON PADDING (OPTIONAL)
EDGE ROLL
STUFFING
BURLAP

upholstery cover and the muslin cover. In other instances it is found between the stuffing and the muslin (Fig. 18).

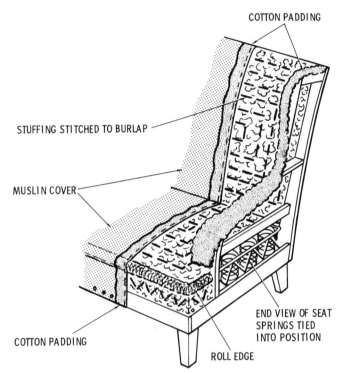

COTTON PADDING

STUFFING STITCHED TO BURLAP

MUSLIN COVER

COTTON PADDING

END VIEW OF SEAT SPRINGS TIED INTO POSITION

ROLL EDGE

Fig. 18. Typical layers of upholstery materials.

10. *THE STUFFING LAYER.* The stuffing layer is either placed directly below the muslin cover or the cotton padding and is sewed to the burlap cover. Cut the threads with a knife or a razor blade, and remove the stuffing. This same construction can be found on the inside back, inside arms, and seat. If the burlap covers a solid-wood frame area (tops of arms, fronts of arms, etc.) rather than an opening in the frame, then it may be tacked down (Fig. 19).

11. *THE ROLL EDGE.* If the chair has a rounded (arched) seat, then the springs are tied to create a rounded seat cushion. Tying the springs back in this manner can cause the

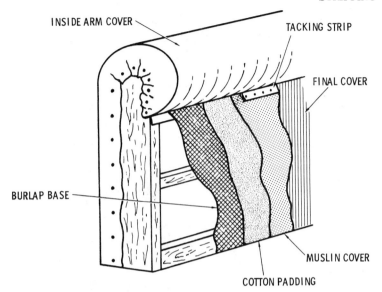

Fig. 19. Cutaway view of the typical construction of an outside arm.

upholstery materials (muslin and outer upholstery fabric) to rub or pull against the seat frame. To prevent excessive strain and wear at this point, a roll-edge is sewn into position on the burlap all along the edge of the wood frame. Use a razor to cut the thread and remove the roll-edge. There may be roll-edges on the arms, too.

12. *THE SPRING EDGE.* If, instead of a round seat, the chair or sofa you are working on has a spring-edge seat, the material must be protected from rubbing against the edge of the springs rather than the seat frame. This is handled in the same way as the frame edge in Step 11. In this case, the protective edging is sewed along the burlap on the edge of the springs. Cut the threads attaching the roll edge to the burlap and remove it (Fig. 20).

13. *THE BURLAP LAYER.* Now that you have removed the stuffing, you can see that the springs and other areas of the frame have been covered with a layer of burlap. The chair illustrated in Fig. 15 indicates how the burlap covers every open portion of the frame.

69

The burlap covering over the springs assists in containing some of the pressure the springs exert against the rest of the upholstery materials. Most upholsterers stitch the burlap to the tops of the springs. Remove all tacks and other fasteners, cut the stitching twine that secures the burlap to the spring tops, and remove all the burlap (see Fig. 20).

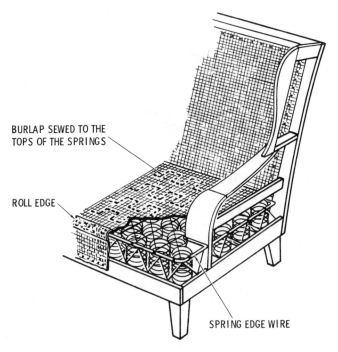

BURLAP SEWED TO THE
TOPS OF THE SPRINGS

ROLL EDGE

SPRING EDGE WIRE

Fig. 20. Removing burlap from springs and frame.

14. *SPRING CONSTRUCTION*. Now that the burlap has been removed, the type of springs used are exposed to view. If some sort of sagless springs were used, there will be no layer of webbing. Nonsag springs are usually attached from the front to back seat rails with metal clips. The rows of sagless springs are joined together with smaller helical springs. Remove the helical springs first. Take the clips off the frame and remove the sagless springs.

If the springs used were coil springs, you will notice that the tops were tied in position and that the twine was also tacked to the rails of the seat frame.

Cut the twine with a razor blade and remove the tacks along the rail. For more information on springs, please refer to Chapter 7.

15. *SPRING EDGE* WIRE. If this was a spring-edge seat, then a wire (usually a No. 9 spring wire) was bent to the exact shape of the frame and attached to the springs with twine or clips (these will have to be pried open). Remove the spring edge wire.

16. *COIL SPRING.* The bottoms of the coil springs will have been sewn to strips of criss-crossed, interlaced webbing. Cut these threads and remove the springs. Sometimes there may be no webbing and the springs have been tacked (or stapled) to wood slats or a solid wood base. Usually a strip of burlap, webbing, or cloth is placed between the coil and the wood to prevent any noise of metal against wood. Remove this noise insulator when you remove the springs.

17. *WEBBING.* Turn the chair or sofa upside down and examine the webbing. If it shows signs of damage or weakness, remove it.

NON-SPRING CONSTRUCTION

Dining room chairs, arm chairs, and side chairs are among the more similar examples of non-spring construction. This type is commonly referred to as the padded seat. No springs are found in either the seat or the back.

The stripping process for furniture of non-spring construction has much in common with that of spring construction. Gimp, welting, and metaline nails are used. The same kinds of upholstery tacks or staples are used to attach the fabric. The major differences between non-spring and spring construction are found internally, and center principally around the use or non-use of springs.

Furniture of non-spring construction can be divided into two types: (1) those with open frames and (2) those with closed frames. The open frames are covered with a criss-crossed, interlaced pattern of webbing tacked to the *top* of the frame to which burlap is sewn (in spring construction, it is tacked to the *bottom* of the frame). The rest of the construction parallels that of spring construction (the stuffing is sewn to the burlap, etc.). With the closed frames, there is no need for webbing. The stuffing materials are tacked to a solid wood base. If foam padding is used, it may be either glued into position or attached with a tacking strip. In many instances, the outer covering holds it in place.

CHAPTER 4

Frame Construction and Repairs

Anyone attempting frame repairs should have some knowledge of basic frame construction. This is particularly important if large sections of the frame have to be replaced due to some form of wood shrinkage or splitting. Such knowledge is indispensable to anyone who wishes to build a furniture frame in its entirety. It is the purpose of this chapter to give the reader some fundamental knowledge of frame construction. More detailed information can be found in any number of modern woodworking texts.

The frame is the basic foundation of the piece of furniture minus its upholstery coverings, stuffing, webbing, springs, and fasteners. In short, it is the bare wood "skeleton".

The frame is generally thought of as a box-shaped seat foundation to which legs, arms, and a back have been attached. However, the shape of the seat foundation is much more varied than the box design. It is possible to find round-shaped ones, horseshoe-shaped ones, and others that do not strictly follow a box shape. (Fig. 1).

Perhaps a better classification of seat foundations (and furniture frames in a more general sense) would be by whether or not they are of closed or open construction (Fig. 2). The former is found more frequently in modern furniture where rubber and polyurethane foam cushions are used. Examples of closed frames not

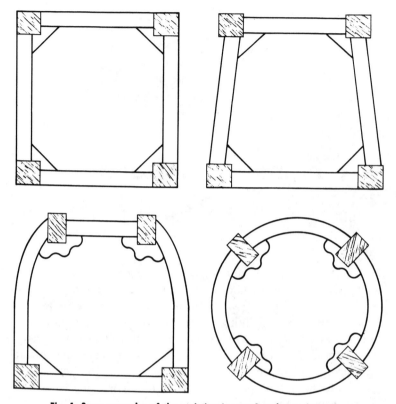

Fig. 1. Some examples of the variation in seat foundation designs.

using upholstery are the typical "captain's chair" or maple desk-chairs.

JOINERY

An important factor in frame construction and repair is how the corners of the frame are joined. This can be as elementary as fastening two boards together or as complicated as the construction of special joints that are secured with wood dowels and glue. This special skill is known as "joinery." Those types of joints best suited to frame construction are (1) the butt joint, (2) the miter joint, (3) the dado joint, (4) the rabbet joint, (5) the mortise and

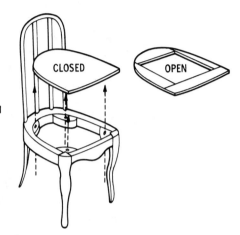

Fig. 2. Examples of open and closed seat frames.

tenon joint, and (6) the dovetail joint. These have been listed in an ascending order of complexity beginning with the most elementary form of furniture joint.

The *butt* joint is the most elementary of the joints to construct. However, in exchange for its simplicity of construction, the butt joint sacrifices strength. This is undoubtedly the weakest of the six joints listed. A butt joint is formed by joining the square end of one piece of wood with another. Because the butt joint is frequently strengthened with wood dowels, it is also called a *dowel* joint. Examples of the butt and dowel joints are illustrated in Fig. 3.

The *miter* joint is similar in many respects to the butt joint, but differs in that the two pieces of wood forming the corner are joined by cutting each at an angle. The butt joint, on the other

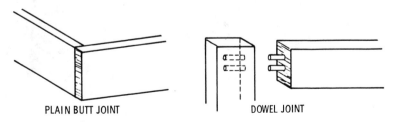

PLAIN BUTT JOINT   DOWEL JOINT

Fig. 3. Plain butt and dowel joints.

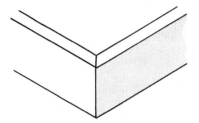

Fig. 4. A miter joint.

hand, is formed by overlapping one of the two pieces with the other (Fig. 4).

A *miter box* (Fig. 5) is often used to cut this type joint. This insures that the two cuts will be accurate and will form a perfect fit. The cut is usually made at a 45° angle on each of the two pieces to be joined. Once joined they combine to form a 90° angle. However, there may be occasions where it is desired to have the angle formed to be smaller or greater than 90°. This will depend upon the style of the furniture being constructed.

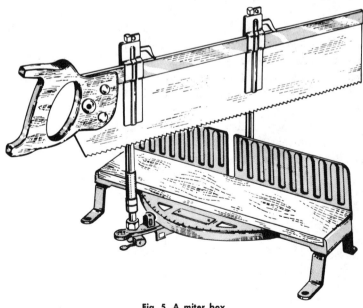

Fig. 5. A miter box.

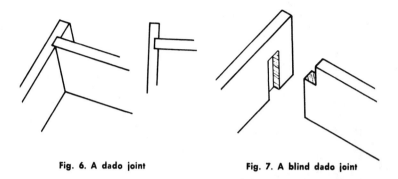

Fig. 6. A dado joint   **Fig. 7. A blind dado joint**

The *dado joint* is formed by cutting a recess or groove in one of the pieces of the frame and fitting the other piece to the cut portion. This is more complicated than the miter joint because it requires some precision cutting (Fig. 6).

The common variations of the dado joint are the *blind dado joint* (Fig. 7) and the dado joint which uses a rabbet cut for the inserted edge (Fig 8).

The *rabbet joint* has a recessed cut made along the end of the piece of the wood (Fig. 9). When the cut is made further in from the end, it is a variation of the dado joint.

The *mortise and tenon joint* is one of the strongest joints used in furniture construction. In the mortise and tenon joint, one of the pieces of wood is cut to form an extension (tenon) that fits

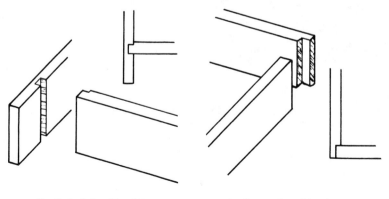

Fig. 8. A dado-rabbet joint   **Fig. 9. The rabbet joint.**

77

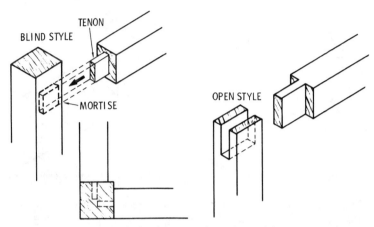

Fig. 10. Blind and open mortise and tenon joints.

snuggly into a recess (mortise) cut into the piece of wood to which it is joined. There are variations of the mortise and tenon joint. Two commonly used in furniture construction are the *closed* (or *blind*) and *open mortise and tenon joint* (Fig. 10).

The *dovetail joint* is the most complicated type used in furniture construction. Essentially it consists of a number of interlocking extensions and recesses cut on the ends of the wood in such a manner that both pieces lock together when joined. The extensions that are formed are called "pins" and "tails." The spaces in between are the "sockets." The pins and tails are similar in appearance except that there is always a half pin on the outside row (never a

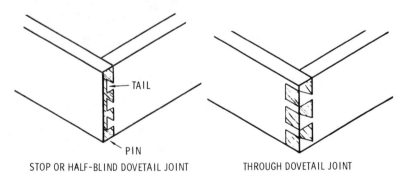

STOP OR HALF-BLIND DOVETAIL JOINT   THROUGH DOVETAIL JOINT

Fig. 11. Examples of dovetail joints.

half tail). The tail-like appearance of the extensions is respon-
sible for this joint being called the dovetail joint. The dovetail joint
is almost always found in quality furniture (Fig. 11).

All of the above-mentioned joints may be strengthened by using
corner blocks, dowels, screws, splines, and various types of fasteners. Surfaces should be glued and not nailed.

Corner blocks are wood supports cut to fit into each corner
of the frame for re-inforcement. The wood support piece must
be cut so that it fits into the corner of the frame. There is no standard size for these corner blocks. Each is made to fit to the dimensions of the frame. These corner blocks are attached with glue
and wood screws. The screws should be sunk so that they penetrate
perpendicular to the frame sides (Fig. 12).

Sometimes wood screws are used from the outside of a chair
rail. That is, they enter from the outside exposed surface of the
rail and screw into a corner block. These screws should be counter-

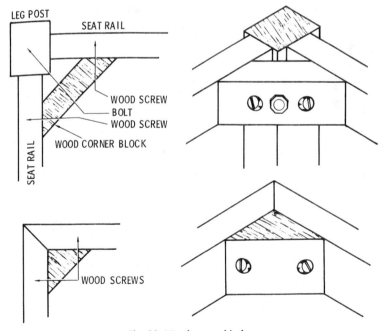

Fig. 12. Wood corner blocks.

sunk at least a quarter of an inch and the holes filled in with plastic wood or a wood plug.

Nails are sometimes used to fasten corners together in cheaper furniture construction. However, their use is not recommended because they form a far weaker joint than other methods available to the craftsman. The use of wood dowels and glue, on the other hand, is an indication of quality furniture and strong construction. Wood dowels that have been glued in place will not work loose as nails do. If you are repairing a piece of furniture and you find that the joints have been nailed together, remove the nails and fill the holes with wood filler. Sand off the excess. Drill new holes for the wood dowels (Fig. 13). Avoid drilling where the old nail holes

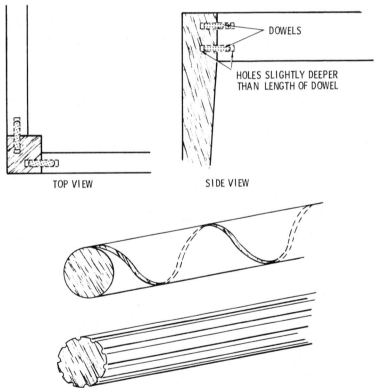

TOP VIEW   SIDE VIEW

DOWELS

HOLES SLIGHTLY DEEPER THAN LENGTH OF DOWEL

Fig. 13. Wood dowels and their use.

were, if possible. Note that the hole for the dowel in Fig. 13 is slightly longer than the dowel itself. Also note that the dowel has spiral grooves (dowels with longitudinal grooves are also available). This enables the glue to flow the length of the dowel. A wood dowel is preferable to a wood screw on an exterior surface.

Dowels for furniture use come in many sizes (diameters of ⅛ to 1 inch, with increases of 1/16 inch between sizes). As a general rule, the dowel should not be more than one half the thickness of the piece of wood into which it is inserted. A ¼ or ½ inch dowel would do for a 1 inch thickness.

The procedure for using wood dowels in the construction of a joint is as follows:

1. Select a dowel with grooves, because these allow excess glue and air to escape as the dowel is inserted into the hole.
2. Use a Try Square and make certain that the two surfaces to be joined are square.
3. Mark off the dowel positions on the edge of each piece of

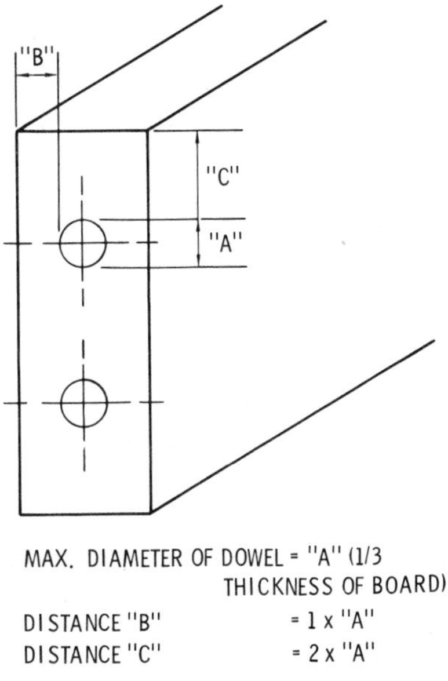

Fig. 14. Selection and positioning of dowels.

MAX. DIAMETER OF DOWEL = "A" (1/3 THICKNESS OF BOARD)

DISTANCE "B"   = 1 x "A"
DISTANCE "C"   = 2 x "A"

wood. Dowel diameter should be selected for the smaller of the two pieces being joined (Fig. 14).

4. Dowels should be from two to three inches in length. Use a drill bit the size of the dowel and make the hole depth one half the length of the dowel plus an additional $\frac{1}{16}$ inch (Fig. 15).

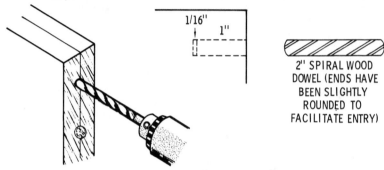

Fig. 15. Drilling holes for wood dowels.

5. Test the fit without glue. The dowel should fit snuggly, but without the need of forcing it in.

6. Dip the dowel in glue and insert it into the hole. Repeat this procedure with all the dowels on the same piece of wood. Wipe away all excess glue.

7. Cover the exposed dowel ends and the joint surface with glue. Insert the glue-covered dowels into the holes on the second piece of wood. Force the joint together, clamp it so that it will not move apart, and allow to set over night.

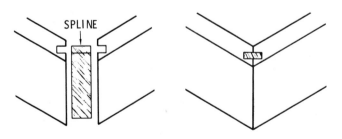

Fig. 16. Spline-reinforced miter joint.

If the holes are too big for the size of the dowels, a tighter fit can be made by gluing a piece of cloth around the dowels before inserting them in the holes. This also works well when repairing loose dowels on existing furniture.

Wood splines are sometimes used instead of wood dowels in the construction of a joint. A spline is a thin, narrow piece of wood often used to reinforce a miter joint (Fig. 16). A groove (kerf) is cut into the end of each piece of wood forming the joint and the spline is inserted and glued into position in much the same manner as the wood dowels are.

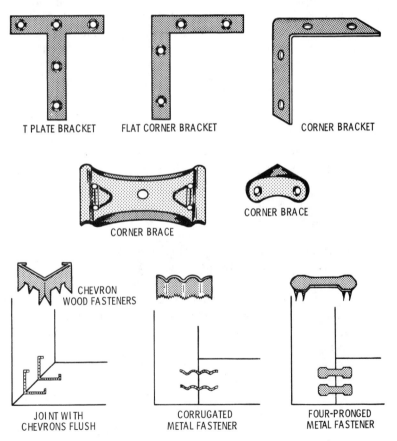

Fig. 17. Metal brackets and fasteners used in furniture construction.

There are a number of metal fasteners on the market that can be used for the reinforcement of miter and butt joints. These come either in the form of metal pieces that are forced into the wood, or metal plates and irons that are screwed into place (Fig. 17).

Such fasteners can be used when originally constructing a new piece of furniture or can be employed to strengthen a weak joint on an existing item.

GLUES AND THE GLUING PROCESS

An important consideration in furniture frame construction and repair is the type of glue used in joining the various pieces.

The glues used in furniture work fall into two large classes: (1) natural glues and (2) synthetic resin glues. Synthetic resin glues are of comparatively recent origin, dating largely from the 1930's. Prior to this time, the natural glues dominated the commercial market.

NATURAL GLUES

Natural glues are those that are processed from the body parts of animals (hides, sinews, bones) or from fish, or from the by-products of animals (casein glues are made from sour milk curds), or from vegetable sources. The list is more extensive than this, but we are essentially interested in those mentioned here because they are used in woodworking. Natural glues have been in use since ancient times. Recently, the synthetic resin glues have begun to replace the natural glues in many aspects of woodworking.

Animal glues can be derived from a number of sources (principally cattle, horses, hogs, sheep, or goats). The common source for animal glue today is the processed body parts of cattle. The best portion of the animal for glue manufacture is the hide, the worst is the bone.

Animal glues are sold as dry flakes, shreds, or ground powders that must be mixed with water and heated before application. They can also be purchased in the form of cold liquids which need no further preparation (Fig. 18).

Before preparing the dry form of the animal glue, read the instructions carefully. Water and glue must be mixed in amounts

Fig. 18. Typical animal hide glues.

Fig. 19. Typical 2-part epoxy glue.

according to the manufacturer's specifications. These amounts may vary between manufacturers. Using the amount suggested in the instructions, mix the glue flakes (or shreds, etc.) with *clean,* cool water. Stir until a creamy, smooth mixture is produced. Be particularly careful about removing all the lumps. Allow this mixture to stand until all the glue particles are completely soaked. Heat the glue in a glue pot at a steady temperature of about 145 to 150°F.

These "hot" glues cannot be used on cold surfaces because the glue will congeal. The wood surfaces must be warmed before the glue is applied. The rapid setting rate for the heated animal glues allows little time to adjust the clamps. Animal glues are weakened by moisture. For this reason, they are not as suitable for gluing outdoor furniture as others. Re-heating animal glues will cause them to lose strength. Consequently, only as much glue as will be used in a work session should be mixed at any one time.

The liquid forms of animal glue do not need to be mixed. They are ready to be applied directly to the surface without any further preparation. Liquid animal glues also suffer from humidity and moisture. They are not recommended for outdoor furniture. Unlike the dry forms, liquid animal glues dry slowly. These glues are easy to apply, inexpensive, and hardly ever stain. Two of the more common names available are *Franklin Liquid Hide Glue* and *Craftsman Hide Glue* (Fig. 19).

85

Fish glue is made from the various parts of the body of the fish (scales, tissue, bones, etc.). This is a liquid glue having many of the same characteristics as liquid animal glue. Fish glue sets slowly and is adversely affected by moisture.

Vegetable glues are derived from starches, dextrin (a starch derivative), and soybeans. They are inexpensive. Like animal and fish glues, they have little resistance to moisture. The strength of vegetable glue is limited and is largely restricted to use in veneering.

Casein glue is derived from the same yellowish curds of sour milk that constitute the basic protein of cheese. These curds are washed, dried, and mixed with hydrated (slaked) lime and sodium. The casein glue powder that results from this processing must be mixed with water before it is ready to be applied.

Casein glue is more water resistant than the other natural glues. However, long exposure to moisture will cause the glue to break down. It will make a joint waterproof for a short period of time. Casein glues are being replaced by other type glues currently available.

SYNTHETIC RESIN GLUES

Synthetic resin glues were developed in the 1930's and became available on a large scale commercially in the second half of that decade. There are two basic categories: (1) thermosetting and (2) thermoplastic. The major distinction between the two is that thermosetting types of synthetic resin glues undergo a chemical change during the bonding process and cannot be softened with heat. Perhaps the best known example of the thermosetting type is the epoxy glue.

Epoxy glue is a thermosetting type glue with an extremely rapid drying time. It is usually packaged in two separate tubes, one containing the synthetic resin and the other a substance that causes hardening when mixed with the resin.

Epoxy glue resists moisture and humidity. It forms an extremely strong bond. It is also expensive when compared to natural glues, which might make it financially impractical for wide application in furniture frame construction. There are several epoxy glues on the market including *Elmer's Epoxy Glue, Devcon Clear Epoxy*

Adhesive, and *Duro Plastic E-Pox-E Glue* (Fig. 19). Epoxy glues are suitable for minor repairs and as a filler around loose joints. For commercial applications where larger quantities of epoxy glues are required, it is recommended to contact a glue manufacturer and explain your requirements. There are many controlable variables to be considered, such as drying time, which the manufacturer can adjust to meet the requirements.

Fig. 20. Typical resorcinol resin glues.

Fig. 21. Typical polyvinyl resin glues.

Other thermosetting types of synthetic resin glues used in furniture construction or the manufacture of related wood products are: (1) *phenol formaldehyde resin glue,* (2) *urea formaldehyde resin glue,* and (3) *resorcinol formaldehyde resin glue.* The phenol resins are used in plywood production, and are available as powders or liquids. They show a strong resistance to moisture, but tend to stain the wood slightly. The urea resins are used primarily for gluing veneer surfaces. They set at room temperatures in about five to seven hours. They also stain wood surfaces slightly. The urea resins are less resistant to moisture than are the phenol resins. Both the phenol and urea resin glues form a strong bond. The resorcinol resin glues have a strong resistance to moisture. They form a very strong bond, but like most of the thermosetting types tend to stain the wood slightly. They also set at room temperatures, but require slightly more time than the urea resins do. Resorcinol resin glues are available only in the liquid form. Two brands currently available on the market are *Elmer's Waterproof Glue* and *Weldwood Waterproof Resorcinol Resin Glue* (Fig. 20).

Polyvinyl resin emulsions are manufactured in the form of a resin glues of the thermoplastic type. These are used quite extensively in furniture construction and are steadily replacing animal and fish glues. The gluing action is produced by the absorbtion of moisture into the wood and the evaporation of moisture into the air. Since this is a thermoplastic type of glue, high temperatures will cause it to soften.

Polyvinyl resin emulsion are manufactured in the form of a white liquid (these glues are frequently referred to as "white glues") under such trade names as *Franklin Evertite, Elmer's Glue-All,* and *Sears Craftsman General Purpose* (Fig. 21).

These glues are easy to apply and are cheaper than any of the other synthetic resin glues. The polyvinyl resins do not stain the wood. They set fairly quickly and can be applied at room temperature without further preparation. They form a strong joint, but are subject to weakening in high temperature, excessive moisture, or stress. A polyvinyl resin glue will dull the surface of metal tools and should be cleaned off as quickly as possible.

PREPARING THE SURFACES FOR GLUING

The strength of a joint does not depend entirely upon the glue that is used. The surfaces to be glued must be properly prepared or the glue (regardless of its merits) will simply not form a lasting bond. The amount of surface area to be glued, the type of joint, and the kind and condition of the wood are also important considerations.

The longer a joint is held in the clamp the stronger it will be. As discussed earlier, the type of joint is also important. Some joints have a greater surface area for gluing than others. This contributes to the strength of the joint.

The following steps outline the procedure for preparing the surfaces for gluing.

1. The wood to be used should have a uniform moisture content. If the moisture content is above 15%, then only water-

resistant glues will perform satisfactorily. Even though such glues are available, it is best to make certain that the moisture content is low. This is not an easy task for the average workman in a small shop. The wood should be a kiln-dried one when it is purchased. However, even here one board may have a moisture content different from another. To ensure some uniformity in moisture content and to possibly lower it, store all the wood in the same place for several days and make certain that the storage area is a dry one.

2. The two surfaces that are to be glued together must be cut so that their fit is tight without extra pressure from the clamps. If the surfaces have been cut inaccurately, the joint will be weak. Fit the two surfaces together without gluing them. They must not be forced together. Any need to force the joint together indicates that it was cut inaccurately. By forcing the pieces together, stress is being placed against various points in the joint. This will eventually weaken it.

3. The two surfaces must be clean and smooth. Fill in and sand all scratches and dents. Take a T-square and make certain that all the corners, edges, and sides are exactly square. Remove all dust, dirt, sawdust, etc.

4. Reassemble all the joints with the necessary clamps in the same position in which they will be glued. If everything fits to your satisfaction, then you are ready to disassemble the pieces and begin applying the glue.

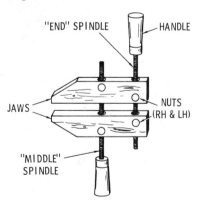

Fig. 22. Wooden hand screw clamp.

Courtesy Adjustable Clamp Co.

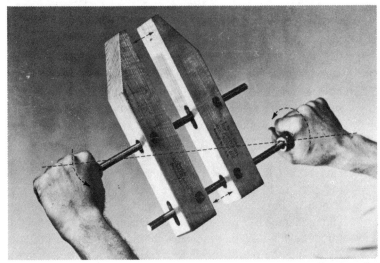

Courtesy Adjustable Clamp Co.

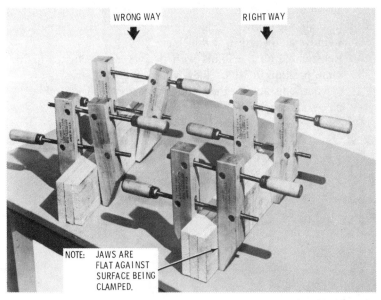

WRONG WAY   RIGHT WAY

NOTE: JAWS ARE FLAT AGAINST SURFACE BEING CLAMPED.

Courtesy Adjustable Clamp Co.

Fig. 23. Use of

5. Methods of reinforcing the joints (dowels, types metal fasteners, glued corner blacks, etc.) were discussed earlier.

A word of caution. Do not glue surfaces that are dirty or still contain traces of the old finish. Also, do not apply glue or allow the glue to set in a cold room.

CLAMPING

Clamping offers the best method of applying pressure during gluing. Simply stated, *clamping* is the procedure for holding the pieces of wood to be joined so that they will not move while the glue is drying. In addition, clamping will give pressure to the two surfaces being glued. The clamping procedure you follow will depend upon whether you are constructing a brand new frame or repairing an old one. Consequently, there are a variety of clamps you can use. Your selection will depend upon the requirements of the particular job.

THIRD CLAMP BEING USED TO PREVENT OTHER TWO CLAMPS ON IRREGULAR SURFACE FROM TWISTING OR CRAWLING.

Courtesy Adjustable Clamp Co.

hand screw clamps.

A clamp commonly found in most workshops is the hand screw clamp. The hand screw clamp (Fig. 22) is generally constructed of two wooden jaws that can be closed or opened by adjusting the two spindles. The maximum openings depend upon the size of the hand screw, and range from four to eighteen inches.

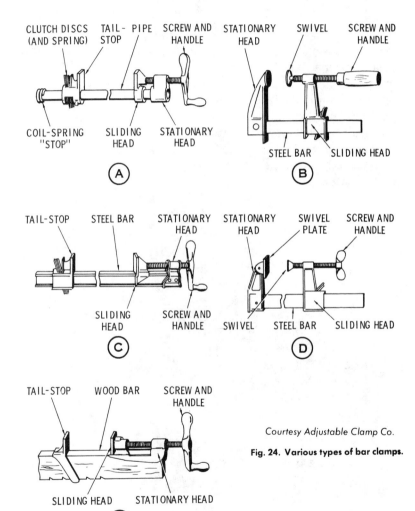

Courtesy Adjustable Clamp Co.

Fig. 24. Various types of bar clamps.

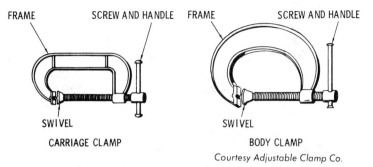

FRAME   SCREW AND HANDLE   FRAME   SCREW AND HANDLE

SWIVEL   SWIVEL

CARRIAGE CLAMP   BODY CLAMP

Courtesy Adjustable Clamp Co.

Fig. 25. Typical "C" clamps.

The hand screw clamp can be used for a variety of small operations in furniture construction and repair (Fig. 23).

For larger operations bar clamps are especially useful when it is necessary to apply pressure over an extended distance (Fig. 24).

Bar clamps are not only capable of expanding over a greater distance but they can also apply more pressure per square inch over this area than any other type of clamp. Remember, the harder the wood (e.g. mahogany) the greater the required pressure for a successful job of gluing.

The C clamp (Fig. 25) exerts pressure in a small, compact area, which assigns to it a function completely opposite to that of the

Fig. 26. Miter clamp.

bar clamp. It is frequently used to supplement bar clamps or to handle small repair jobs.

The pressure points of a miter joint are so placed that a frame using this type of construction requires a special clamping device. The miter clamp (Fig. 26) was designed for this purpose.

Band clamps (Fig. 27) are used in furniture construction for clamping shapes that are neither square nor rectangular. The bands of these clamps are either steel or heavy cloth. These bands are drawn taut by various tightening devices. The entire procedure is similar to tightening a belt on a pair of pants (Figs. 28 & 29).

Sometimes clamps are not available. If this is the case, wood screws can be used as substitutes. It should be pointed out that this procedure is inferior to clamping. The screws should be countersunk so that the holes may be filled in with wood plastic.

A word of caution about clamping. Do not mark the surface of the wood with the clamp. To avoid this, place a piece of paper next to the sanded surface and a block of wood between the paper and the clamp to spread the pressure. Also, do not apply too much pressure or you will risk crushing or warping the wood.

FRAME REPAIRS

Not everyone will be involved in constructing an entirely new frame. There are those who may simply want to repair a piece of furniture and restore it to its former condition.

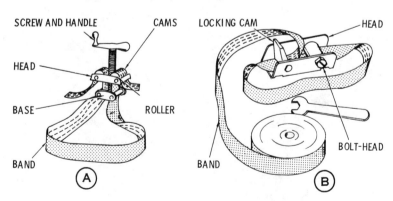

Courtesy Adjustable Clamp Co.

Fig. 27. Examples of band clamps.

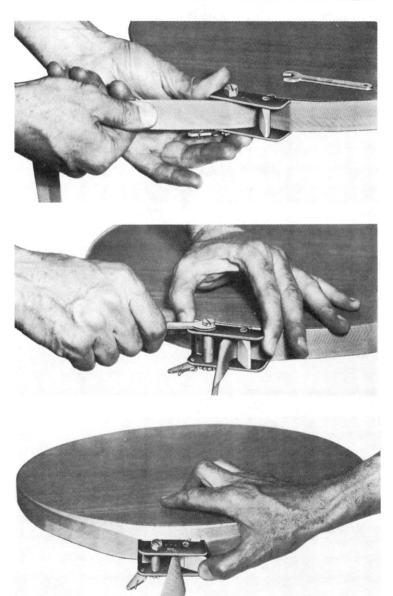

Fig. 28. Employing a band clamp.

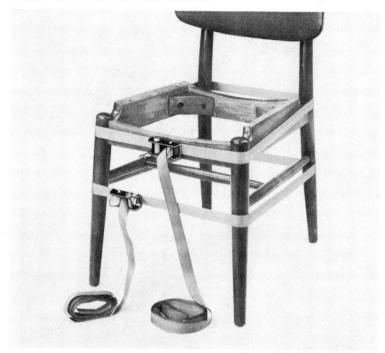

Courtesy Adjustable Clamp Co.

Courtesy Adjustable Clamp Co.

Fig. 29. Using cloth and metal band clamps.

There are a number of repair and restoration problems that we can consider here. These range from total repair to something as minor as removing scratches or dents. We will begin with the major problems and work down to the minor ones.

If any portion of the wood frame has been split, it is best to remove that particular section and replace it with a new piece of wood. It is important that this new piece of wood be seasoned lumber (kiln dried), because unseasoned wood will shrink. This could result in unsightly gaps after the glue has dried.

All of the old glue must be removed from the surfaces to which the split section was attached (a new coat of glue applied over an older one will result in a weak joint). A glue used in furniture construction must penetrate the wood in order to set properly.

It is not difficult to replace pieces of the seat-foundation or the back, because they are, for the most part, hidden from view. However, arms and legs present a totally different problem. This is largely because they may be in full view and must therefore be identical in appearance to the original after the repairs have been completed.

Some legs and arms are quite ornate and consequently difficult to replace. If they are badly broken, it may be possible to obtain a matching piece from an identical piece of furniture in a similar condition. For example, it may be possible to make one good chair from two damaged ones.

If the entire frame is loose, it would be best to completely disassemble it, remove all the glue from the exposed surfaces, and then re-glue it.

Whether or not you are re-assembling the entire frame, or simply re-attaching a certain piece (arm, leg, etc.), the following steps are recommended:

1. Remove all glue from both surfaces. Never place a new layer of glue over an older one.
2. Before re-gluing, test the pieces for fit.
3. Do not use nails in the re-assembly. If these were used in the previous construction, remove them, and fill in the holes with wood filler. Should you feel that a re-inforcement is needed in adding to gluing, see the sections of this chapter

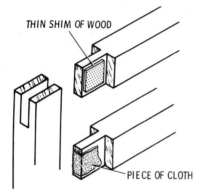

Fig. 30. Methods of tightening a loose joint.

dealing with wood corner blocks, wood screws, wood dowels, and metal fasteners.

4. If the frame fits together too loosely (in the case of mortise and tenon joints), use thin pieces of wood or cloth glued to the tenon to tighten the fit (Fig. 30).

5. Re-glue the frame. Remember that clamping pressure is necessary.

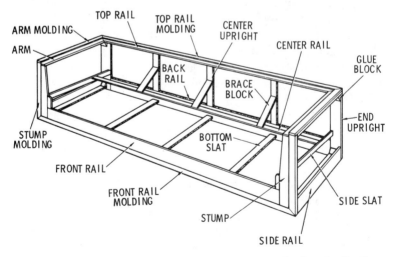

Courtesy   Kroehler Corp.

Fig. 31. Sofa frame.

CONSTRUCTING A NEW FRAME

Up to this point we have been discussing frame strengthening and repairs. Generally speaking, it is not usually necessary to replace the entire frame. The replacement of several small sections will, in most cases, adequately strengthen a damaged frame.

Constructing an entirely new frame requires a more extensive knowledge of woodworking than simple repairs do. In addition, the craftsman must have a knowledge of frame design. A few samples of the many variations of frame designs are given in Figs. 31 thru 35.

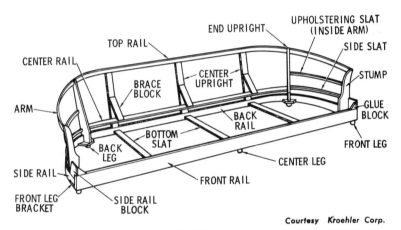

Courtesy Kroehler Corp.

Fig. 32. Sofa frame.

In constructing a new frame, several important points should be kept in mind.

1. Frame wood must be selected with care. It cannot be too hard, or it may develop a tendency to split (this is particularly true of black walnut, oak, and ash). If it is too soft the tacks will probably pull loose when tension is placed on them. Then, too, there are some soft woods that have a tendency to split. Consequently, a wood of moderate hardness is desired. Maple, white pine and yellow poplar are recommended. Both the white pine and yellow poplar are easier to

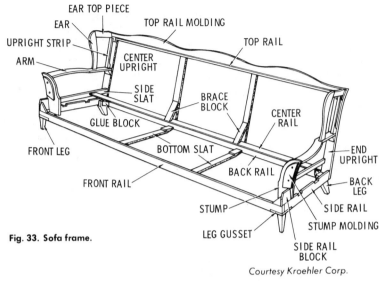

Fig. 33. Sofa frame.

Courtesy Kroehler Corp.

work with, although with yellow poplar you run a greater risk of splitting the wood. Maple has an even greater tendency to split, and is more difficult to work with than either white pine or yellow poplar. On the other hand, maple has greater strength. These recommendations for wood selections certainly do not exhaust the matter, and it is suggested a careful study be made of the attributes and characteristics of several types of wood before a final selection is made.

2. Bear in mind that the exposed parts (legs, arms, etc.) should be composed of a wood that will take a stain well. Walnut and mahogany are two examples of woods that are extremely attractive when stained. Those parts of the frame that will be covered by upholstery fabric can be constructed from a less expensive wood that may lack the staining properties of walnut and mahogany. Be sure to select seasoned wood (kiln dried is preferable). Unseasoned wood may warp or shrink. Also, glue will not stick properly to green wood.

3. Do not nail your frame pieces together. Always use a suitable glue. The frame can be made stronger by using wood dowels or flat-head screws and corner blocks for re-inforcement.

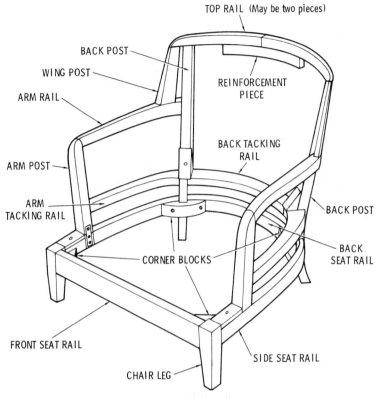

TOP RAIL (May be two pieces)

BACK POST

WING POST

ARM RAIL

REINFORCEMENT PIECE

ARM POST

BACK TACKING RAIL

ARM TACKING RAIL

BACK POST

CORNER BLOCKS

BACK SEAT RAIL

FRONT SEAT RAIL

SIDE SEAT RAIL

CHAIR LEG

Fig. 34. Chair frame.

FRAME RESTYLING

Sometime you may be confronted with the possibility of re-styling a frame. You may want to modernize an older piece or take a conventional piece of furniture and give it the style of an older period.

Although this is really no more difficult than frame repair, many people hesitate when faced with the desire to restyle a piece of furniture. They really shouldn't, because it is simply a matter of determining the type of chair or sofa that is wanted and estimating which portions of the frame will have to be altered. The frame alterations may consist of (1) adding portions to the frame (adding

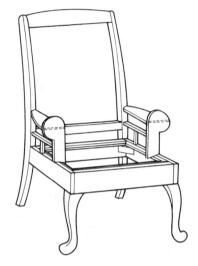

Fig. 35. Chair frame.

wings to a conventional chair to create an Early Colonial piece; raising a seat rail; closing off arms, etc.), or (2) subtracting portions from the frame (removing wings to make a conventional chair; reducing seat height; cutting back arms, etc.).

FRAME MEASUREMENTS

If you are making your own furniture, you might as well make it so that it is comfortable. You may have noticed that chairs come in various sizes. Many short people find it very uncomfortable to sit in chairs whose height does not allow their feet to touch the floor. Therefore, the seat should be at a level to allow proper support for the thighs and to permit the feet to rest on the floor. If you are short (or tall), you will want to construct your chair frame so that it is comfortable for your own particular measurements. However, most chair frames are constructed from what have become accepted as standard measurements. For example, the average measurement for the height of the seat above the floor is 18 inches. The seat depth is usually placed at 18-20 inches, and is slanted very slightly downward toward the rear (less than ½ inch). This directs the sitter's weight away from the front edge

102

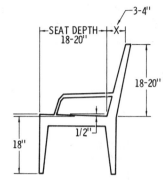

Fig. 36. Standard measurements for chair.

of the frame. The back of the chair is also 18-20 inches in height (measuring from the seat foundation) and is slanted 3-4 inches back from the perpendicular (Fig. 36).

SANDING

Sanding is considered in greater detail in the next chapter (Chapter Five: Finishing and Re-Finishing Wood Surfaces). At the early stage of frame construction, sanding is used primarily to smooth rough edges and surfaces, However, there are three important points to remember at this stage:

1. Sanding should be done after all work with tools having cutting edges has been completed. Otherwise, the grit left in the wood pores may dull the cutting edges.
2. Sand with the grain. Cross-grain strokes will leave scratches. Straight (forward and backward) strokes, not circular ones, are required.
3. Begin with a coarse grade of sand paper. Generally this will not be higher than a No. 2 grade. Coarser grades will tend to leave deep stratches on the surface that will be difficult to remove when sanding for a finish.

MAIL ORDER SUPPLIES

There are a number of mail order houses through which you can place orders for supplies needed in frame construction and repair. The total list of these supplies is too extensive to individually describe each item, but among others it includes (1) rare woods, (2) veneers and inlays, (3) various types of hardware for furniture, (4) furniture legs in both metal and wood, (5) wood carvings, and (6) woodworking tools.

Three well-known mail order houses are:

1. Albert Constantine and Sons, Inc., 2050 Eastchester Road, Bronx, New York 10461, Dept. H-18.
2. Craftsman Wood Service Company, Dept. EX-99, 2729 South Mary Street, Chicago, Illinois.
3. H. L. Wild, 510 East 11th Street, New York, New York 10003.

CHAPTER 5

Finishing and Re-finishing Wood Surfaces

This chapter is concerned with an examination of the basic steps to be followed in producing a number of different finishes on wood surfaces. It includes both the finishing of new wood surfaces as well as the re-finishing of old ones. There are a number of books available that give much more detailed information on the subject of wood finishing. This chapter is intended only as an introduction and guide for the layman.

TOOLS AND MATERIALS

There are a number of abrasive materials available for preparing the surface of the wood before the finish coats are applied as well as for smoothing and polishing these finish coats to obtain a uniform, attractive surface. These abrasive materials can be divided into the following three categories: (1) sandpaper (abrasive paper), (2) steel wool, and (3) rubbing compounds (powders) and their solvents.

Sandpaper is sold in grades ranging from extra fine to extra coarse. These grades are also identified by grit numbers that begin with number 12 (extra coarse) and extend to number 400 (extra fine). The word "grit" refers to the hard granules that forms the cutting surface of the sandpaper. These granules are derived from *flint* (a quartz), *garnet, aluminum oxide,* or *silicon carbide.*

105

Strangely enough, no sand is used in making sandpaper. The distribution of the granules on the backing of the abrasive determines the grit number.

An older classification system for sandpaper—the "ought" number system—is still in use. Table 1 illustrates the correspondence between the two numbering systems.

Table 1. Suggested Grades of Sandpaper To Be Used in Woodworking and Wood Finishing.

PURPOSE	GRADE TITLES	OUGHT NUMBER SYSTEM	GRIT NUMBERS
Rough Sanding	Medium	1/0	80
Preparing The Surface	Fine	2/0	100
Preparing The Surface	Fine	3/0	120
Preparing The Surface	Fine	4/0	150
Preparing The Surface	Fine	5/0	180
Finish Sanding	Very Fine	6/0	220
Finish Sanding	Very Fine	7/0	240
Finish Sanding	Very Fine	8/0	280

Note that the examples illustrated in the table are those that are recommended for woodworking and wood finishing. The most widely sold sandpaper is made with aluminum oxide granules.

Sanding blocks come in a variety of sizes and shapes. It is important that you select the size and shape most suited for the particular surface area being sanded. For example, a square or rectangular block is recommended for large, flat surfaces. On the other hand, a curved block is preferable for rounded surfaces.

Steel wool is also used as an abrasive in finishing. It is available in a number of grades ranging from coarse to fine. Steel wool can be used after the sanding to produce an even smoother surface. It can also be used in place of sandpaper. This abrasive is very useful for preparing carved surface areas. Steel wool is adaptable to many different phases of the finishing process. One should be cautioned about the fine, metal particles that break loose from the steel wool pad when it is being used. These can be quite irritating to the eyes, skin, and lungs.

A final rubbing of the finish is done to produce a smooth uniform polished surface. The best materials for this are pumice (FFF grade) or rottenstone powder mixed with a solvent (water, raw linseed oil, or a light mineral oil), and rubbed with a heavy felt pad.

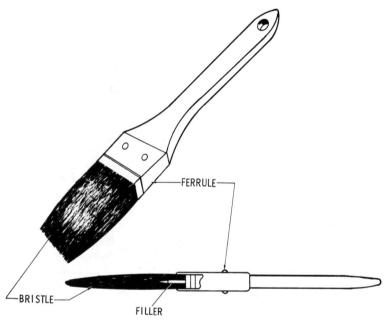

FERRULE

BRISTLE

FILLER

Fig. 1. The brush and its principal parts.

Sprinkle the powder across the surface. Dampen the cloth in the liquid you intend to use and rub the area covered by the powder. Wrapping the pad in a sanding block is advised. This will give better control and will reduce surface scratches.

The brush should be selected with as much care as the finish. It is to your advantage to purchase the most expensive brush that you can afford. It will last longer (if it is properly cleaned and stored), and it will produce a better finish.

A typical brush with the basic parts labelled is illustrated in Fig. 1. The *ferrule* is a metal (sometimes leather) band wrapped around the brush and fastened to the handle. A good brush will have a tightly fastened ferrule. The bristles are made from either

107

natural animal hair (usually hog bristle) or a synthetic material (nylon).

Brushes may be purchased with flat, round, or oval shapes. The last two are used primarily for trim.

A good quality brush will have the following characteristics:

1. The tip-edge of the bristles will be cut to form a wedge or chisel shape. A blunt edge is an indication of a cheap brush.
2. The tip of the bristles will taper to a fine, narrow, almost invisible edge.
3. The bristles will be securely fastened to the handle, and will not come loose while the finish is being applied.
4. The bristles will have a good flex to them (that is, they will be firm without being stiff and they will be flexible without being excessively loose or floppy).

Carefully clean your brushes after you use them. Clean them in the solvent recommended for the finish or a commercial brush cleaner and then wash them in soap and water.

Brushes should be stored so that the bristles retain a flat, tapered shape. This can be accomplished by wrapping them in paper and laying them flat, or by hanging the brush by the handle so that the bristles do not touch any surface. Brush storage containers can be purchased in paint or hardware stores.

PREPARING THE SURFACE

The first step to be considered in any finishing or re-finishing procedure is the preparation of the surface for the final finish. If this is not done properly at this stage, the results will be very disappointing. This cannot be emphasized strongly enough.

You will be faced with either one of two possible situations: (1) an old finish that needs to be removed or covered over or (2) a new wood surface that requires finishing.

The decision of removing or covering an old finish depends upon the type finish desired, and, upon the condition of the piece on which you are working. To a certain extent, the decision could rest upon how ambitious you are. Removing an old finish can be quite complicated, but correctly done gives satisfying results.

COVERING AN OLD FINISH

If the old finish is still in good condition, then you can save yourself a great deal of time and trouble by simply covering it with paint or enamel. By "good condition," it is meant that the finish is not cracking, is not brittle, and still adheres strongly at every point on the surface. Run your hand over the surface of the old finish. If it feels smooth to the touch, then it will probably accept a covering coat well. If even minor repairs (small areas of cracking, etc.) are required, it is recommended to refinish the article. The time spent preparing the area so that it will match the rest of the covering coat would be better spent completely stripping away the old finish.

The procedure for covering an old finish is as follows:

1. Thoroughly clean the surface of the old finish. This means removing all the dirt and furniture wax that has accumulated over the years. It is quite possible that a good cleaning will restore the surface to a condition that will not require re-finishing or covering. Use warm water and a home detergent for cleaning. Work quickly—do not allow water to soak in or stand on the surface. If you have done your job well, the water will run off the surface without beading (an indication of a layer of wax is the formation of moisture beads on the surface). Decorative carvings can be cleaned with a soft tooth brush. Wipe the surface with a clean, soft dry cloth and allow the piece to air dry.

2. If the old finish has a gloss, it must be removed. The new finish will not adhere to a surface with a gloss. A very fine grade of sandpaper can be used to remove the undesired gloss.

3. It may be necessary to re-glue joints loosened by the cleaning. Refer to the section on gluing in the previous chapter. When the repairs have been completed, make certain that no glue film is found on the surface to be finished. If there is, then remove it.

4. Brush on the first coat of paint. Allow it to dry for twenty-four hours and apply a second coat.

REMOVING THE OLD FINISH

If the old finish shows signs of brittleness, cracking, and poor adhesiveness, it is best to completely remove it.

Select a liquid paint-and-varnish remover you feel would best satisfy your needs, *read the instructions carefully,* and apply it to the surface in the manner suggested by the manufacturer. Use generous amounts of the remover. Because of its ingredients, a remover tends to evaporate quickly. The evaporation of the remover reduces the efficiency of its loosening action on the old finish. The only way to counter-balance this is to use a lot of remover.

The procedure for removing an old finish is as follows:

1. Apply the liquid remover to the surface in liberal amounts. It can be applied by flowing it on with an old, *clean* brush or a new inexpensive one. Allow the remover several minutes to work down into the old finish. When you feel that you have allowed enough time for the remover to penetrate the finish layers (there will be visual clues such as wrinkling of the surface), gently remove the old finish with a paint scraper. Do *not* bear down with force, because you will run the risk of gouging or scratching the surface of the wood. If some of the old finish proves stubborn, apply another coat of remover and repeat the process.

2. Now that you have pushed away the bulk of the dissolved finish with the paint scraper, wipe it free with clean rags and then rub the surface with a fine grade of steel wool and some alcohol. This will not only enable you to remove the last traces of the old finish from the open surfaces, but also from corners, carved designs, and other difficult-to-reach spots.

3. Take a clean, soft cloth, soak it in a solvent, and wipe the entire surface. After you have finished, take a clean, dry cloth and wipe the surface dry.

DENTS AND SCRATCHES

This stage in the preparation of the wood surface is an important one. Regardless of whether or not you have an old furniture frame from which a finish has been removed or a new one that has never had a finish, the wood surface probably has some dents and scratches. These must be removed now.

Raise the dents by applying a wet cloth to the area of the dent or by applying an iron to a wet cloth held over the dent. This causes the wood fibres to swell and raise above the surface.

Scratches, pit marks, old nail and screw holes, or gouges can be eliminated by filling them in with wood filler or a shellac stick. These latter items are recommended for using beneath natural finishes. The stick shellacs are particularly useful, because they come in a number of different colors.

After the filler has dried, sand off any excess.

SANDING

There are several stages of sanding in furniture construction and wood finishing. In the previous chapter, we were concerned with a very basic form of sanding that was related to frame construction rather than the special attention demanded in sanding a surface for the application of finishes. That type of sanding emphasized shaping and rough smoothing. However, sanding preparatory to the application of a finish requires much more exact care taken to insure that the surface will be completely smooth, leaving no marks that will detract from the final finish. For this reason, the major portion of this sanding is done *after* dents, scratches, gouges, etc. have been eliminated and *before* the bleaching, filling, and finishing procedures.

Normally, a satisfactory surface can be produced by starting with a 3/0 sandpaper (fine grade), switching to a 4/0 sandpaper, and finishing with a 6/0 (very fine grade).

Use a sandpaper block and sand with the grain. Change your sandpaper frequently. If you continue to use it after it has become worn smooth, it will smear the surface of the wood. This will prevent stains from penetrating into the wood, because the pores will have become blocked. This can also occur if you are using too fine a grade of sandpaper.

Use a clean, dry brush to clean the dust off the surface of the wood.

111

As a final touch, pass a damp, clean cloth over the surface of the wood. This will cause the wood grain fibres to swell and raise slightly. Sand these down level with the surface, and brush away the sawdust.

BLEACHING

Examine the surface of the wood. Sometimes an old finish has penetrated deeply into the wood pores. This stains the wood, making it somewhat darker than its original, natural color. Bleaching is a remedy for this.

Although both one- and two-solution bleaches are available commercially, the latter is by far the more effective form with woods that resist lightening. In the two-solution bleaches, the first solution produces the chemical change in the pigments and the second solution removes the residue.

Wood surface colors can be permanently whitened or lightened by bleaching. The hoped-for result is a lighter, uniform wood surface color.

Bleaching should be used only as a last result, because (unless extreme care is taken) the strong chemicals used in the bleaching process can harm the skin or ruin the wood surface by destroying the fibres.

The procedure for mixing and using your own bleach to lighten a wood surface is as follows:

1. Use a brush with a synthetic fibre. Natural fibre brushes disintegrate under the action of the bleach solution. Wear rubber gloves to protect the hands.
2. Apply an oxalic acid-water solution to the surface of the wood. A mild bleach can be formed from three ounces of oxalic acid (usually obtained in crystal form) dissolved in a quart of hot water and allowed to cool.
3. Mix sodium hypochlorite (household bleach) with hot water in the same proportions as the oxalic acid solution. Allow it to cool before application.
4. After the two solutions have been prepared and cooled, apply the oxalic acid solution. After it has dried, then apply the second solution.

5. As soon as the sodium hypochlorite has dried, wipe the surface with a solution of borax and water (one ounce of borax to a quart of hot water. Again, allow the solution to cool before applying it to the surface). The borax will neutralize the acid in the bleaching operation.

Step three will further lighten the wood, though it is not absolutely necessary to apply sodium hypochlorite after the application of the oxalic acid solution. Household bleaches work best at lightening natural wood colors, although they can also be used with success on water stains and ink. Oxalic acid-water solutions also work on water stains, chemical stains, and as a color lightener. If you would prefer not mixing your own bleach solution, there are a number of commercially-prepared bleaches available.

Commercially prepared two-solution bleaches enjoy widespread use. A popular brandname is *Dexall,* a commercial wood bleach manufactured by the Sherwin-Williams Company. Other reliable two-solution bleaches are *Albino* and *Blanchit.*

Clorox is a commonly known one-solution bleach. It is a chlorinated liquid form that will continue to lighten the wood with successive application

A special word of caution should be given about bleaches. Do not allow them to come into contact with your skin. The ingredients in the bleaches will frequently cause extreme skin reactions. This can be avoided by wearing rubber gloves and using some caution. Bleaches using oxalic acid solutions are particularly dangerous to the eyes and lungs. The threat is greatest when sanding a wood surface that has been treated with an oxalic acid bleach solution. The dried oxalic acid adheres to the sawdust particles and is easily inhaled and brought into contact with the eyes. Excessive inhalation can cause the throat muscles to contract. It is recommended that you wear some sort of protective face mask (with goggles) when working with this type of bleach.

STAINING

Stains are used to enhance otherwise dull natural finishes (e.g. birch), to highlight good finishes (e.g. oak), and to imitate the

113

finishes of other woods (e.g. gumwood can be stained to resemble cherry).

Stains are frequently used to add color to a wood by darkening areas so that they match other equally dark areas of color. Using stains to add color to the wood *before* a final finish is applied gives to staining a function exactly the opposite of bleaching (that is, the removal of coloring).

Stains can also be used as a clear, natural finish without any other finish being added. In this case, only a thin shellac sealer coat is brushed over the stain. A stain finishing schedule is given further on in this chapter.

FILLERS

Open grain woods (those having large pores) must have their pores filled before the finish coats are applied. Otherwise, the finish will seep down into these large pores, resulting in a very uneven coat.

Fillers are produced in either a paste or liquid form. Both are manufactured from a base which includes quartz silica mixed with some sort of drier, a thinner (usually turpentine or oil), and a vehicle.

The procedure for applying a filler to a wood surface is as follows:

1. Apply a washcoat of shellac to the untreated wood surface. A washcoat of shellac can be made by mixing 50% shellac with 50% alcohol.
2. Thin the filler to the thickness you find suitable for working. Follow the manufacturer's advice for the selection of a thinner.
3. Brush in the filler in the direction of the grain. Allow the filler to dry until its sheen has become dull.
4. Rub the filler *across* the grain with a burlap.
5. Take a clean burlap cloth and rub across the grain a second time.
6. Take a clean, soft cloth and wipe the surface in the direction of the grain.

7. Allow the filler to dry completely and then sand lightly to restore the smooth surface.

SEALERS

After a filler has been applied and sanded, a sealer should be used. Sealers or sealing coats are also applied to the surfaces of close-grained woods (those having small pores) that do not require the use of a filler. Finally, a sealer should be used over stains that have been used to color the wood.

A sealer or sealing coat acts as a base for the rest of the finishing coats. It also functions as a barrier to the bleeding-through of fillers or stains.

An excellent sealer is a thin coat of shellac.

SHELLAC

Both orange and white shellacs are readily available. White shellac will add almost no color tone to the wood. For this reason, it is especially good for highlighting the grains of light colored woods. Orange shellac, on the other hand, adds an attractive tone to darker surface colors. It is frequently used to highlight the grains of mahogany and similar woods.

Shellac is often sold in four-pound cuts. The four-pound cut is dissolved in one gallon of pure denatured alcohol. The amount of alcohol used depends upon how thin you wish to make the shellac solution. The amount can be increased or decreased depending upon the thickness you find easiest to work with. It is better to apply several thin coats of shellac than it is to work with a solution that is too thick. The best formula for a shellac solution in wood finishing is one having a mixture of 50% shellac. The alcohol is also the solvent in which the shellac brushes should be cleaned.

Purchase the best grade of shellac possible and in small quantities. Do not store shellac for a long period of time, because its shelf life is measured in months. Always keep shellac in the original container and tightly sealed. Do not use shellac in a room in which there is any appreciable amount of humidity. Moisture in the air will affect the finish.

SHELLAC FINISHING SCHEDULE

1. Prepare the wood surface according to the instructions given in this chapter. It is important to use a filler on open grained woods and to cover this with a sealer *before* applying the finish (see the discussion on fillers and sealers elsewhere in this chapter).
2. Thin the shellac (50% shellac and 50% denatured alcohol).
3. Apply the first coat of shellac.
4. Allow the first coat to thoroughly dry.
5. Sand the first coat smooth with 3/0 sandpaper or fine steel wool.
6. Brush away any dust on the surface caused by Step Five.
7. Apply the second coat of shellac.
8. Allow the second coat to dry.
9. Rub the second coat with 6/0 sandpaper or extra fine steel wool.
10. Brush away any dust on the surface.
11. Apply the third coat of shellac.
12. Repeat Steps Eight through Ten.
13. Apply the fourth coat of shellac.
14. Repeat Steps Eight through Ten.
15. If you wish, a hard paste wax can be added to the surface after the fourth coat has had about a week to dry. Buff the wax well.

VARNISH

Varnish was developed in an attempt to obtain a finish with greater resistance to moisture than shellac possesses. Originally derived from natural resins, most varnishes today are manufactured with a synthetic resin base.

Varnish is not an easy finish to use. It is slow to set and requires at least one day of drying for each coat used. Because of its slow drying speed, varnish is susceptible to dust.

A shellac washcoat usually works well under most varnishes as a sealer. A varnish washcoat (4 parts varnish to 1 part turpentine) is even more suitable.

Select a room to work in that is relatively dust free. Keeping dust off the drying surface will be one of your greatest problems.

Your gloss to semigloss varnishes are the best to use, and they are recommended for use in the two finishing schedules below. *Never* use a spar varnish for a furniture finish.

VARNISH FINISHING SCHEDULE NO. 1

1. Prepare the wood surface according to the instructions given in this chapter (also see Step One of the Shellac Finishing Schedule).
2. Brush on a sealer coat of varnish. This should be thinned with 1 part turpentine to 4 parts varnish.
3. Allow about two days for the varnish sealer coat to dry. This will dry faster than a full strength coat of varnish because of the turpentine.
4. Sand the surface lightly with 6/0 sandpaper.
5. Brush away the dust and wipe clean with a cloth.
6. Apply a first coat of *full strength* varnish. This and subsequent coats are not thinned.
7. Allow this first coat two days to dry.
8. Sand the surface lightly with 6/0 sandpaper.
9. Brush away the dust and wipe clean with a cloth.
10. Apply a second coat of full strength varnish.
11. Allow the second coat two days to dry.
12. This final coat can be lightly rubbed with a 6/0 (very fine) steel wool, brushed clean, and dusted with a tack rag.
13. Apply two well-buffed coats of a paste wax for additional protection.

VARNISH FINISHING SCHEDULE NO. 2

1. Follow the wood surface preparation instructions in Step One of Varnish Finishing Schedule No. 1.
2. Brush on a first coat of shellac (50% shellac and 50% denatured alcohol).
3. Allow the shellac coat at least five hours to dry.
4. Sand this first coat with 3/0 sandpaper.

5. Brush away any dust on the surface.
6. Repeat Steps 3 through 5 with a second coat of shellac.
7. Brush on a coat of semigloss or gloss varnish.
8. Allow the varnish coat two days to dry.
9. Follow Steps 12 and 13 of Varnish Finishing Schedule No. 1.

For extra smooth and high gloss finishes, a hand-rubbing with pumice and/or rottenstone used with linseed oil will result in a superior finish.

LACQUER

Clear lacquer is a very quick drying finish that has been popular for the past forty to fifty years. It was developed as a substitute for both varnish and shellac in an attempt to increase both the drying time and the resistance to moisture. Because of its extremely fast drying time, it is better to use it in a spray gun than it is to brush it on.

Whenever you use a clear lacquer finish, make certain that any of the layers beneath it (fillers, strains, sealers) will not react to the chemicals in the lacquer and dissolve, causing blistering and an unsightly finish. N.G.R. stains are safe, as is shellac and fillers developed especially for use with lacquer.

Use thinners and solvents recommended by the manufacturer of the lacquer you are using.

LACQUER FINISHING SCHEDULE

1. Prepare the wood surface according to the instructions given in this chapter. (See also Step One of the Shellac Finishing Schedule.)
2. Apply the first coat of lacquer.
3. Allow this first coat at least eight hours to dry.
4. Sand the surface with 6/0 sandpaper.
5. Brush off the dust.
6. Apply the second coat of lacquer.
7. Allow the second coat eight hours to dry.
8. Sand lightly with 6/0 sandpaper.
9. Brush off the dust.

10. Rub with 3/0 steel wool.
11. Brush off the dust.
12. Rub the surface with pumice and linseed oil.
13. Remove granular residue with soft clean rags. This can be facilitated by liberally rinsing with linseed oil only and soft clean rags.
14. Rub the surface with rottenstone and linseed oil.
15. Remove granular residue as in Step 13.
16. Remove all traces of the linseed oil.
17. Apply a paste wax and buff well.

Steps 12 through 16 are optional and are offered simply as an illustration of how these two abrasive powders could be used in a finishing schedule.

LINSEED OIL

Linseed oil is a plant derivative that is used not only as a binder and vehicle in paints, but also as a clear finish. It is produced in two forms: *raw* linseed oil and *boiled* linseed oil. The former is used in paints, particularly the exterior kind. Boiled linseed oil can be used in wood finishing.

Never leave linseed oil on the surface to dry. It must always be rubbed until no oil moisture is left on the surface.

LINSEED OIL FINISH SCHEDULE

1. Prepare the wood surface according to the instructions given in this chapter (see also Step One of the Shellac Finishing Schedule). DO NOT use a sealer.
2. Prepare the linseed oil solution. The linseed oil is combined in varying amounts (depending upon the consistency desired) with distilled spirits of turpentine. The mixture may be 3, 2, or 1 part linseed oil and 1 part turpentine. Place the mixture in a container. Place the container in a larger one filled with water. Heat the mixture over a flame (about 15 minutes). Since this mixture is highly flammable, hold the containers far enough away from the flame to heat and still prevent any accidents.

3. Spread the linseed oil over the surface (a cloth is best for this) and allow the mixture to stand for about 20 minutes.

4. Rub the surface (with a lint free cloth) until all signs of the oil have disappeared. *Do not* leave any oil to dry on the surface.

5. Polish the surface with lint free cloth.

6. Allow this first coat of linseed oil to dry for two or three days.

7. Apply a second coat (following steps One through Five). Allow two weeks for this coat to dry.

8. Successive coats are optional, but should be applied at least at one week intervals and preferably at one month intervals.

9. A paste wax should be applied once a year and buffed well.

STAIN

There are a number of different stains available for use in wood finishing. Some are very difficult to use; whereas, others are so easy to apply that even the beginner will have no difficulty. Each type of stain has advantages and disadvantages that become apparent with use.

Water and spirit stains are made by dissolving the desired color of aniline dye powder in water or alcohol. A spirit stain has the advantage of a much faster drying time than does a water stain. On the other hand, a water stain is cheaper, easier to use, and provides truer color tones (the colors of spirit stains appear paler by contrast).

One of the problems encountered when using water or spirit (alcohol) stains is that the moisture in the base causes the finer hair-like fibers of the wood grain to swell and extend above the surface. These always have to be sanded smooth with the surface before successive layers of finish can be applied. For this reason N.G.R. stains (non-grain raising stains) were developed. A non-grain raising substance is added to either a water or spirit stain to prevent the grain from raising.

Oil stains are made by dissolving aniline dye powder in an oil solution. However, these are seldom used today because they have a tendency to fade more than the other stains.

Wiping stains are also available, and are the easiest for the beginner to use. Because they contain color pigments, they are perhaps closer to a paint or other opaque finishes than they are to a true stain. They tend to darken the wood color and will obscure the wood grain if too much is applied.

These wiping stains are usually applied to the surface with a soft lint-free cloth or pad. The stain is allowed to penetrate the pores of the wood for about 15-20 minutes and the excess is wiped away. Never allow portions of the stain to dry on the surface. Successive coats of stain may be applied and wiped away until the desired color tone is reached. However, be sure to allow at least 24 hours for each coat to dry before applying the next one.

A lighter color tone may be achieved by wiping the stain off sooner. Some wiping stains can be thinned for the same effect (follow the instructions suggested by the manufacturer).

A sealer coat of thinned shellac applied before the stain will reduce penetration. This is particularly important for the edge-grains, which will otherwise absorb more stain and become darker than the rest of the wood surface. This advice holds true for all stains—not just the wiping stains.

ENAMEL

Enamel is an opaque finish. It is produced in gloss, semigloss, and flat types. As with varnishes, gloss enamel is the most durable of the three, but due to the hardness of its finish is more subject to chipping.

Enamel is a pigmented varnish, the opaque counterpart of a clear varnish finish. It completely covers and obscures the grain characteristics of the wood. For this reason it is ideal to cover unattractive wood grains.

Pigmented lacquers are also frequently referred to as "enamels" and are most commonly manufactured and sold as sprays.

ENAMEL FINISHING SCHEDULE

1. Prepare the surface according to the instructions given in this chapter (see also Step One of the Shellac Finishing

121

Schedule). A washcoat of shellac (50% shellac and 50% denatured alcohol) is suggested as a sealer coat beneath the enamel.

2. Prepare an undercoat. It is best to use a primer, although a substitute undercoat can be made by a thinned enamel (four parts enamel to one part recommended solvent).
3. Apply the undercoat.
4. Allow the undercoat to thoroughly dry.
5. Sand the undercoat with 6/0 sandpaper.
6. Brush away all dust.
7. Apply the first coat of enamel. Thin the enamel with turpentine to a good brushing consistency.
8. Allow the first coat to dry.
9. Sand the first coat of enamel with 6/0 sandpaper.
10. Brush away all dust.
11. Apply the second coat of enamel.
12. Allow the second coat to thoroughly dry.
13. Rub the second coat with a fine steel wool.
14. Brush away all dust.
15. Apply a paste wax (if desired) and buff thoroughly.

The purpose of this chapter is to outline the basic steps involved in the finishing process, and to offer several finishing schedules as illustrative examples. It is not the intention of this chapter to present a detailed study of wood finishing and its products. There are hundreds of finishing schedules and a vast number of products and materials available for use. If additional information is desired, it is suggested that books concerned exclusively with wood finishing be consulted. Local paint and hardware store dealers can also be quite helpful.

SOME WORDS OF CAUTION

Finishing contains many pitfalls for the unwary craftsman. A principal difficulty encountered in finishing is the chemical formula of the finish itself. There is no uniformity in the formulas used by the various manufacturers. Consequently, when different finishes, thinners, solvents come into contact with one another, there are often strange and unwelcomed reactions. With this in mind, following are several cautionary reminders which should help to avoid some very discouraging results.

1. *Always* carefully read the manufacturer's instructions for using his product.
2. *Always* use the solvent or thinner recommended by the manufacturer for his finish product. If you mix products, you run the risk of chemical reactions that may damage the surface (or, at the very least, create a mess that will have to be removed).
3. *Never* use a lacquer over fillers, washcoats, and stains that will react with the lacquer. N.G.R. stains fill this requirement as do certain fillers and washcoats.

CHAPTER 6

Webbing

Webbing is used to provide support for the upholstery materials from which the seats of *open* furniture frames are constructed. Because of this central role in the construction of the seat, a high grade of webbing must be selected and properly attached to the frame. To settle for less is to invite trouble later on. Using a low grade of webbing or attaching the webbing incorrectly (or both) will result in an uncomfortable piece of furniture at best. Other complications such as a sagging seat will most likely develop. The life of such poor webbing is guaranteed to be short.

TYPES OF WEBBING

Jute webbing is sold in 3, 3½, and 4 inch widths, with 3½ inch width being the most commonly used. The average chair requires 10-12 yards; the average sofa, 30-35 yards. Jute webbing may be purchased by the yard, and in rolls of 72 yards or more.

The color of jute webbing is a khaki or tan and is sold in three grades indicated by the color of the stripe running along each edge. Red indicates the highest grade; black the lowest.

If the jute webbing has been sized (that is, stiffened with some sort of glaze), then it is more than likely an inferior grade of webbing. Check the weave. A good quality webbing will have a close, tight weave (Fig. 1).

Fig. 1. Jute webbing.

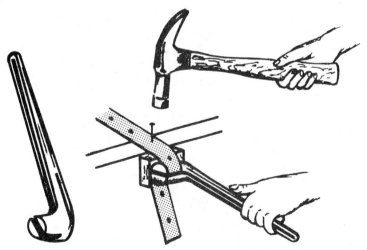

Fig. 2. Flat steel perforated webbing and steel webbing stretcher.

Steel webbing is sold in ⅝, ¾, and 1 inch widths, with the ¾ inch width occurring more frequently. Steel webbing is usually sold in 75 foot rolls, although larger rolls can be purchased.

Steel webbing is used in cheap grades of furniture (it does not have the resiliency of jute webbing), and as additional support when repairing a weak section of jute fiber (See Fig. 23).

Steel webbing is most often attached to the frame with 1-inch nails. The webbing is perforated so that the nails may be inserted. It is also possible to purchase steel webbing with a corrugated surface to facilitate the attachment of springs. It can also be purchased in plain strips which are neither perforated or corrugated. (Fig. 2).

Cotton webbing can be purchased in a number of widths ranging from as narrow as ½ inch to as wide as 2 inches. It is not as strong as jute webbing and should not be used to support the seat. It cannot carry as much weight as jute webbing (a good quality jute webbing will support 500-600 pounds with no difficulty). Cotton webbing is most suitable for arms and backs where there is not as much pressure exerted.

Plastic webbing is a decorative webbing designed to be exposed to view. It functions not only as the webbing, but as the seat itself. It may be purchased in several widths ranging from ¾ to 5 inches, and in a variety of colors. It is specially treated to resist the effects of weather, and for this reason it is used extensively in outdoor furniture.

Rubber webbing is usually purchased in 1¾ inch widths. It is used in some furniture (usually the cheaper modern or contem-

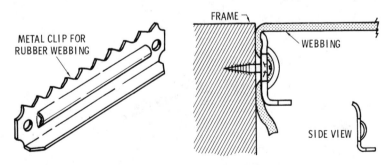

METAL CLIP FOR RUBBER WEBBING

FRAME

WEBBING

SIDE VIEW

Fig. 3. Metal clips for rubber webbing.

porary styles) in place of jute webbing. The method of attachment is far simpler, but is subject to relatively rapid deterioration. There are several methods of attachment. A metal clip can be attached to the frame and the webbing inserted through an opening in the clip. The webbing is held in place with teeth on the edge of the clip. (Fig. 3).

One of the problems with this kind of construction is that the edge of the metal clip wears against the rubber webbing and rips it.

Rubber webbing may also be tacked into place. Since the pressure placed against the webbing tends to rip the rubber where the tacks have been inserted, certain precautions should be taken. If the wood frame will allow it, cut a groove deep enough for the webbing and a narrow strip of wood to lock the webbing in place (Fig. 4).

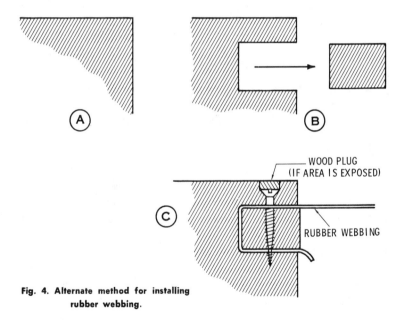

Fig. 4. Alternate method for installing rubber webbing.

If the frame is constructed so that the rails lie flat, then holes or slots may be cut through the wood. The webbing is then inserted and tacked (or stapled) to the bottom (Fig. 5).

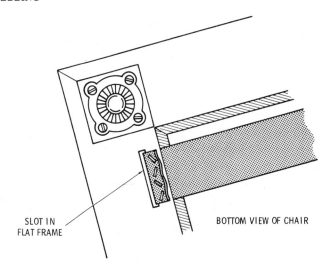

SLOT IN
FLAT FRAME

BOTTOM VIEW OF CHAIR

Fig. 5. Stapling rubber webbing to bottom of a flat frame.

THE WEBBING PROCEDURE

Regardless of the shape of the seat frame (it may be square, rectangular, round, or semi-round), it is viewed as having four sides whose boundaries are determined by the four leg posts. These four sides are referred to as the front rail, the back rail, and the two side rails (Fig. 6).

Padded seats and those that use coil spring units require webbing across the opening of the frame. The webbing strips for padded seats are tacked to the *top* of the seat rails. On seats using coil spring units, the strips are tacked to the *bottom* of the seat rails. The latter procedure is due to the fact that the coil springs must be so placed as to allow approximately 2½ inches of spring to extend above the top edge of the seat rails (Fig 7).

The following steps in the webbing procedure are used for either padded seats or those using coil spring units.

1. The webbing should be attached to the front rail first and then stretched to the back rail. This step protects the wood surface of the front rail of the frame, because the webbing stretcher never comes in contact with it.

128

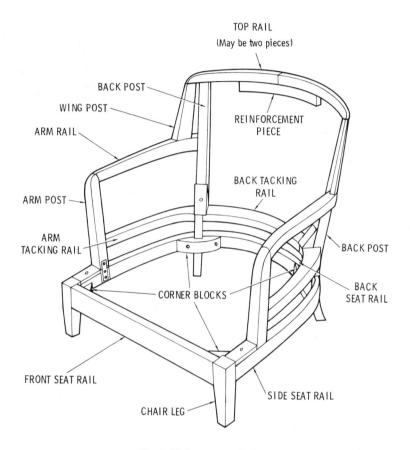

TOP RAIL
(May be two pieces)

BACK POST

WING POST

ARM RAIL

REINFORCEMENT
PIECE

BACK TACKING
RAIL

ARM POST

ARM
TACKING RAIL

CORNER BLOCKS

BACK POST

BACK
SEAT RAIL

FRONT SEAT RAIL

SIDE SEAT RAIL

CHAIR LEG

Fig. 6. Chair parts terminology.

2. Measure and find the center of the width of the frame. Mark the center point with a pencil on the *inside* surface of both the front and the back rails (Fig. 8.)
3. Ideally, a strip of webbing should be centered on this mark with the rest of the webbing divided on either side of it. To determine if this is possible, temporarily secure a strip of webbing in position and space out the rest of them. For a seat opening these strips of webbing should be from ½

129

WEBBING

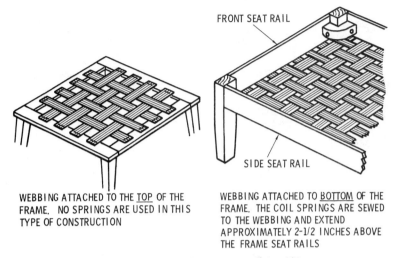

WEBBING ATTACHED TO THE <u>TOP</u> OF THE FRAME. NO SPRINGS ARE USED IN THIS TYPE OF CONSTRUCTION

FRONT SEAT RAIL

SIDE SEAT RAIL

WEBBING ATTACHED TO <u>BOTTOM</u> OF THE FRAME. THE COIL SPRINGS ARE SEWED TO THE WEBBING AND EXTEND APPROXIMATELY 2-1/2 INCHES ABOVE THE FRAME SEAT RAILS

Fig. 7. Different methods of placement of webbing.

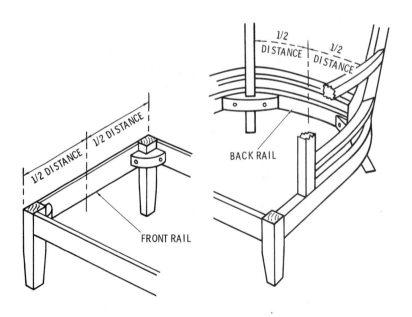

1/2 DISTANCE   1/2 DISTANCE

1/2 DISTANCE   1/2 DISTANCE

BACK RAIL

FRONT RAIL

Fig. 8. Marking the frame for centering the webbing.

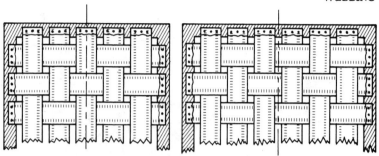

Fig. 9. Spacing of webbing, using one as a center strip.

Fig. 10. Spacing of webbing on both sides of a center mark.

to 1½ inches apart. Mark the position of these strips on the inside of the front rail. Do *not* under any circumstances cut a strip of the webbing length-wise to create the suggested arrangement. This would only weaken the webbing strip. If the webbing cannot be arranged with a strip placed in the center of the frame opening, then arrange them evenly on either side of the center mark. The center mark will then appear half-way between the center-most spacing (Fig. 10).

Fig. 11. Comparative view of webbing tacks and regular upholstery tacks.

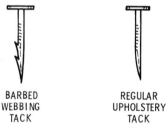

BARBED WEBBING TACK

REGULAR UPHOLSTERY TACK

4. Use number 12 upholstery webbing tacks for tacking the webbing strip to the front rail. Webbing tacks have barbs on the shank which grip the wood better than the ordinary smooth-shanked upholstery tacks (Fig. 11).

5. Position the webbing and tack it to the front rail with three webbing tacks (Fig. 12). Make certain that the tacks are placed so that they enter the exact center of the rail.

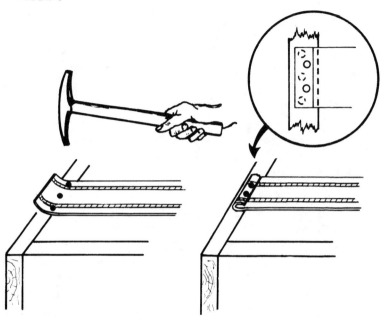

Fig. 12. Attaching the webbing to the bottom of the front frame.

Fig. 13. Folding the webbing back and tacking it.

The closer they are placed to either the front or back edge, the greater the possibility of splitting the wood. This must be avoided at all cost.

6. Cut the webbing strips so that only about 1½ inches of webbing extends beyond the front rail. Fold the end of the webbing back so that it is recessed from the outer edge and tack it to the seat rail with two more webbing tacks (Fig 13), but *not* in a parallel line with the three tacks under the fold of the webbing. Staggering the line of tacks reduces the danger of splitting the frame wood. The last two tacks should be placed ⅛ inch toward the inside of the front rail. Since most furniture rails are at least 1 inch in width, these tacks are still far enough from the inner edge to avoid splitting the wood.

The three tacks, then two arrangement may be reversed to two tacks, then three if desired (see Fig. 14). Addition-

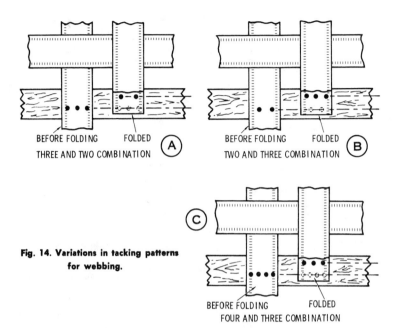

Fig. 14. Variations in tacking patterns for webbing.

BEFORE FOLDING   FOLDED   (A)
THREE AND TWO COMBINATION

BEFORE FOLDING   FOLDED   (B)
TWO AND THREE COMBINATION

BEFORE FOLDING   FOLDED
FOUR AND THREE COMBINATION

ally, some upholsterers prefer a four-and-three arrangement. Recessing the end of the webbing strip hides it from view. There is no danger of unsightly bulges once the cambric and upholstery covering are attached.

7. Stretch the webbing across the frame opening. Place the rubber end of the webbing stretcher against the wood frame with the other end slightly higher. Pull the webbing taut and down over the other end of the webbing stretcher, inserting the nails through the webbing. If additional protection to the frame surface is required, place a block of wood, heavy cloth, or piece of old carpet between the frame and the webbing stretcher.

8. Keeping the rubber edge of the webbing stretcher against the wood frame, force the nail end (the end closest to you) downward until the webbing is taut. The problem here is to determine how taut the webbing should be. There should be some give to the pressure of the hand. Webbing must give under the weight of the individual sitting in the chair.

133

The amount of "give" is directly related to the natural resilience the jute fiber. If the webbing is pulled too tight, the tacks may be pulled loose or the jute fibers in the webbing may begin to weaken under the strain. On the other hand, a webbing that is too loose will not provide a secure seat foundation. Springs will eventually slip out of place, and the stuffing will begin to fall through.

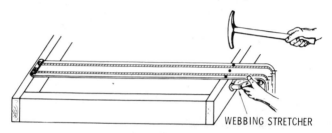

WEBBING STRETCHER

Fig. 15. Stretching the webbing.

9. Use number 12 upholstery webbing tacks and tack the webbing strip to the back rail of the frame. Be certain that the webbing strip is parallel to the side rails. The webbing tacks should be evenly spaced and in a row. Cut the webbing strip off about 1½ inches beyond the frame and fold

Fig. 16. Completing the webbing (front to back).

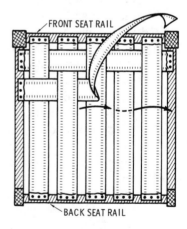

Fig. 17. Interlacing the webbing (side to side).

back. The edge of the fold should run next to the parallel line of tacks. The fold of the webbing strip will then be recessed from the outside edge of the back rail of the frame. Tack the folded webbing in place being careful to stagger the tacks in relation to those beneath the fold (Fig. 15).

10. Follow the same procedure and tack the rest of the webbing strips in place between the front and back rails (Fig. 16). Keep the webbing strips straight and evenly spaced. The webbing will later be used as a guide for the attachment of the springs.

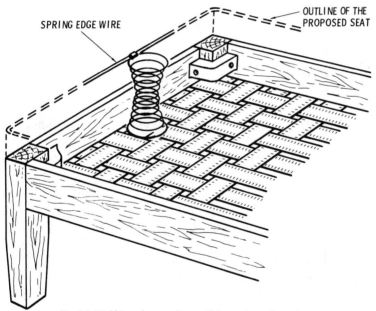

Fig. 18. Webbing close to front rail for spring edge wire.

11. The webbing strips running parallel to the back and front seat rails must be interlaced with those already tacked in place (Fig. 17). If the seat is to have spring-edge construction, then the first strip of webbing must be placed as close to the front rail as possible (Fig. 18). This will give additional support to the front row of springs.

12. Select either side rail and tack the end of the webbing strip in place. Use the same procedure as outlined in Steps Five through Eleven. Remember that each strip must be interlaced to give greater strength and better weight dispersement.

WEBBING THE BACKS

Backs, particularly padded backs, do not need the webbing strength required for the seat. Most of the pressure of weight is

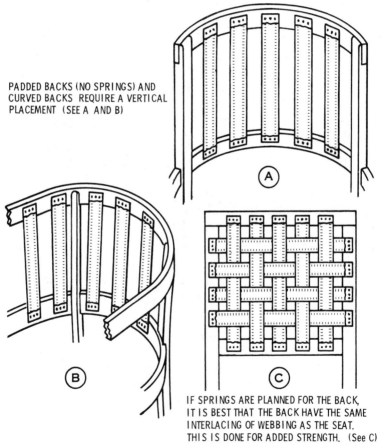

PADDED BACKS (NO SPRINGS) AND CURVED BACKS REQUIRE A VERTICAL PLACEMENT (SEE A AND B)

Ⓐ

Ⓑ

Ⓒ

IF SPRINGS ARE PLANNED FOR THE BACK, IT IS BEST THAT THE BACK HAVE THE SAME INTERLACING OF WEBBING AS THE SEAT. THIS IS DONE FOR ADDED STRENGTH. (See C)

Fig. 19. Webbing on various types of chair backs.

exerted downward toward the floor. The direction of the pressure is primarily through the seat frame opening. However, some pressure is exerted against the back. Since the webbing in the back does not need to be as strong as the seat webbing, it can be stretched by hand rather than using the webbing stretcher tool. In addition, a lighter weight of jute webbing may be used or cotton webbing may be substituted.

The same procedures for attaching the webbing to the seat rails is used on the back. Here, horizontal interlaced strips are used only when marshall spring units are part of the back construction. This gives additional support. One or two horizontal webbing strips are also used when the back is a particularly high one. When the curve in the back is a particularly strong one (as in barrel-back chairs), the horizontal webbing should be avoided since it tends to distort the form (Fig. 19).

WEBBING THE ARMS

Attaching webbing to arms offers little difficulty. No particular pressure is exerted against the webbing. The primary purpose of arm webbing is to provide a stiff background as support for the layers of stuffing and upholstery material added to complete the upholstering of the arm. The webbing strips are always tacked to the *inside* of the frame. They may be stretched by hand (that is without a webbing stretcher), but should not be cut to length. Use the same procedures for attaching the webbing as outlined in Steps Five through Eleven (Fig. 20).

In some instances, a solid piece of burlap is used on the arms instead of individual webbing strips.

WORKING WITHOUT WEBBING

There are methods for avoiding the use of webbing in open frame construction. Two of these are found in the use of bar spring units or sagless springs. Bar spring units are so named because rows of springs are attached to a metal bar which is then attached to the frame (Fig. 21). Sagless springs are strips of spring wire bent to form a zigzag pattern and coiled so that when straightened the

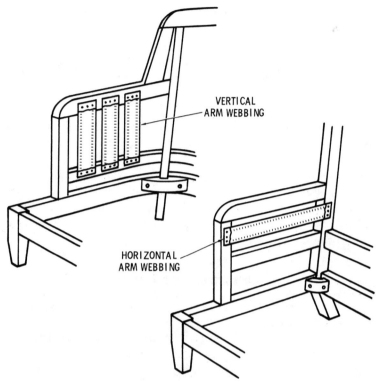

VERTICAL
ARM WEBBING

HORIZONTAL
ARM WEBBING

Fig. 20. Arm webbing.

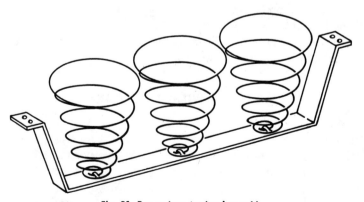

Fig. 21. Bar springs (spring bar unit).

138

wire attempts to return to the coiled position. This zigzag-coiled form of the spring produces the spring action for the seat. The sagless springs are attached to the frame with special metal clips (Fig. 22).

Both bar spring units and sagless springs are discussed in greater detail in the next chapter.

REPAIRING THE WEBBING

All webbing is subject to deterioration over a period of time. The rate of deterioration depends, of course, upon many factors among which the quality of the webbing is foremost. A high grade of jute webbing, for example, will last longer than a low grade.

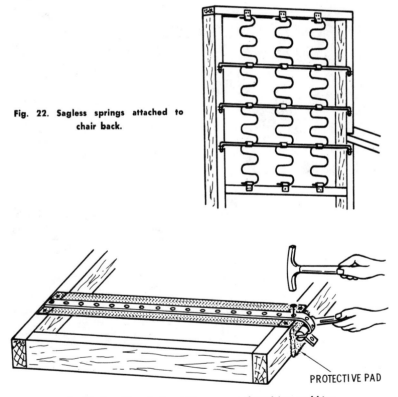

Fig. 22. Sagless springs attached to chair back.

PROTECTIVE PAD

Fig. 23. Attaching steel webbing over weakened jute webbing

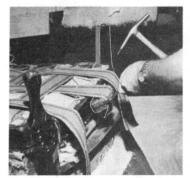 

Courtesy Kwik-Bed Sofa Corp.

Fig. 24. Typical installation sequence of webbing.

As the webbing becomes weaker it loses its resiliency. It no longer is capable of returning to its original position when the weight of the sitter is removed from the seat. This causes the springs that are attached to the weakened webbing to sag.

Remove the cambric dust-cover on the bottom of the frame and examine the webbing. If some of the webbing has deteriorated, there is good reason to believe that the remainder of the webbing is also close to doing so. The question is whether or not all the webbing should be removed and replaced or only the weakened section.

The jute webbing can be reinforced with steel webbing which is attached to the frame over the original webbing. The steel webbing should be interlaced and crisscrossed.

Unlike jute webbing the steel webbing used as reinforcement is precut to a length of three to four inches longer than the frame on either side. A webbing stretcher designed to be used with steel webbing is used to stretch the webbing across the frame opening. Once the metal webbing strips are tacked in place the excess is cut off. (Fig. 23).

Before the steel webbing is attached, it might be wise to examine the springs. If the weakened jute webbing had caused any of the springs to sag, then the twine used to tie the springs in place may have loosened. If this is the case, securely re-tie the springs before tacking the metal webbing in place.

Replacing or reinforcing only a portion of the webbing is not recommended. Although the remaining webbing may appear to be in good condition, it is older than the new webbing and there is no longer any uniformity of strength. It is advised to either employ a total reinforcement (as described above) or to do a complete stripping of the webbing and install new material.

The chair used to illustrate the stripping process in Chapter Three was shown to have damaged webbing (Figs. 12, 13, 14 of Chapter 3). Because the undamaged webbing was also considered likely to be close to decay, it was advised that all the webbing be replaced. The task was made easier by the fact that the bottoms of the coiled seat springs were not sewed to the webbing, but to a burlap layer placed on top of the webbing.

The new webbing was first attached from the back to the front seat rails. Horizontal strips of webbing were then stretched from side to side and interlaced with the webbing connecting the back and front rails (Fig. 24).

CHAPTER 7

Springs

Springs are devices designed to give under pressure and to regain their former shape once the pressure is removed. By this simple process, springs have the major responsibility for providing seating comfort in upholstered furniture. Seating comfort, then is directly related to the quality of spring construction.

Springs are made from steel wire that is highly tempered and coated with a substance to prevent corrosion. They are manufactured in a number of gauges and a variety of sizes.

The three types of springs discussed in this section are: (1) coil springs (both single and double coil); (2) innerspring units or marshall springs; and (3) sagless-wire or sinuous coil springs.

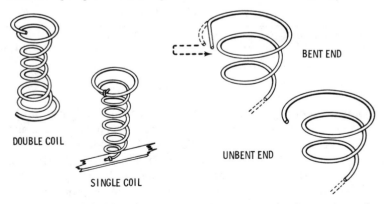

DOUBLE COIL

SINGLE COIL

BENT END

UNBENT END

Fig. 1. Single and double coil springs.   **Fig. 2. Bent and unbent spring ends.**

143

COIL SPRINGS

Coil springs can be purchased either with single or double coils (Fig. 1). The single coil type is shaped like a cone and is used in the construction of bar spring units (see the section on bar spring units in this chapter). These normally are used in cheaper grades of furniture. Better quality furniture will use double coil springs, which generally must be attached one by one.

Double coil springs can be used in the seat, back, arms, or cushion. Their method of attachment depends upon the type of base provided (wood board, jute webbing, or steel webbing). This is discussed a little further on in the chapter. It was indicated above that double coil springs were superior in quality to the single coil type. The reason for this (an important consideration in furniture construction) is that they provide greater seating comfort. Even among double coil springs there is a variety of types that display varying degrees of comfort. The seating comfort provided by a spring is related to the degree of firmness it is capable of giving. The firmness is based upon the gauge of the wire or the width of the coil at the center of the spring.

Double coil springs used in seats range in height from 4 (11 gauge) to 14 (8 gauge) inches. They are made so that the spring wire is left open at both ends (Fig. 2). The end that is to be placed up is bent so that it will not tear the fabric.

Table 1. Coil Spring Dimensions.

Spring Number	00	0	1	2	3	4	5	6
Height (inches)	4	5	6	8	9½	10½	12	14
Wire Gauge	11	11	11	10½	9½	9½	8½	8

Each height represents a different size spring. Each size can be obtained in three different grades of firmness: hard, medium, and soft. The different grades are determined by the width of the center portion of the double coil (Fig. 3). The hard grade is represented by springs with the narrowest center width; the soft grade has the widest center width. The most commonly used springs range in height from 7 to 10½ inches with a medium firmness.

COIL SPRINGS IN THE SEAT

Heavy gauge (9 to 11 gauge wire) double coil springs are used for seats because they can take the greatest punishment and still produce

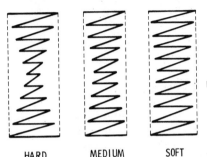

HARD   MEDIUM   SOFT

Fig. 3. Construction shapes for the three degrees of spring softness.

the most comfort. The top wire is bent to prevent it from ripping the fabric. It is not necessary to do this with the bottom end of the wire since it is attached to the webbing.

As mentioned previously, seat springs are sold in soft, medium, and hard sizes (the size is determined by the width of the center portion of the coil, *not* the height. A hard spring has a narrow center width; whereas a soft spring has a wide one). These "sizes" are actually the degrees of compression each spring is subjected to when pressure is placed upon it. They are very important to consider when tying down the springs.

PILLOW SPRINGS

The name may be misleading for pillow springs are not used in pillows. Pillow springs are made from a lighter gauge wire. These are generally obtainable in heights ranging from 4 inches (14 gauge wire) to 10 inches (12 gauge wire) (Table 2).

Table 2. Pillow Spring Dimensions.

Height (inches)	4	6	8	10
Wire Gauge	14	14	12	12

Both ends of the spring wire are attached to the coil. This is a precaution taken to protect the fabric from being ripped by the exposed wire. Because of their light weight, pillow springs are used in backs and arms—never in seats (Fig. 4).

145

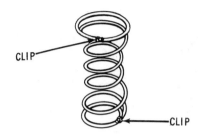

Fig. 4. Pillow spring.

CUSHION SPRINGS

Cushion springs are sometimes used in automobile, truck, and bus seats. They can be purchased in either 4 inch (11 gauge) or 6 inch (10 gauge) heights with one or both ends tied. The gauge wire used in cushion springs is a bit heavier than that used in pillow springs. Note that a 4 inch pillow spring is made from a 14 gauge wire and a 4 inch cushion spring uses an 11 gauge wire. There is no inconsistency here. The height of a spring does not necessarily have any relationship to the gauge of the wire used.

INNERSPRING UNITS

Innerspring (or marshall spring) units are used in backs, cushions, the seats of overstuffed furniture, and sometimes arms.

The springs are 3 inches in diameter and are individually sewn into burlap or muslin pockets. The marshall spring units used in backs contain springs with a height of 6 inches. Those in the cushion units are smaller, usually only 3½ inches.

Innersprings can be purchased as ready-made units or in strips. If they are purchased in strips, they must be sewn together to form the size or shape unit desired. These strips consist of groups of springs (usually six to a group) sewn into their burlap or muslin casing. The groups are separated by a space of 2½ to 3 inches. These are the bending sections of the strip. The strip can be bent or folded back on itself at these points to form a square or rectangular spring unit. The successive strips are sewn together with stitching twine (Fig. 5). Sew along both the bottom and top of the springs.

Innersprings are sometimes used as the second layer of seat springs in overstuffed furniture. Generally, they are used in the loose cushion, but from time to time they are sewn into position over the

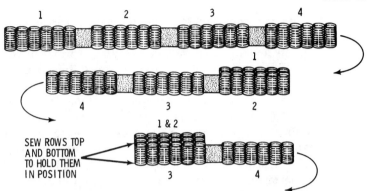

SEW ROWS TOP
AND BOTTOM
TO HOLD THEM
IN POSITION

Fig. 5. The construction of an innerspring unit.

first layer of springs (which is constructed in the form of a spring edge seat). Before constructing and attaching the innerspring unit, finish upholstering the inside arms and the back. This is important because you will now be able to gauge the size of the innerspring unit required. Use paper to measure and cut a pattern for the springs. The pattern should be about 1 inch less than the area covered by the seat.

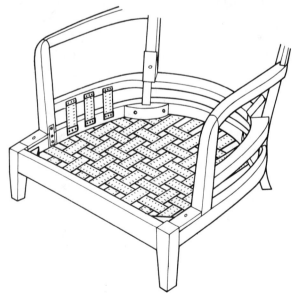

Fig. 6. Webbed base for coil springs.

147

This 1 inch difference will be filled by the cotton lining surrounding the spring unit beneath its muslin cover.

Place a burlap covering over the bottom layer of springs. If you wish, spread a thin layer (about ½ inch) of loose stuffing over the burlap and sew it down with a random stitch.

Using the paper pattern you just made, construct the innerspring unit. When you have finished sewing it together, test it for fit. Do you still have your 1 inch clearance on all sides? If so, center the innerspring unit and sew it in place. Next, take strips of cotton (the height of the innerspring unit) and fill in the 1 inch allowance around the springs. Place two layers of cotton in place (see Chapter 10—Cushions—for greater detail).

ATTACHING COIL SPRINGS

The method used to attach double coil springs depends upon the type of base. The four most common types are:

1. the webbed base
2. the web panel base
3. the slat base
4. the solid wood base

The webbed base (Fig. 6) consists of parallel, interwoven rows of webbing stretched from side to side and from back to the front. The springs are usually attached to the webbing by sewing.

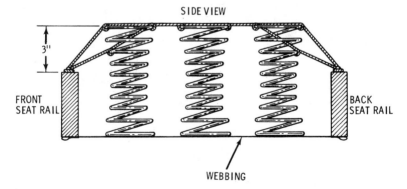

Fig. 7. A typical method of tying down coil springs.

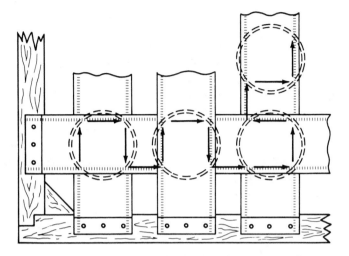

BOTTOM VIEW OF THE FRAME. THE TWINE
USED TO STITCH THE SPRINGS TO THE WEBBING
IS EXPOSED TO VIEW FROM THIS SIDE

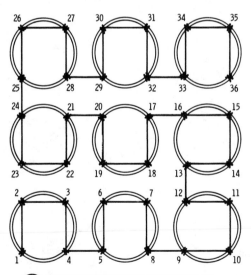

THE STITCHING PATTERN USED TO STITCH THE
COIL SPRINGS TO THE WEBBING.

Fig. 8. Stitching coil springs to the webbing.

149

As soon as the webbing is attached, the number of springs needed for the seat can be estimated. Usually this amounts to three rows of three springs each for a total of nine springs. However, the total number of springs will, in the long run, be determined by the size of the frame opening. The springs should be spaced so that they are (1) evenly distributed (the same distance apart); (2) not too close together (results in a hard uncomfortable seat); and (3) not too far apart (results in a loose, lumpy seat).

The type of spring you select (that is, the height of the spring and the gauge of its wire) is determined by the amount of resiliency you want in the seat. The degree of resiliency increases the higher the spring is tied *above* the top of the seat rail. The lower you tie the spring, the lower the resiliency. Generally, you are safe if you keep the top of the spring at least 3 inches above the top of the seat rail (Fig. 7).

Thread a double-pointed straight needle (or a comparable curved needle, if you prefer) with stitching twine. Take four stitches for each spring. The final stitch on each spring should

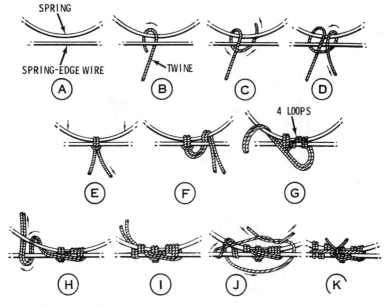

Fig. 9. Using the clove-hitch knot to tie a spring edge wire to a coil spring.

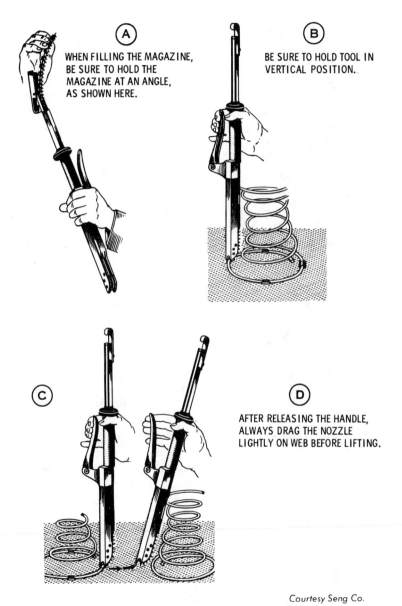

WHEN FILLING THE MAGAZINE,
BE SURE TO HOLD THE
MAGAZINE AT AN ANGLE,
AS SHOWN HERE.

BE SURE TO HOLD TOOL IN
VERTICAL POSITION.

AFTER RELEASING THE HANDLE,
ALWAYS DRAG THE NOZZLE
LIGHTLY ON WEB BEFORE LIFTING.

Courtesy Seng Co.

Fig. 10. Using the hand-operated "Klinch-It" tool.

151

be directly opposite the next spring to be stitched. Your stitching pattern should be planned as illustrated in Fig. 8.

Make certain to carefully align the springs in rows before final attachment. Springs to which spring-edges are attached are generally placed against the seat rails of the frame.

Spring-edge wire is purchased in a 9 or 10 gauge wire for seats. Its primary purpose is to strengthen the edge of the seat and to create the desired contour. Fig. 9 indicates how and where the spring-edge wire is sewn with heavy cord to the tops of the double coil springs.

Double coil springs can also be attached to webbing with staples. The Klinch-It Tool (manufactured by The Seng Company) is a labor-saving device used to fasten springs to webbed bases Fig. 10. It is available in either hand-operated or air-powered models. The advantages of stapling the springs to the webbed base are: (1) the time saved by not having to stitch each spring to the webbing and (2) the replacement of stitching twine with the longer lasting steel staples. Fig. 11 illustrates the method for using the hand-operated model (the one most likely to be found in the smaller shops).

Webbed panel bases are made from a single piece of webbing material (although burlap is sometimes used) large enough to fit inside the furniture frame with about a 2½ to 4 inch gap between the panel end the frame on all sides.

Helical springs are attached to the frame with metal clips and to a wire imbedded in the edge of the webbed seat panel. The springs are sewn or stapled to the panel (Fig. 11).

The slat base is used in the cheaper lines of furniture. It naturally does not have the resiliency of a webbed base. Springs can be attached to it with staples, tacks, or folded strips of material (Fig. 12). Springs are attached to solid wood bases in the same manner. However, in the case of these wood bases, it is necessary to add a cloth "silencer" to reduce the noise made by the metal spring striking the wood (Fig. 13).

TYING COIL SPRINGS

Earlier it was pointed out that a spring had three degrees of compression, and that these were expressed it terms of firmness—

soft, medium, and hard. It was also pointed out that the degree of firmness was an important factor to consider when tying springs down.

All springs are tied down in such a way that they will not slip sideways out of position. They must also be tied according to a uniform height so that each spring has a maximum limit to its upward expansion. Springs are tied to the frame with a stitching twine. Generally, this twine is a 6-ply hemp with a wax coating to give it longer life.

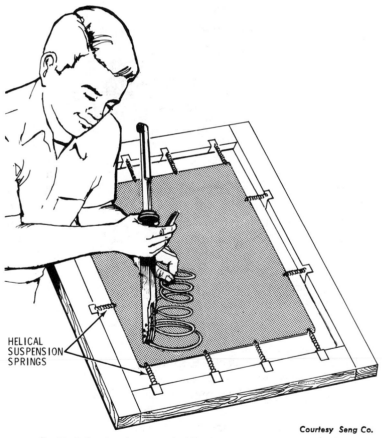

HELICAL
SUSPENSION
SPRINGS

Courtesy Seng Co.

Fig. 11. Coil springs being attached by staples to a webbed-panel base.

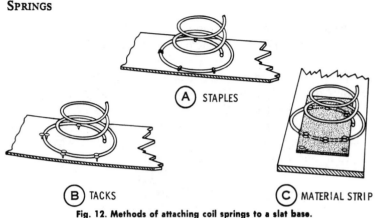

Fig. 12. Methods of attaching coil springs to a slat base.

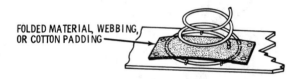

Fig. 13. The use of a "silencer."

Both single coil (those used in spring bars) and double coil springs must be tied down to the frame. The level at which a spring is tied depends upon whether it is a hard, medium, or soft grade of firmness. Before tying, each spring is completely free of any restraint and stands at a height approximately 1 to 1½ inches above its "normal" height. The *hard* springs are tied at this height (i.e. 1 to 1½ inches above normal height). *Soft* springs, on the other hand, are tied 2 inches below normal height, while *medium* springs are tied 1 inch below.

TYING THE ROUNDED SEAT

The two-way (or four-knot) tie is the tying pattern recommended for rounded seats. There are no diagonal rows of twine in the two-way pattern—only cross-ties and the back-to-front rail rows (Fig. 14).

A return tie is used in the two-way pattern to cant or tip the tops of the outer coil springs to round the edges of the rounded

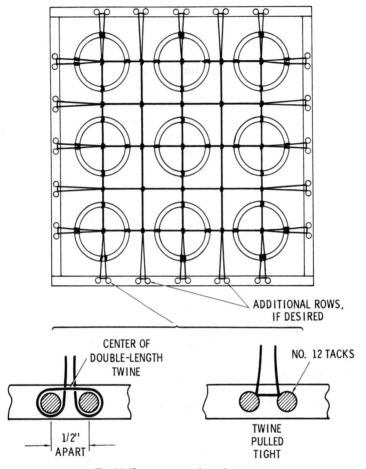

CENTER OF
DOUBLE-LENGTH
TWINE

NO. 12 TACKS

1/2"
APART

TWINE
PULLED
TIGHT

ADDITIONAL ROWS,
IF DESIRED

Fig. 14. The two-way spring tying pattern.

seat. This consists of a length of twine looped around the upper coils of the springs closest to the frame edge and parallel to a second length of twine attached to a lower coil of the same spring. Occasionally, the twine is doubled in length for the two-way tying pattern. As a result, the construction of the return tie differs from that used when a single length of twine is used to tie the springs.

155

The procedure for tying a rounded seat with a twine and no return is as follows:

1. Drive No. 12 tacks into the frame opposite the *center* of each row of springs. The tacks should be about ½ inch apart. Do not drive them all the way in. If you plan to have additional rows of twine between the spring rows, then place two more No. 12 tacks in the frame opposite the point of which each row of twine will be located (Fig. 14).

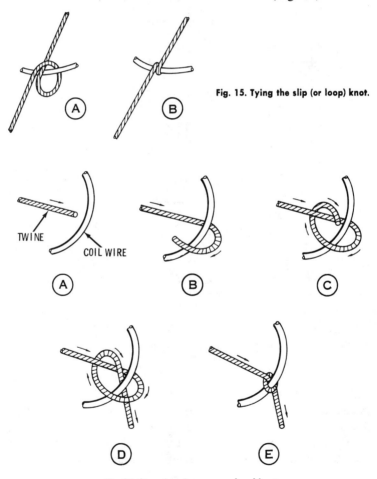

Fig. 15. Tying the slip (or loop) knot.

TWINE

COIL WIRE

Fig. 16. Steps in tying an over-hand knot.

2. Measure the distance across the frame from side to side and from back to front. Double the amount and add about ten inches for knots. Cut a length of twine with these measurements for each row in your tying pattern.

3. The two types of knots most commonly used in spring tying are (1) loop (or slip) knots and (2) overhand knots (Figs. 15 and 16). Some prefer to use the loop knots because it is easier to adjust the springs while each row is being tied. An overhand knot, however, results in a more permanent type knot that is not as prone to slip as the loop knot.

4. Begin at the back and loop the centers of each of the twines around each of the pairs of tacks (point "a"—Fig. 17) in the frame. Drive the tacks in tight against the twine.

5. Begin with the center-most row of springs. Take the doubled length of twine and loop it to the top section of the coil directly opposite the tacks on the seat rail (point "b").

6. Push the edge of spring down to the desired height above the frame and pull the twine so that all slack is removed. Extend the twine to the inside of the top coil and make a knot (point "c").

7. Extend the twine to each of the springs in the center row repeating the knots on each coil that is crossed (points "d" thru "g"). When the spring closest to the front rail is reached, tie it down to the same height as you did the first spring you tied in Step Six. Attach the doubled twine to the tacks in the front seat rail (point "h") and cut off the excess.

8. Before driving in the tacks on the front seat rail, check to see that the springs are all correctly aligned. If not, loosen the knots and straighten them. Once you are satisfied with their alignment, drive the tacks in tight against the twine and frame.

9. Repeat Steps One through Eight for each row of springs until all the rows extending from the back to the front rails are completed.

10. Repeat Steps One through Nine for each of the cross-ties (rows running from side rail to side rail). Tie an additional knot in each twine running from the back rail to the front rail that you cross (points "x"—Fig. 18).

157

11. Additional ties between rows may be added as illustration in Fig. 14.

A return tie was defined previously as a length of twine looped around the *top* coils of the springs closest to the frame edge and parallel to a second length of twine attached to a *lower* coil of the same spring. The return tie is designed to round the edge of the seat and to provide less opportunity for the springs to become loose and move out of position. The procedure for tying a rounded seat with a return tie depends upon whether a double-length or

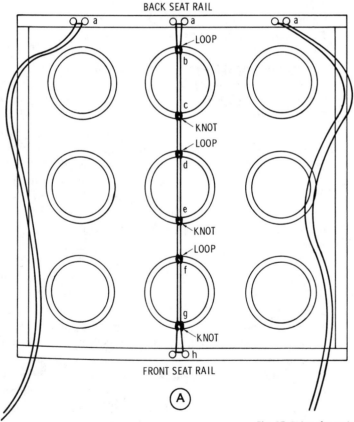

Fig. 17. Tying the springs

single-length twine is to be used for the tying. The method for tying the two types of return ties is as follows:

1. For a double-length twine, the twine should be twice the distance from front to back plus an allowance of 10 or 12 inches for knots. After cutting the twine to proper length (make enough lengths for each row of coils), tie one end of the twine to one of the two rear tacks in each coil row (point "a"—Fig. 19). Then, beginning with the center row of springs, loop the twine around the second coil from the top of the spring nearest the back rail (point "b"—Fig. 19).
2. Push the spring down to the desired height above the frame

BACK SEAT RAIL

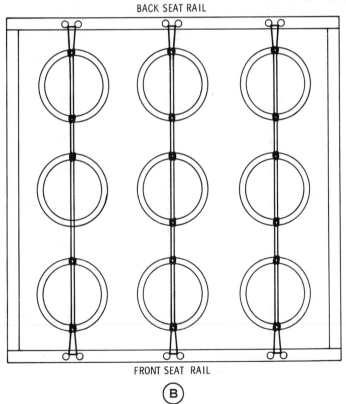

FRONT SEAT RAIL

(B)

(back to front rows).

and pull the twine through so that all the slack is removed. Tie a secure knot at point "b." Extend the twine up through the same spring to the inside top coil and make a second knob (point "c"—Fig. 19).

3. Take the twine across the entire row tying a knot on each coil.
4. At the spring nearest the front rail, tie a knot to the inside top coil (point "f"—Fig. 19). Take the twine down through the spring and tie another knot to the outside coil second from the top (point "g"—Fig. 19).

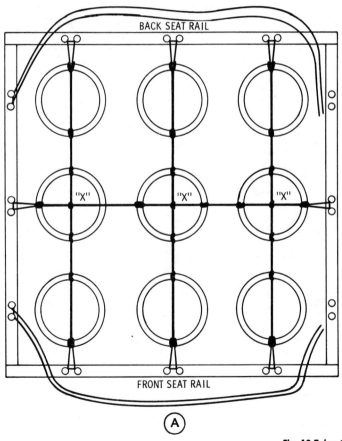

BACK SEAT RAIL

"X"   "X"   "X"

FRONT SEAT RAIL

(A)

Fig. 18 Tying the

5. Pull the twine down to the pair of tacks on the front seat rail and loop it around both tacks (points "h" and "i"). Check for spring alignment and drive in the tacks. DO NOT cut the excess twine.

6. Repeat Steps One through Five for each spring until all the rows extending from back to front rails are completed.

7. Take the excess length of twine left at the end of Step 5 and continue the tying from points "j" through "p" back across the top of the coils. Note particularly points "j" and "o" where this return line will be tied to the top coil of the springs nearest the seat rail. These points should be pulled taut so the outside edge of the coil is pulled downward toward the rail to give the rounded effect desired.

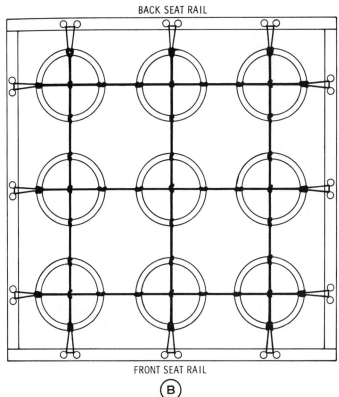

BACK SEAT RAIL

FRONT SEAT RAIL

(B)

springs (side to side).

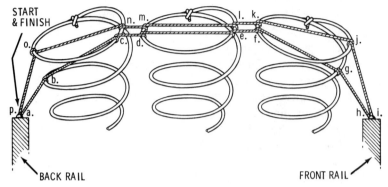

Fig. 19. Tying a return tie with a double-length twine.

8. Repeat the procedure just described for the remainder of the rows extending from the back to the front rail. When you have completed this, do the cross-ties using twine of a length twice the width plus knot allowance.

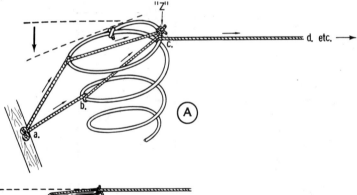

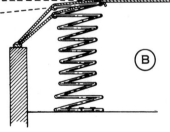

Fig. 20. The return tie on the rounded seat using a single-length cord. Note the degree of depression on the top coil.

For tying a rounded seat with a single crossing of the twine, it is necessary to add (after having made the initial measurements across the frame opening) enough twine at both ends to account for the return tie. This will usually amount to about 10 to 12 inches. Fig. 20 illustrates the tying of a rounded seat with a return tie using only a single crossing of twine.

1. Loop the twine around the tack pairs with one end of the twine being 5 to 6 inches long and the balance of the twine with the other end. Drive the backs down securing the twine.
2. With the longer piece of twine, starting at "a" proceed to "b," then "c" as explained in the previous procedure.
3. When the other side is reached, wrap the twine around the tacks and drive them down.

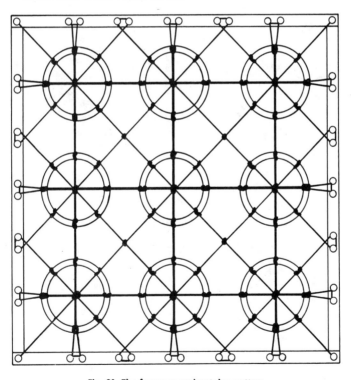

Fig. 21. The four-way spring tying pattern.

4. Now pull the outer edge of the top coil down as noted in Fig. 20 and tie the other end of the twine securely at point "z."

TYING THE FLAT SEAT

The flat seat is tied in the same manner as described for the rounded seat with the following exceptions: (1) a single length of twine is used for tying the springs; (2) a diagonal row is sometimes

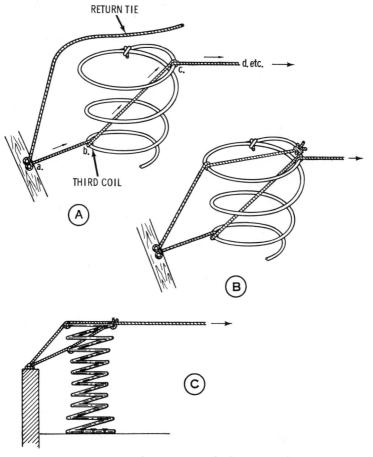

Fig. 22. The return tie on the flat seat.

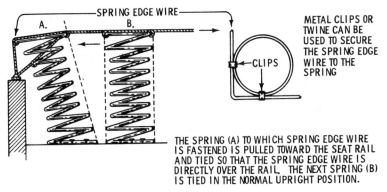

SPRING EDGE WIRE

A.   B.

METAL CLIPS OR TWINE CAN BE USED TO SECURE THE SPRING EDGE WIRE TO THE SPRING

CLIPS

THE SPRING (A) TO WHICH SPRING EDGE WIRE IS FASTENED IS PULLED TOWARD THE SEAT RAIL AND TIED SO THAT THE SPRING EDGE WIRE IS DIRECTLY OVER THE RAIL. THE NEXT SPRING (B) IS TIED IN THE NORMAL UPRIGHT POSITION.

Fig. 23. Tying a spring which is attached to a spring edge wire.

used (this results in a four-way or eight knot tie on each spring. See Fig. 21); and (3) the return tie is made with the lower length of twine tied initially to the outside edge of the *third* coil (rather than the second coil (down from the top of the outer springs. (Fig. 22).

A spring edge wire is occasionally added to the front and sometimes to the sides of a flat seat. The front row of springs must be uniformly tipped forward so that the top outermost edge of each coil is in line with the outside front edge of the frame. If the spring edge extends around to the sides of the chair, the same must be done with the coil springs to which the spring edge is to be attached. Fig. 23 illustrates how these springs are to be tied.

The tying of the spring edge wire to the coil springs was described earlier in this chapter.

TYING THE BACK

Backs are tied with the two-way or four knot tying pattern. Both the rounded and flat styles (usually with a spring edge wire) are used. The return tie is also included in the tying pattern. Tying begins at the center row bottom. The vertical rows are tied first; the cross-ties next.

SPRING BAR UNITS

Spring bar units consist of conical, single coil springs attached to a bar in evenly spaced groups of two, three, or four. These

165

springs form an inverted cone with the small end being attached to the bar. The bar itself varies in length from 16 to 26 inches (Fig. 24).

Springs bar units are used to take the place of webbing. Because of their type of construction, they need no further support. The spring bars can be attached to the frame with nails, tacks, or screws. One of the advantages of spring bar units is that the springs have already been spaced and attached to the steel bar.

Spring bar units do not have the resiliency of double coil springs and are considered by some to not be as comfortable.

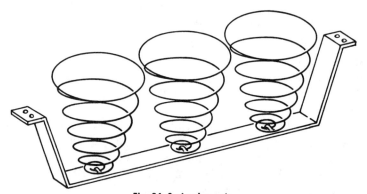

Fig. 24. Spring bar unit.

SAGLESS WIRE SPRINGS

Sagless wire springs are easier and quicker to install than the coil variety. Unlike coil spring construction, no webbing is used and it is not necessary to tie the springs down to any particular height

The lengths of sagless spring wire are attached to the front and back seat rails (and to the top and bottom rails on the back) with special metal clips. The rows may be joined together with helical springs. Sometimes metal connectors or links are used instead of helicals on the interior rows (Fig. 25).

Sagless springs are made from a continuous length of spring wire that has been bent into a zig-zag shape and rolled into a coil. When a length of this spring wire is removed from the coil, cut to size, and attached to the frame, we have an example of sagless (sinuous) wire spring construction. The resilience is produced by the steady pull of the spring wire in its attempt to regain its former coiled shape.

Sagless springs are normally sold in bundles of 10 coils or in boxes of cut lengths (standard radii). Pre-cut lengths with special radii can also be ordered. These special radii are used for furniture pieces that require a lower crown. Generally, the larger the radii, the lower crown. However, an increase in the radius requires

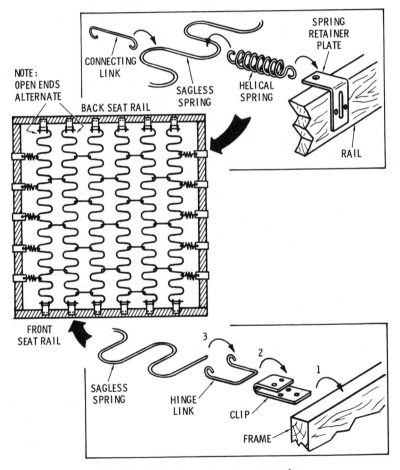

Fig. 25. Typical sagless wire spring construction.

167

an adjustment in the wire gauge (the gauge must be increased correspondingly) and another adjustment in the spring length (it must be shortened). If these adjustments are not taken, the support characteristics will be much lower.

A 7 to 8 gauge wire is generally recommended for chair seats and a 10 to 12 gauge wire for backs. A well-known brand name of sagless springs, "No-Sag," is sold in three different types: (1) Original "No-Sag," (2) "XL," and (3) "Supr-Loop." Table 3 illustrates the size requirements for a variety of seat and back dimensions.

These springs can also be purchased in custom configurations that can be adapted to special furniture designs.

Table 3. "No-Sag" Spring Sizes for Seat and Back Applications.

ORIGINAL NO-SAG

SEATS				BACKS			
Inside Rail Dimension	Standard Crown	Gauge No-Sag	Length	Inside Rail Dimension	Standard Crown	Gauge No-Sag	Length
12"	1¼"	11	11¾"	16"	1½"	12 or 13	16"
13	1¼	10½	12¾	17	1⅝	12 or 13	17
14	1⅜	10	13¾				
15	1½	10	14¾	18	1¾	12 or 13	18¼
16	1⅝	10	15¾	19	1⅞	12	19¼
17	1⅝	9½	16¾				
18	1¾	9	17¾	20	2	12	20¼
19	1¾	9	18¾	21	2	12	21¼
20	1⅞	9	20				
21	1⅞	9	21	22	2	12	22¼
22	1⅞	8½	22	23	2¼	11½ or 12	23½
23	2	8½	23				
24	2	8½	24	24	2¼	11½	24½
25	2	8	24⅞	25	2½	11	25½
26	2	8	25¾				
27	2	8	26¾	26	2½	11	26½

Courtesy No-Sag Co.

"Modu-Loop" is another trade name of the No-Sag Company. This is a high carbon steel spring which is produced in a square, flat surface (Fig. 26). The dimensions of "Modu-Loop" springs used in backs and seats are given in Table 4.

Sagless wire springs are attached to the frame with metal clips. "No-Sag" offers a variety of these clips. Some clips are designed specifically for use on back frames (Fig. 27), while others are used on seats (Fig. 28). A large number of miscellaneous clips are available that can be used in various furniture construction (Fig. 29).

It was mentioned earlier that the rows of sagless wire springs were tied together with either metal connecting links or helical springs (the helicals are *always* used to tie side of the spring rows

Table 3 (Cont.) "No-Sag" Spring Sizes for Seat and Back Applications.

"XL"

SEATS

Inside Seat Dimension	Standard Crown	Gauge XL	Length
12"	1⅞"	11½	11¼"
13	1	11	12¼
14	1⅛	10½	13¼
15	1⅛	10½	14¼
16	1 3/16	10½	15¼
17	1⅜	10	16¼
18	1¼	9½	17¼
19	1¼	9½	18¼
20	1½	9½	19½
21	1 9/16	9½	20½
22	1¾	9	21½
23	1 13/16	9	22½
24	2	9	23½
25	1½	8½	24⅜
26	1 9/16	8½	25¼
27	1¾	8½	26¼

BACKS

Inside Back Dimension	Standard Crown	Gauge XL	Length
16"	1⅛"	12	15½"
17	1⅜	12	16½
18	1½	12	17¾
19	1⅝	12	18¾
20	1⅞	12	19¾
21	1⅝	12	20¾
22	1⅝	12	21¾
23	1¾	12	23
24	1¾	12	24
25	1⅞	11½	25
26	2	11½	26

Courtesy No-Sag Co.

next to the frame edge regardless of how the inner rows are tied). Metal connecting links provide a cheaper method of tying the inner spring rows (Fig. 29). They are sold in standard sizes of 1 inch to 6 inches with ⅛ inch increments. It is recommended that each link be 1⅜ inch shorter than the spacing of the metal clips holding ends of the rows of sagless wire springs. This will reduce noise to a minimum and provide a taut, firm seat.

Hinged links (Fig. 29) can be inserted between the clips on the back seat rail and the sagless wire spring to create movable pivots that increase the arc of the spring up to as much as 2½ inches. Hinge links are sold in three lengths: (1) regular (1 1/16 inch); (2) medium (1 7/16 inch); and (3) long (1 13/16 inch).

Table 3 (Cont.). "No-Sag" Spring Sizes for Seat and Back Applications.

SUPR-LOOP

SEATS				BACKS			
Inside Seat Dimension	Standard Crown	Gauge Supr-Loop	Length	Inside Back Dimension	Standard Crown	Gauge	Length
12"	1¼"	10	11½"	16"	1⅜"	11½	15½"
13	1¼	10	12½				
14	1¼	9½	13½	17	1½	11½	16½
15	1½	9½	14½	18	1¾	11½	17¾
16	1¾	9	15⅝				
17	1¾	9	16⅝	19	2	11½	19
18	1¾	9	17⅝	20	2	11½	20
19	1⅞	9	18½				
20	1⅞	9	19½	21	2	11	20⅞
21	1⅞	9-8½	20½	22	2	11	21⅞
22	1⅞	8½	21½				
23	1⅞	8½-8	22¼	23	2¼	11	22¾
24	2	8	23½	24	2¼	11	23¾
25	1¾	8	24½				
26	1¾	8	25⅛	25	2¼	11	24¾
27	1¾	8	26⅛	26	2¼	10½	25⅞

Courtesy No-Sag Co.

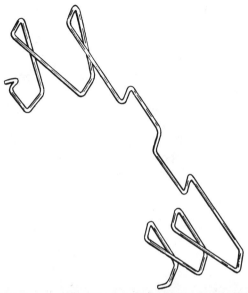

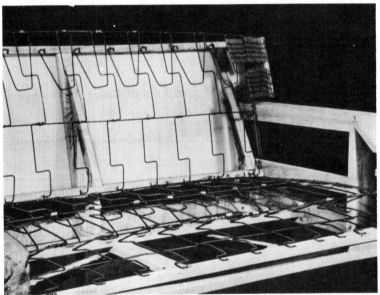

Fig. 26. The "Modu-Loop" construction.

Flat links (Fig. 29) are used to fasten sagless wire springs to one another or to a border wire. They are available in four sizes depending upon the gauge of the wires to be connected. Pilers are used to close the open ends.

Borderwire (Fig. 30), the equivalent to spring edge wire in coil spring construction, is available in gauges 6 to 12 and any specified length. It is used to shape and add support to edges or corners.

Torsion springs (Fig. 31) are available in 10 and 11 gauge wire. They are used to support borderwire in the construction of spring-edge seats and backs employing sagless springs.

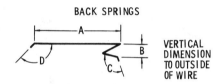

BACK SPRINGS

VERTICAL DIMENSION TO OUTSIDE OF WIRE

Table 4. "Modu-Loop" Spring Sizes for Seat and Back Applications.
BACK SPRINGS
DIMENSIONS

A	B	C	D	Gauge
18½"	5¼"	125°	105°	11½
19½"	5¼"	125°	105°	11
16"	5¼"	125°	105°	11½
14¾"	5¼"	125°	105°	11½
20½"	4½"	125°	105°	11
21"	4½"	125°	105°	11
22¾"	4½"	125°	105°	11
8½"	5¼"	125°	No D-End	11½
17"	4½"	125°	105°	11½
11"	5¼"	125°	No D-End	11½
17¾"	4½"	125°	105°	11½
17¾"	4½	125°	105°	11½

Courtesy   No-Sag Co.

Although it is not necessary to purchase special tools for working with sagless wire springs, a few suggestions should be made at this point that may contribute to making the work easier. Two types of tools for stretching the springs (particularly the heavy duty types) are very valuable (Fig. 32).

The ends of the springs must be bent so that they will not slip from the clips. This can be done with a vise and a hammer or with a tool specifically designed to do the job (Fig. 33).

Table 4 (Cont.). "Modu-Loop" Spring Sizes for Seat and Back Applications. SEAT SPRING DIMENSIONS

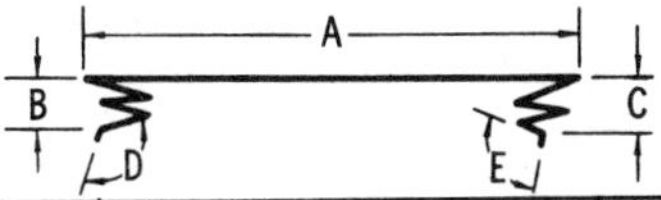

A	B	C	D	E	Gauge
22"	5¼"	6"	107°	90°	8
20¼"	5¼"	6"	107°	90°	8
22"	4½"	4½"	90°	90°	7½
21"	4½"	4½"	90°	90°	7½
22"	4½"	4¼"	107°	90°	7½
21⅞"	6¼"	5½"	107°	90°	8
20⅛"	5¼"	6¼"	107°	90°	8
21"	5¾"	5"	107°	90°	8
21"	2½"	4½"	107°	90°	7½
14¼"	4½"	90°	—	—	7½
10¼"	4½"	90°	—	—	7½

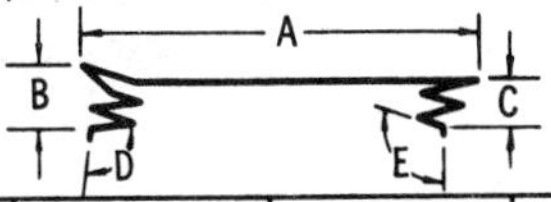

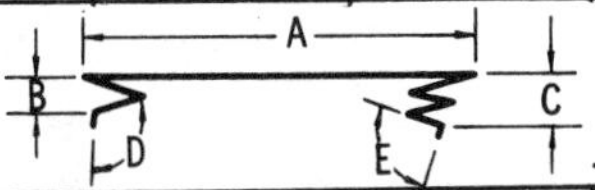

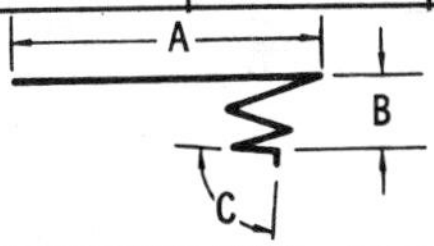

Courtesy   No-Sag Co.

173

SPRINGS

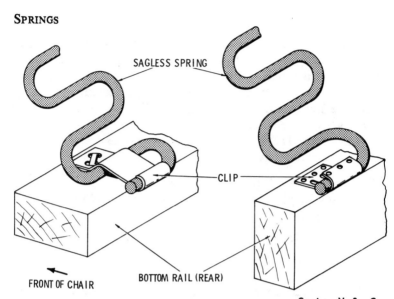

SAGLESS SPRING

CLIP

FRONT OF CHAIR

BOTTOM RAIL (REAR)

Fig. 27. Types of back clips used with No-Sag springs.

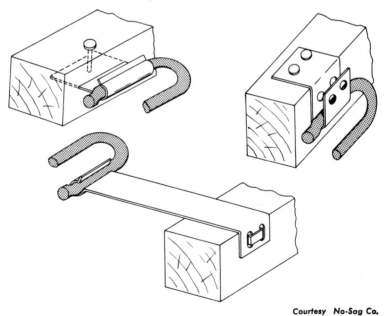

Fig. 28. Types of seat clips used with No-Sag springs.

174

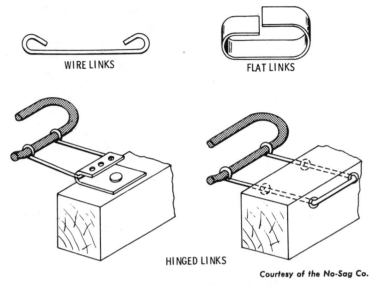

WIRE LINKS

FLAT LINKS

HINGED LINKS

Courtesy of the No-Sag Co.

Fig. 29. Types of links used with No-Sag springs.

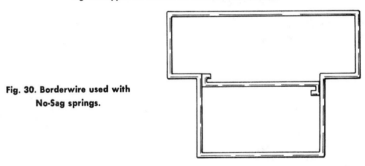

Fig. 30. Borderwire used with
No-Sag springs.

Courtesy No-Sag Co.

Helical springs are short (1⅜ to 6 inches), lightweight springs used to connect the outside rows of sagless wire springs to the side rails and sometimes to inter-connect the spring rows. They contribute to an even distribution of the seating load and provide more comfort than the metal connecting links are capable of doing. It is recommended that 2 inch lengths be used for 4 inch spacings 3 inch lengths for 5 inch; and 4 inch lengths for 6 inch spacings of the rows of sagless wire springs.

175

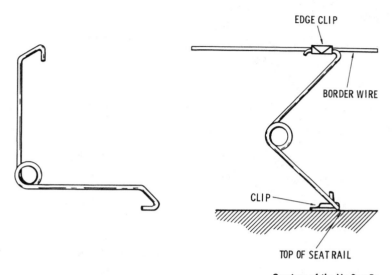

EDGE CLIP

BORDER WIRE

CLIP

TOP OF SEAT RAIL

Courtesy of the No-Sag Co.

Fig. 31. Torsion springs and their use.

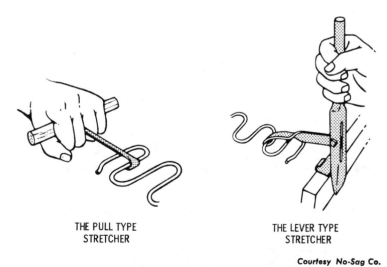

THE PULL TYPE
STRETCHER

THE LEVER TYPE
STRETCHER

Courtesy No-Sag Co.

Fig. 32. Two spring-stretcher tools used with sagless springs.

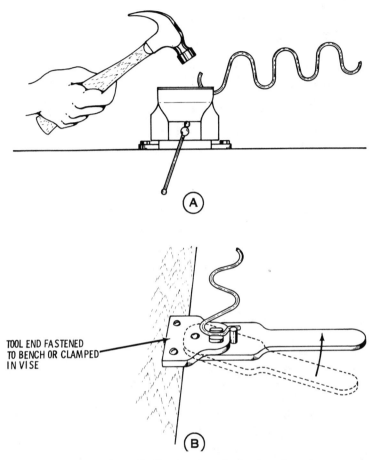

TOOL END FASTENED
TO BENCH OR CLAMPED
IN VISE

Fig. 33. Two methods of bending the ends of sagless wire springs.

The No-Sag Company produces several types of helical springs for use in furniture construction (Fig. 34). Note that all are open wound except the seat springs.

Standard sizes for the more popular type helicals are shown in Table 5. Retainer clips for helical springs are shown in Fig. 35.

Before installing sagless wire springs, it is wise to check the condition of the frame. A weak frame will not be able to withstand the steady pull of the sagless wire springs. It may be necessary to strengthen the frame before the springs can be used.

177

SPRINGS

SEAT HELICALS

CLOSELY WOUND,OPEN HOOK TYPE
15 GAUGE WITH 1/2" OD

USE:

FOR SECURING OUTSIDE
ROWS OF SINUOUS WIRE
TO SIDE RAILS OF WOOD
SEAT FRAMES. THESE
HELICALS MAY ALSO BE
USED AS SPRING INTER-
TIES TO PROVIDE BETTER
FILLING SUPPORT AND
MORE EVEN DISTRIBUTION
OF LOADS.

BACK HELICALS

(OPEN HOOK AND OPEN WOUND,
17 GAUGE, 1/2" OD)

USE:

USE TO UNITIZE SINUOUS
WIRE BACK SPRINGS AND
TO PROVIDE A BETTER BASE
FOR FILLING THESE MAY ALSO
BE USED TO PROVIDE SOFTER
SEATS.
AVAILABLE IN STANDARD
LENGTHS AND CAN BE SUPPLIED
IN OTHER SIZES TO MEET SPECIAL
REQUIREMENTS.

SNAP-END HELICALS

(OPEN-WOUND 19 GAUGE
WITH 3/8" OD)

THESE SMALLER HELICALS ARE
USED TO PROVIDE MORE TIES
AND ACHIEVE FULLER SUPPORT
FOR FILLING. ENDS SNAP
EASILY AND PERMANENTLY ON
SINUOUS SIRE.

BEDDING HELICALS

(OPEN HOOK AND OPEN WOUND -
11 AND 12 GAUGE WITH 11/16" OD)

THESE ARE USED AT CRITICAL
POINTS REQUIRING EXTRA
STRENGTH OR RIGIDITY (SUCH
AS BED ENDS AND FLOATING
DECK SEATS).

Courtesy No-Sag Co.

Fig. 34. Four types of helical springs.

Corner blocks should be used for re-inforcement, particularly if there is no overlap of seat rails. If at all possible, the front and back seat rails should overlap the side rails. The pulling force of the springs is naturally between the two rails to which they are attached. See Fig. 36. The wood used for constructing these rails should be at least 1 inch thick. Long frames (sofas, loveseats, etc.) should have one or two center braces (Fig. 37).

Sagless wire springs are normally installed from the back to the front rails on seats and from the bottom to the top rails on backs. However, side to side attachment is possible and produces satisfactory results. For the purposes of our explanation here, the conventional method will be described.

The step-by-step procedure for installing sagless wire springs is as follows:

1. Measure the frame for the length of spring to be used. Measurements are taken from the inside of the seat rails (Fig. 38). These measurements will help to determine the

Table 5. Helical Spring Sizes. (Other sizes available on special order.)

Seat Helical Springs	Back Helical Springs	Snap-End Helical Springs
1-⅜ inch	2-0 inch	1-½ inch
1-½	2-½	1-¾
1-⅝	3-0	2-0
1-¾	3-½	2-¼
2-0	4-0	2-½
2-½	5-0	2-¾
3-0		3-0
3-½		3-¼
4-0		3-½
		3-¾
		4-0
		4-¼
		4-½
		4-¾
		5-0
		5-¼
		5-½
		5-¾
		6-0

correct arc (crown) to be used, the length, and the gauge of the wire. When you have taken the measurements for the distance between seat rails, use these dimensions in referring to Table 3 to determine the crown (arc of the spring), the wire gauge, and the length of the spring.

2. To determine the number of rows of sagless wire spring to be used, measure the distance between the arms and refer to Table 6.

3. A "standard" crown (that is, one with the arc of the spring above the seat rail) is normally 1¼ to 2 inches. The total deflection will be about twice the dimension of the crown. Therefore, if the crown is 2 inches, the total deflection will be 4 inches.

The height of the crown can be increased by adding ¼ to ½ inch to the length of the spring. A lower crown can be created by subtracting the same amount. Generally, each

Table 6. Seat Dimensions for Sagless Springs.

Distance Between Arms Along Front Seat Rail	Number of No-Sag springs	Center to Center Spacing of Clips	Center Spacing of Two Outside Clips From Inside Arm Posts	Size of Connecting Links
21" Chair	5	4¼"	2"	2⅝"
22" Chair	5	4½"	2"	2⅞"
23" Chair	5	4¾"	2"	3⅛"
24" Chair	5	5"	2"	3⅜"
25" Chair	6	4¼"	1⅞"	2⅝"
40" Sectional	9	4½"	2"	2⅞"
50" Love Seat	11	4½"	2½"	2⅞"
52" Love Seat	11	4¾"	2¼"	3⅛"
58" Sofa	12	5"	1½"	3⅜"
59" Sofa	12	5"	2"	3⅜"
60" Sofa	13	4¾"	1½"	3⅛"
61" Sofa	13	4¾"	2"	3⅛"
62" Sofa	13	4¾"	2½"	3⅛"
63" Sofa	14	4½"	2¼"	2⅞"
64" Sofa	14	4½"	2¾"	2⅞"
65" Sofa	14	4¾"	1⅝"	3⅛"
66" Sofa	14	4¾"	2⅛"	3⅛"

½ inch change in spring length will result in a similar ¼ inch change in the crown measurement. Thus, reducing the length by ½ inch will reduce the crown by ¼ inch.

4. Unwind the length of sagless wire spring and press it flat on your work area on top of a yardstick. Take particular care in doing this. Sagless wire springs will snap back into a coiled position if you release them. This could cause injury. The distance between each of the outside edges (Fig. 39) is the true length of the spring as required in Table 3.

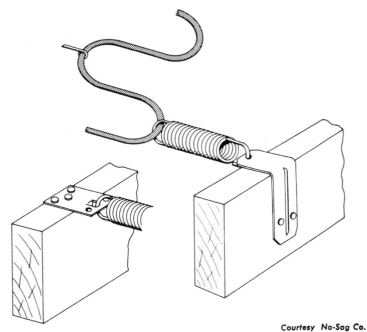

Courtesy No-Sag Co.

Fig. 35. Helical spring retainer clips.

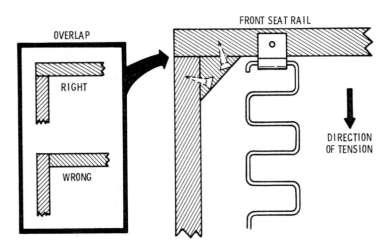

OVERLAP

RIGHT

WRONG

FRONT SEAT RAIL

DIRECTION
OF TENSION

Fig. 36. Frame overlap detail.

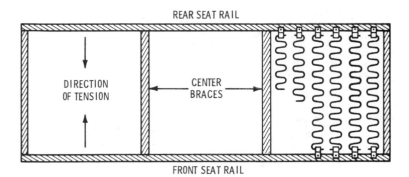

REAR SEAT RAIL

DIRECTION
OF TENSION

CENTER
BRACES

FRONT SEAT RAIL

Fig. 37. Center braces used to reinforce a long frame.

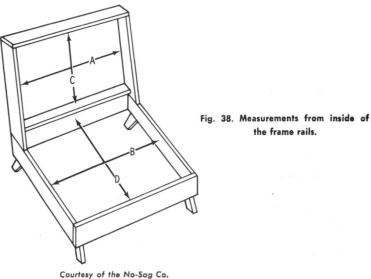

Fig. 38. Measurements from inside of
the frame rails.

Courtesy of the No-Sag Co.

5. Cut the spring ½ loop longer than the measured length of
the spring (This small additional amount may be removed
once the exact height of the crown is determined). Since this
is spring steel, the surface of the sagless wire spring can be
notched with a file or hacksaw and snapped off at the
desired point.

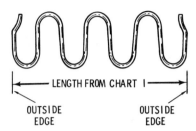

LENGTH FROM CHART I

OUTSIDE
EDGE

OUTSIDE
EDGE

Fig. 39. Measuring sagless wire springs.

6. File the cut end of the spring smooth to remove any burr and bend it as shown in Fig. 33. The ends are bent so that they will not slip out of the clips or hinge links.

7. Cut as many lengths of sagless wire springs as the measurements in Step Two require.

8. Locate and mark the positions for the metal clips. Nail the clips in place with webbing tacks or barbed nails.

9. Attach the lengths of sagless wire springs to the metal clips on the frame so that the open ends alternate (Fig. 25).

10. Locate and mark the positions for the helical springs on each side rail of the frame. The number and location is an arbitrary decision depending upon the weight loads anticipated and the size of the frame.

11. Tie the inner rows together with either helical springs or metal connecting links.

12. In Steps Ten and Eleven locate the helicals (or metal connecting links) so that they alternate positions in each row (Fig. 25). Turn the open end of the helical spring down when attaching it to prevent the loose wire from snagging in the padding and materials which will be over it.

Follow Steps One through Twelve for attaching the sagless wire springs to the back. Remember that the wire gauge will usually be different.

A square edge can be constructed if so desired with the use of borderwire, flat links, and torsion springs.

183

CHAPTER 8

Burlap, Stuffing, and Muslin

The burlap, stuffing, padding, and muslin combine to form the central core of an upholstered piece of furniture. Each layer performs a practical function essential to the strength and comfort of the piece. Burlap serves as the base for the stuffing. The principal function of the stuffing and padding is to provide the softness of the seating comfort. The muslin cover is an optional layer of material that provides a protective barrier for the outer upholstery fabric, preventing the stuffing (particularly down, feathers, and animal hair) from working through to the surface.

BURLAP

Burlap has three important functions in upholstery: (1) it is used to cover the springs in furniture having spring construction; (2) it covers the webbing and serves as a foundation base for furniture having no springs (open frame construction); and (3) it is used to make edge rolls.

Burlap is a strong, coarse fabric of plain design woven primarily from jute fibers (Fig. 1). It is graded by the weight per yard. These grades start as low as 5-oz. per yard and extend as high as 14-oz. The widths will range from 36 to 100 inches. The most common width used in upholstery is 40 inches. The weights commonly used will range from 8 oz. to 14 oz. depending upon their particular function. For example, the inside of a wing would only need a burlap weighing 8-10 oz., whereas the frame opening

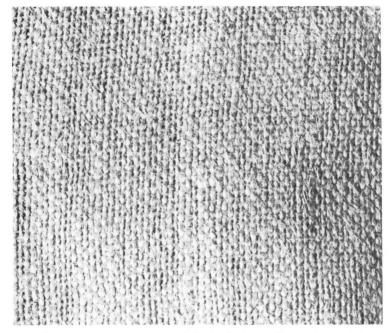

Fig. 1. Upholstering burlap.

in a piece of furniture of non-spring construction would require a 12-14 oz. heavy duty grade.

MUSLIN

Muslin is a light-to-medium-weight, plain fabric that is sometimes used between the stuffing and the outer upholstery cover for additional protection. The most common width sold for upholstery work is 36 inches. In the case of a pile fabric, the muslin protects the pile from the constant rubbing of the stuffing against it. (Fig. 2)

STUFFING

The quality of a stuffing is determined by its resilience. That is, by its ability to spring back into its original shape after having

185

been depressed by some sort of pressure. The better the quality of the stuffing, the more quickly it will resume its original shape. Inferior grades of stuffing will pack if pressed down.

Tow is made from the stems of flax plants. These stems are crushed and processed until a hairlike fiber is produced. Tow is cheap and easy to work with. Unfortunately, it packs (that is, compresses into lumps) very easily. It probably has the lowest resiliency of any of the stuffing materials. For this reason, it is frequently used as a base for a better quality stuffing. Tow is spread evenly across the burlap and stitched into place (use a 4 inch curved needle for this). A better quality stuffing is spread across the tow base.

Tow is also used on a solid base (seat or arm top). It is spread evenly across the surface to be covered and is then secured in position with a piece of burlap. The burlap is stretched across the tow and tacked in place. Tow is also frequently used

Fig. 2. Upholstering muslin.

in making edge rolls. Because it packs so easily, it is best to err on the side of "too much" rather than "too little." Tow comes in three grades and is sold by the pound.

Sisal is even cheaper than tow. For that reason, sisal is frequently used as a substitute for tow. Whereas tow is derived from the fibrous stem of the flax plant, sisal finds its beginnings in the large leaves of the sisal hemp plant. Like tow, sisal is easy to work with. Unfortunately, it also has the same tendency to pack down, and is best used as a base for better grades of more resilient stuffing materials. Sisal fibers are white, long, and coarse. Sisal can be rubberized, (i.e., the fibers receive a thin coating of rubber) and manufactured in pad form or sold loose as a filler. Sisal can be found in the seat, arms, and back.

Palm leaf fiber is produced through the processing of palm leaves and has only slightly more resilience than either sisal or tow. Best results are obtained if palm leaf fibers serve as a base for a stuffing of better quality. Like sisal and tow, palm leaf fibers have a tendency to pack down and form lumps.

Coconut shell fiber or *coco fiber* has the same characteristics as palm leaf fiber. It is processed from the coir—the coarse fiber found in the outer coconut husk.

Rubberized coconut fiber is produced by impregnating the coir with a synthetic rubber latex. The result is a mildew and odor-resistant pad of uniform density. Blocksom & Company manufactures rubberized coconut fiber pads, under the trade name of "Coirtex," as a furniture insulator for use in mattresses, automobile and airplane seats. The "Coirtex" pads are sold in thicknesses of ¼ to ½ inch. They may be purchased by the roll or in specific sizes to meet the particular furniture requirement.

Excelsior is a stuffing produced from such woods as eastern cottonwood and black willow. The wood is shredded in much the same manner as the palm leaves. Excelsior will pack down when new and crumble into small pieces after a period of time.

Kapok is a seed fiber resembling cotton to some extent. It is derived from the seed pods of the kapok tree. Kapok is very soft and is frequently used as a stuffing for cushions and life preservers. It can also be used alone or mixed with other stuffing materials in pillows. Unfortunately, kapok tends to separate and pack down into uncomfortable lumps. Kapok is usually purchased by the pound.

Cotton is also a seed fiber, but it finds much greater use in upholstery than kapok. It is used both as a stuffing for cushions and pillows as well as a protective layer between the outer upholstery cover and the stuffing material. It is also used to stuff arms, channels (pipes), tufts, and corners. As a stuffing for cushions and pillows, cotton is decidedly inferior. It has a tendency to pack down and form uncomfortable lumps. The cotton used in upholstery is derived from the linters—short fibers remaining on the cotton seeds after the ginning process. These short fibers are removed and woven into pads. Cotton is purchased by the roll (27 inch width) in several weights.

Moss (or Spanish Moss as it is commonly known) is not a true moss. It hangs in long strands from trees, taking both moisture and nourishment from the air. It is not parasitic; that is, it in no way lives off the body of the tree to which it attaches itself.

Moss is second only to animal hair as a stuffing for upholstered furniture. Since moss is somewhat less resilient than hair, it should be built up to a level higher than called for when used as a stuffing. This will allow for the slight packing that will occur.

The moss that is gathered from trees must be processed before it can be used commercially. This processing not only cleans it (removing dirt, twigs, etc.) but also removes the outer bark of the moss, leaving the fine hair-like inner fiber. The more times the moss is run through the process, the better the grade. The processing will also change the color of the moss. Consequently, the grades are easily recognized by their color.

The number of times that moss has been processed is indicated with the symbol x. Moss can be purchased by the pound. It is very easy to work with.

Animal hair is a better quality of material for stuffing upholstered furniture than any of those previously discussed. It is very resilient and ages well (outlasting most substitutes). There is little tendency to pack down or form uncomfortable lumps. Moreover, it can be easily and economically restored. Its major drawback is that it must be moth proofed before being used as a stuffing.

The four types of hair used in stuffing are: (1) horse hair, (2) cattle hair, (3) hog hair, and (4) rubberized hair. The term *curled hair* is frequently encountered and should not be considered a type of hair. Rather, it is a process to which hair (any hair) is submitted. The hair is soaked in large vats of water at a temperature of over 200°F. This gives the hair a long lasting curl and, as a result, greater resiliency. The earliest records of the use of curled hair in upholstering date from the seventh century in England.

Horse hair (from both the mane and the tail) is the best type of hair for stuffing. Only hair from the tails of cattle is as long as horse hair (those from the tail). The XXXX grade of moss is frequently used as a substitute. Horse hair is purchased by the pound. The grade-quality (and this is true of other types of hair) is based primarily on color and length. *Cattle hair* (from the tail) is second to horse tail hair in quality, lacking only the hardness of the latter. It stands above horse mane hair and below horse tail hair. The former is shorter and softer than cattle hair in overall quality. The finest grade of cattle hair is taken from the switch or tassel at the end of the tail. *Hog hair* is as hard as horse

Courtesy Blocksom & Co.

Fig. 3. Rubberized hair.

tail hair, but softer than cattle hair. Because hog hair is so short, it is mixed with some other longer hair (either horse or cattle). See Table 1.

Rubberized hair is produced through a process whereby each individual hair (it can be any kind of hair) is covered with rubber. It is lightweight and comes in three grades—soft, medium, and firm. Only the "firm" grade is generally recommended for use in upholstery. (Fig. 3)

TABLE 1. Hair Characteristics.

TYPE	LENGTH	STRENGTH
Horse tail hair	Long	Hard
Cattle tail hair	Long	Soft
Horse mane hair	Short	Softer than cattle hair
Hog hair	Short	Hard

"*Paratex*" is the trade name of a rubberized curled hair product manufactured by Blocksom & Company. It consists of 20% horse hair and 80% hog hair impregnated with rubber. It equals foam rubber and plastic polyurethane in resilience. It is also moth proof, non-allergenic, and resistant to mildew.

"Paratex" can be laminated to any thickness. It conforms to all contours (including sharp bends around corners and edges) without separating. Attaching this material to the frame offers no difficulty. It can be tacked, stapled, sewed, hog-ringed, or button-tufted. (See Fig. 4)

"Paratex" is manufactured in four grades of density—soft, medium, medium-firm, and firm. The firm density is recommended for seats and where heavy and hard usage is expected to occur. The manufacturers suggest a firmer density whenever there is any doubt. "Paratex" is sold in sheets, rolls, or in pieces cut to size. This is a slab stock, and is worked in much the same manner as is foam rubber or plastic polyurethane. It can be cut with scissors, knife, or a band saw.

Down is the short, fluffy feather found in young birds or close to the skin of grown birds. It is lightweight and an excellent in-

190

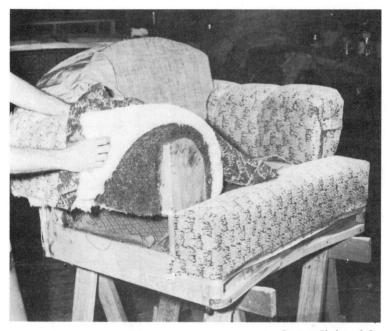

Courtesy Blocksom & Co.

Fig. 4. "Paratex' installed beneath cotton padding.

sulator. Down can be purchased by the pound, and is frequently used as a mixture (55-65%) with feathers.

Duck feathers and *goose feathers* are recommended for upholstery work; *chicken feathers* and *turkey feathers* (although they are both found as a stuffing) are not. Goose feathers have the most resilience; duck feathers are next, with chicken feathers and turkey feathers a poor third. Feathers can be purchased by the pound.

ATTACHING THE BURLAP (SPRING CONSTRUCTION)

The burlap cover serves two functions in spring construction. Primarily, it provides a foundation for the stuffing above it, a surface over which the stuffing can be spread evenly and sewed down. Perhaps equally important, is the fact that burlap prevents the stuffing from spilling down into the springs.

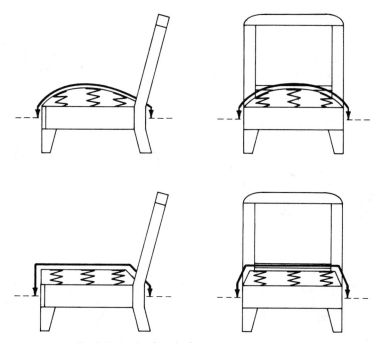

Fig. 5. Measuring for a burlap cover over seat springs.

The following outline details the steps in the application of burlap over the seat springs.

1. Measure across the frame opening and allow for ¾ to 1 inch overlap for tacking to the frame. Do not depress the springs with the measuring tape when taking the measurements. The burlap must be applied in such a way that there is no depression of the springs. Depressing the springs causes a continuous pressure to be placed against the burlap. In time, this will cause the burlap to tear, weakening the upholstery (see Fig. 5).

2. Cut a heavy-grade burlap according to the measurements you have just taken for the seat with a ½ inch allowance along the edges. This will be turned under to give an unfraying hem for tacking. A lighter grade of burlap can be used on backs, arms, and side panels. Be sure to cut along the weave.

3. Center the burlap over the seat springs and the frame opening. Make certain that an equal amount of burlap overlaps each side.

4. Fold about ½ inch of burlap under and place a temporary tack in the middle of the burlap at the center of the back seat rail (Fig. 6).

5. Pull the burlap tight (as tight as you can without depressing the springs) and place a tack through the middle of the burlap at the center of the front seat rail. Again, fold the burlap under about ½ inch before tacking (Fig. 7).

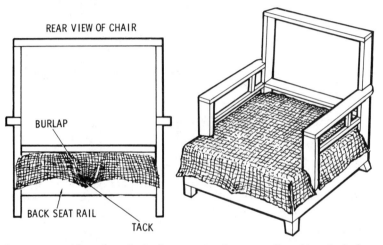

REAR VIEW OF CHAIR

BURLAP

BACK SEAT RAIL

TACK

Fig. 6. Temporarily tacking the burlap to the back seat rail.

Fig. 7. Temporarily tacking the burlap to the front seat rail.

6. Cut each corner of the burlap back to a point equal to the overlap on the sides. Cut and fit the burlap for arm and back posts. Pull the burlap tight on the sides and place a tack through the middle of the burlap at the center of each side rail. Fold under ½ inch before tacking. Begin tacking toward corners and posts away from the center-tack on each seat rail (Fig. 8). This will be temporary slip-tacking.

7. Once you have completed slip-tacking the burlap around all four sides of the frame, check the surface over the tops of the springs. If the burlap is smooth and tight, then you

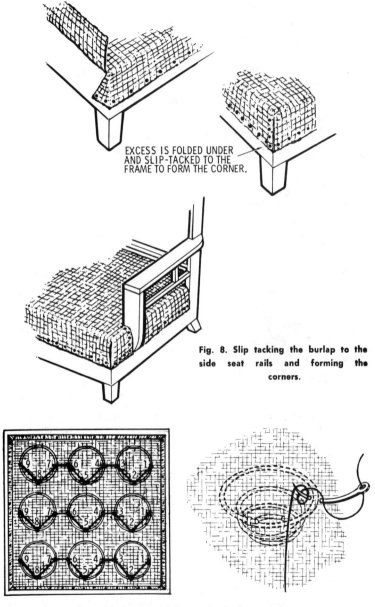

EXCESS IS FOLDED UNDER
AND SLIP-TACKED TO THE
FRAME TO FORM THE CORNER.

Fig. 8. Slip tacking the burlap to the side seat rails and forming the corners.

Fig. 9. Stitching pattern for sewing burlap to springs.

194

are ready to stitch the burlap to the top coils of the springs. Use a curved needle with stitching twine and follow the pattern illustrated in Fig 9.

8. Permanently tack the burlap in position. Begin at the center of each frame rail and move toward the corners and posts. Smooth out all wrinkles in the burlap as you tack. Remember to keep ½ inches of burlap turned under at the bottom as you tack.

9. Fold excess burlap under at the corners and tack them down. Make certain that the folded-under material is smooth flat before the burlap is tacked. If it is bunched, unsightly bulges and wrinkles may occur. You may also wish to sew the corner seams.

Sewing burlap to sagless wire springs offers no great problem. The knots must be spaced and sewed to the spring in such a manner that they will not slip along the spring wire.

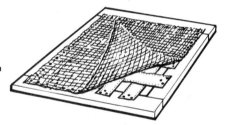

Fig. 10. Attaching burlap over an open frame without springs.

ATTACHING THE BURLAP (NON-SPRING CONSTRUCTION)

Non-spring construction can be divided into two types: (1) those having open frames and (2) those having a wood base or closed frame. In either case, a padded seat must be constructed to provide comfort for the sitter. A variation of the open-frame, non-spring type of construction is the removable or slip-seat. Because it shares construction similarities with the wood based, closed-frame types, we will examine it in greater detail in another chapter (see Chapter Fourteen: Slip Seats and Padded Seats).

Open frames in which no springs are used still require the attachment of crisscrossed lengths of webbing. Burlap (usually a heavy grade) is then placed over the webbing, covering the frame open-

195

ing to provide a stronger base and a surface to which the stuffing can be attached (see Fig. 10). In order to construct a piece of furniture of this type, the following procedure should be followed.

1. Center the burlap over the frame opening. Cut off enough burlap to allow some overlap. The amount of overlap depends upon whether or not an edge roll is to be used. This can be determined by fashioning a mock-up of an edge roll. Construct this edge roll from heavy paper, staple the edges, and stuff it with cotton. Lay the piece of burlap across the opening and slip tack it into position. Now place the paper edge roll where you plan to locate it, slip tack it into position, and pull the burlap over it. You can now get a rough idea of how much allowance to provide (see Fig. 11).

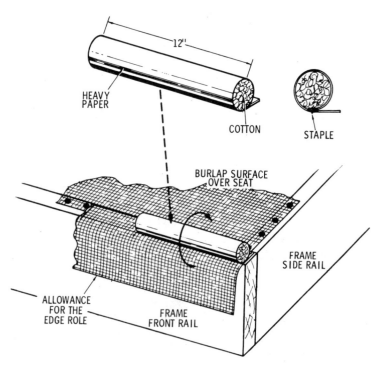

Fig. 11. Using a paper edge roll to determine allowance.

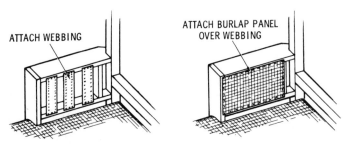

Fig. 12. Burlap cover on inside arm.

If no edge roll is to be used on a frame rail, then an overlap of only about an inch or two is necessary. These areas are at the back of the frame and in some cases along the sides closest to the back.

2. Cut the burlap to your rough measurements and slip tack it to the frame. Is it centered properly? If so, remove the slip tacks from the front, pull the burlap so that it is taut, and permanently tack it into position. It is advised to place a tacking strip (usually a thin strip of cardboard) along the surface of the frame. This will prevent the tacks from slipping through the wide weave of the burlap. Tack from the center outward toward both sides, pulling the burlap tight and smoothing out all wrinkles as you go.

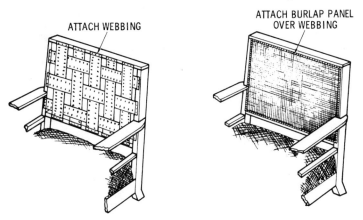

Fig. 13. Burlap cover on inside back.

197

3. Repeat the same procedure for the back of the frame.

4. Follow the same procedure for each side of the frame. Where you do not intend to use an edge roll, fold the excess burlap back and tack it to the frame. Take care to stagger these tacks (as you would if you were tacking webbing) since you are tacking over another row of tacks.

5. The construction of the edge roll is described in the next section.

6. Measuring, cutting, and attaching the burlap to the other portions of the frame (wings, arms or side panels and backs in which no springs are used) is identical to the procedure followed in covering the seat portion (see Figs. 12 and 13).

ATTACHING EDGE ROLLS

Rolls of burlap, filled with stuffing, are tacked along the edges of the wood frame or stitched to the burlap at the point that the

Courtesy Sackner Products, Inc.

Fig. 14. Roll edge applied to chair frame.

springs exert the most pressure. Thus, edge rolls function as buffers between the edge of the frame or springs (in a spring-edge seat) and the outer upholstery cover. A second but equally important function is that it prevents the stuffing from working it way down over the edge to the frame. Finally, the shape of the edge roll contributes to the contour of the chair.

Edge rolls can be purchased ready-made or constructed from burlap and stuffing. Ready-made edge rolls are sold by the foot or in large coils. Edge rolls are made in several sizes ranging from ½ to 1½ inches in height. There are also a number of different shapes that can be purchased. The shape of the edge roll usually depends upon the use to which it is put. Edge rolls that are used to close the gap between the seat foundation and the cush-

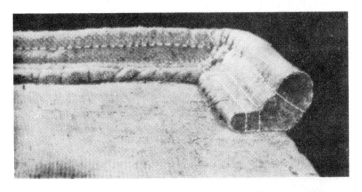

Fig. 15. Ready-made, stitched edge roll.

Courtesy Sackner Products, Inc.

199

ion in the front of chairs and sofas are generally larger than those that are tacked to frame edges (Fig. 14). The former are stitched to the burlap above the spring unit (and directly over the spring edge wire, if one is used). For this reason, they are frequently referred to as *spring* edge rolls or *stitched* edge rolls (Fig. 15).

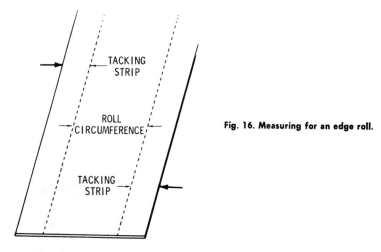

Fig. 16. Measuring for an edge roll.

All edge rolls must be well-packed with stuffing so that they give a continuous, firm surface. You are always assured of this with ready-made edge rolls.

Larger edge rolls tend to break down after a period of time. Tow produces the firmest stuffing, but other fillers are frequently used. The edge roll is either tacked to the frame or—in the case or spring edge seats or especially large edge rolls—sewed to the burlap.

If ready-made edge roll is not being employed, then the following procedure for forming a handmade edge roll should be used.

1. Estimate the diameter of the edge roll required for the seat. This will depend upon the projected height of the finished seat from the floor. If, for example, the height of the finished seat is to be 18 inches from the floor, and the top of the seat rails is 16½ inches then the edge roll will have a diameter of 1½ inches.

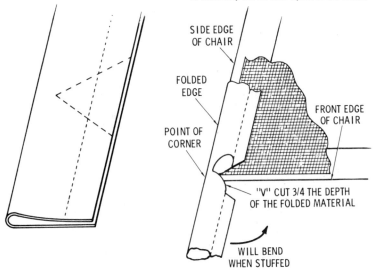

SIDE EDGE
OF CHAIR

FOLDED
EDGE

FRONT EDGE
OF CHAIR

POINT OF
CORNER

"V" CUT 3/4 THE DEPTH
OF THE FOLDED MATERIAL

WILL BEND
WHEN STUFFED

Fig. 17. Folding and cutting for a corner.

2. Measure and cut a piece of burlap wide enough to create the required diameter with enough excess for at least a 1-inch tacking strip and long enough to reach around the seat circumference. (Fig. 16).

3. Determine where the corners are to be. Fold the roll edge strip and make a V-cut at the proper point for the corner. See Fig. 17. Cut through no more than ¾ of the folded, flat material. After the roll is stuffed, the V-cut can be made a little deeper to eliminate any unevenness.

4. Attach the bottom edge of the burlap to the frame with No. 6 upholstery tacks.

5. Begin forming the roll. Start with a small amount of stuffing, fold the burlap around it, pack the stuffing firmly in place, and tack down this first section of edge roll. This will be the shorter section on the side. Sew the corner seam before beginning the next section of edge roll. Continue to proceed in this fashion around the edges of the frame until the entire edge roll is completed (Fig. 18).

The method of forming an edge roll that is stitched in place follows a slightly different procedure. The stuffing within the edge roll

201

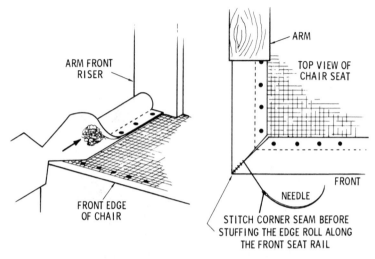

Fig. 18. Forming and stuffing the edge roll.

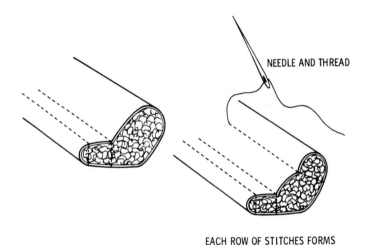

EACH ROW OF STITCHES FORMS
A TIGHTER, HARDER ROLL

Fig. 19. Stitching pattern on an edge roll.

should be stitched to prevent it from moving about. This can be a problem with larger (1¾ to 2 inch diameters or more) edge rolls. A suggested stitching pattern is illustrated in Fig. 19.

202

Ready-made edge rolls also form their corners with a V-cut. Fig. 20 illustrates a V-cut made in a ready-made edge roll, and gives examples of several types of shapes that can be purchased.

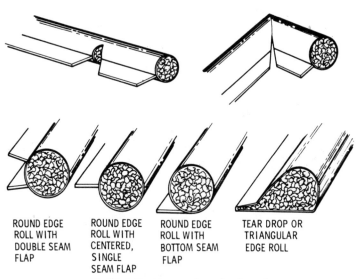

| ROUND EDGE ROLL WITH DOUBLE SEAM FLAP | ROUND EDGE ROLL WITH CENTERED, SINGLE SEAM FLAP | ROUND EDGE ROLL WITH BOTTOM SEAM FLAP | TEAR DROP OR TRIANGULAR EDGE ROLL |

Fig. 20. A V-cut in a ready-made edge roll.

ATTACHING THE LOOSE STUFFING AND PADDING

We have already discussed the properties of various types of stuffing and padding materials used in upholstering. In the previous section, we described the attachment of the burlap cover. It was also explained how and when it was necessary to use the roll edge.

A procedure for spreading and attaching the loose stuffing is as follows:

1. Determine the depth of the stuffing. Some upholsterers suggest at least 1 inch. Others advise using enough so that the springs cannot be felt when the stuffing is pressed down with the hand.
2. Make certain that there are no lumps in the stuffing when you spread it. Any lumps should be picked apart.

3. Spread the stuffing evenly over the surface to be covered.
4. Stitch the stuffing to the burlap (use 2-3 inch stitches). See Fig 21 for some suggested stitching patterns.
5. Distribute at least 25% more loose stuffing over the surface than has been sewed down. This should be a more expensive type (e.g. curled animal hair). DO NOT cover the edge roll (Fig. 22).

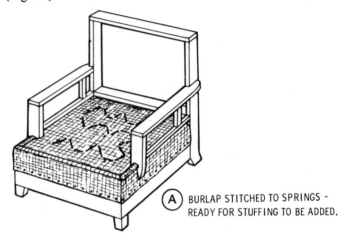

A BURLAP STITCHED TO SPRINGS - READY FOR STUFFING TO BE ADDED.

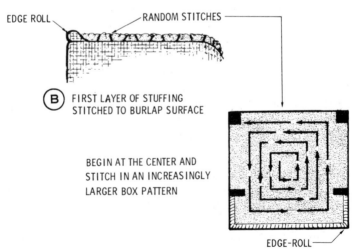

EDGE ROLL — RANDOM STITCHES

B FIRST LAYER OF STUFFING STITCHED TO BURLAP SURFACE

BEGIN AT THE CENTER AND STITCH IN AN INCREASINGLY LARGER BOX PATTERN

EDGE-ROLL

Fig. 21. Stitching first layer of stuffing over burlap.

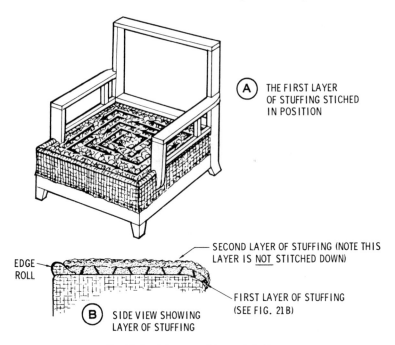

A — THE FIRST LAYER OF STUFFING STICHED IN POSITION

SECOND LAYER OF STUFFING (NOTE THIS LAYER IS <u>NOT</u> STITCHED DOWN)

EDGE ROLL

FIRST LAYER OF STUFFING (SEE FIG. 21 B)

B — SIDE VIEW SHOWING LAYER OF STUFFING

Fig. 22. Applying second layer of stuffing.

6. Covering the stuffing with a layer of cotton padding (Fig. 23). This layer does cover a roll edge if used.

A variation of the above procedure is to cover the stuffing with a layer of lightweight burlap which in turn is attached to the stuffing with a number of random stitches before the placing of the cotton padding (Fig. 24). Do not pull the stitches too tight.

The next step is to cover the stuffing and cotton padding with a muslin cover.

THE MUSLIN COVER

Using a layer of muslin is optional, but it does provide an excellent base for the final cover. You will usually find it easier to position the stuffing with a regulator beneath a muslin cover than through the outer upholstery fabric. Then, too, cutting and sewing

205

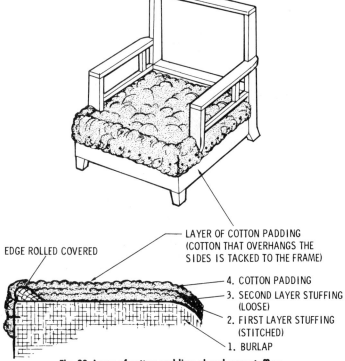

EDGE ROLLED COVERED

LAYER OF COTTON PADDING
(COTTON THAT OVERHANGS THE
SIDES IS TACKED TO THE FRAME)

4. COTTON PADDING

3. SECOND LAYER STUFFING
(LOOSE)

2. FIRST LAYER STUFFING
(STITCHED)

1. BURLAP

Fig. 23. Layer of cotton padding placed over stuffing.

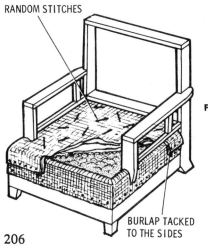

RANDOM STITCHES

**Fig. 24. A cover of lightweight burlap
over the stuffing.**

BURLAP TACKED
TO THE SIDES

206

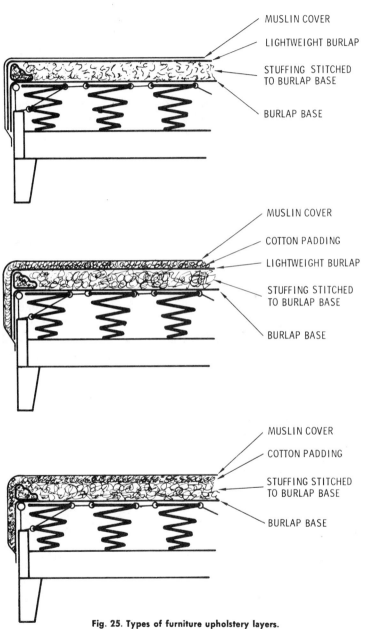

MUSLIN COVER

LIGHTWEIGHT BURLAP

STUFFING STITCHED
TO BURLAP BASE

BURLAP BASE

MUSLIN COVER

COTTON PADDING

LIGHTWEIGHT BURLAP

STUFFING STITCHED
TO BURLAP BASE

BURLAP BASE

MUSLIN COVER

COTTON PADDING

STUFFING STITCHED
TO BURLAP BASE

BURLAP BASE

Fig. 25. Types of furniture upholstery layers.

207

the muslin pieces in place will give you some practice for doing the same with the more expensive surface fabric.

In cheaper grades of furniture and in better quality, mass-produced types, the muslin cover is frequently omitted altogether. When a muslin cover is used, it forms the upper-most layer of three types of construction: (1) muslin, lightweight burlap, stuffing; (2) muslin, cotton, lightweight burlap, stuffing; and (3) muslin, cotton, stuffing (Fig. 25).

MEASURING AND CUTTING MUSLIN FOR THE SEAT

Select enough muslin to cover the piece of furniture you are upholstering. This will, of course, be a rough estimate at this point in your work (fairly accurate guess can be made by referring to Fig. 1 in Chapter Nine—Pattern Layout). The procedure for taking the measurements is as follows:

1. Measure across the width of the seat down over to the sides to a bit past the center of the side rail. This is approximately the line along which the muslin will be tacked. However, you will need an additional inch of fabric on each side to be folded double for tacking. This will protect the muslin from

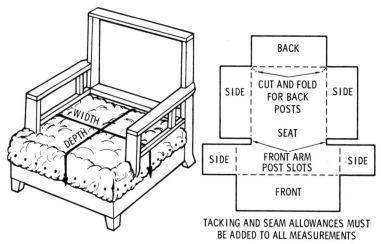

Fig. 26. Measuring for the muslin cover.

ripping when tension is placed upon it. If the entire side of the chair is to be upholstered, then the measurement may be extended to the bottom of the side rail plus a tacking allowance for the material to extend underneath the chair to permit tacking to the bottom edge of the side rails. This will give additional protection to the outer cover at the sharp edge of the side rail.

2. Measure the front-to-back depth of the seat making the same allowance for tacking and folding. Remember to make both the width and depth measurements across the *center* of the seat (Fig. 26).

3. Mark your measurements on the muslin and cut the piece to cover the seat. Be sure to add tacking and seam allowances to all measurements.

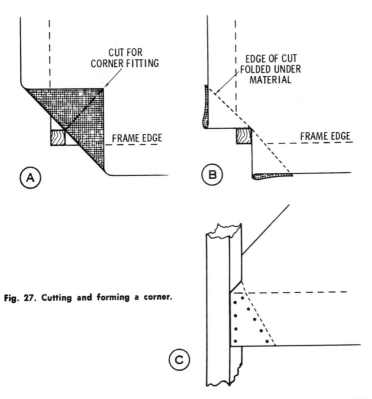

Fig. 27. Cutting and forming a corner.

4. Slip tack the muslin cover to the back seat rail. Place the first tack in the center and space the others on either side of it (smoothing out the wrinkles in the muslin as you proceed).

5. Pull the muslin so that it is tight against the seat (but not so tight as to depress the springs) and slip tack it to the front seat rail. Again, tack from the center out toward the sides smoothing the wrinkles out of the material as you do so.

6. Pull the muslin tight against any corner posts and cut the material to fit the post (Fig. 27).

7. Pull the muslin cover down to the side rails and slip tack it into place. Tack it in the same manner as you did in Steps Four and Five.

8. If you are satisfied with the way the muslin cover looks, permanently tack it in place (fold the muslin for tacking as you did with the burlap).

MEASURING AND CUTTING THE MUSLIN FOR THE ARMS AND SIDE PANELS

The variety of styles in arms (and the side panels) make this a comparatively more difficult pattern to measure and cut.

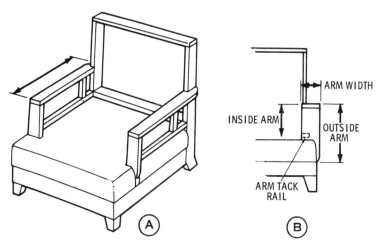

Fig. 28. Measuring the arm.

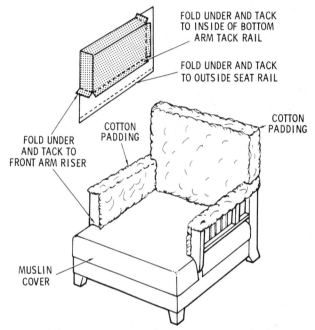

FOLD UNDER AND TACK
TO INSIDE OF BOTTOM
ARM TACK RAIL

FOLD UNDER AND TACK
TO OUTSIDE SEAT RAIL

COTTON
PADDING

COTTON
PADDING

FOLD UNDER
AND TACK TO
FRONT ARM RISER

MUSLIN
COVER

Fig. 29. Muslin cover for a modern, square-arm style chair.

A muslin cover is particularly important for the arms since it gives added support to keeping the cotton layer in place. This is especially true along the curve or corner of the edge. The procedure for taking the measurements and sewing together the muslin cover of a modern, square-arm style chair is as follows.

1. Take a measurement along the top of the arm from the very back to the very front (Fig. 28A). Add at least 1½ inches to each end for seams and tacking. For example, if the measurement in Fig. 28A is 33 inches, add 1½ inches to both ends for a total of 36 inches.

2. Take an arm width measurement and add 1½ inches to both sides for seams which will be formed with the edges of the arm side panels.

3. Measure the side panels. (Note: There probably will be differences in the measurements between the inside panel

211

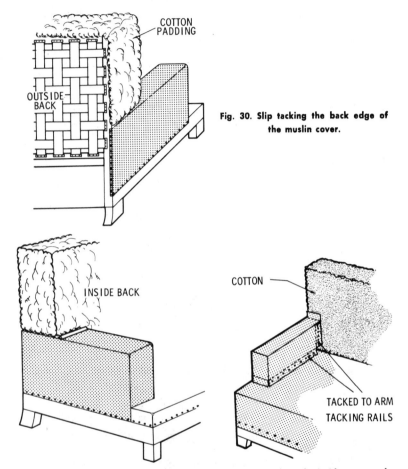

Fig. 30. Slip tacking the back edge of the muslin cover.

Fig. 31. Tacking the outside arm panel.

Fig. 32. Attaching the inside arm panel.

and the outside panel.) See Fig. 28B. Allow an extra 1½ inches on each side and each end for seams and tacking.

4. Sew all the pieces together so that the seams are on the inside. Slip the muslin cover over the arm and tack the front bottom edge. Again, fold the muslin under for tacking (Fig. 29).

5. Pull the muslin cover toward the back, smoothing out all wrinkles and lumps as you do so. Temporary tack it in back

(Fig. 30). Now, take the bottom of the outside arm panel and tack it to the underneath edge of the side rail (Fig. 31).

6. The inside panel of the muslin cover is stretched tight, folded under, and tacked to the tack rail (Fig. 32). At this point the muslin should be securely tacked along the bottom front edge and along the bottom edges of the side panels. Remove the temporary tacks at the back and pull the muslin cover tight (smoothing out wrinkles or lumps), and permanently tack it in place along the back rail.

There are several arm styles that present more difficulty in measuring and cutting the muslin cover than does the simple box-style just described. A common feature of these non-box styles is a roundness or curvature to the surface.

In Fig. 33A we have a typical rolled-arm type arm with the roll extending to the outside. Measure the distance between B1 and B2.

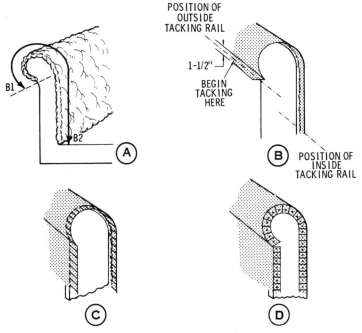

Fig. 33. Measuring, cutting, and attaching muslin to a rounded arm.

213

Make sure that the measuring tape extends under the roll of the arm to the point where the side panel begins. Allow 1½ inch extra at both ends of this piece and along both sides. Spread the muslin over the top of the arm and allow it hang down the inside arm. Tack the upper end of the muslin (do not fold) along the upper tacking rail just below the arm. Begin tacking at the center (Fig 33B) and move toward either side, smoothing out the wrinkles in the muslin. Pull the muslin down over the inside of the arm and tack the other end to the lower tacking rail, beginning at the center and working outward. Be sure the lumps are smoothed out of the cotton as you pull the muslin cover tight.

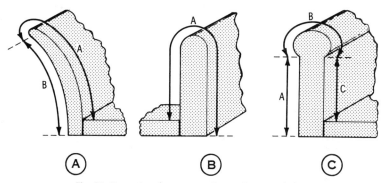

Fig. 34. Measuring three types of curved or rounded arms.

An excess of 1½ inches of muslin will extend beyond the front of the arm. Make cuts every inch around the curve (Fig. 33C) and fold the excess over the front of the arm (Fig. 33D). Pull it tight and tack it in place. These tacks will be covered by a welt-edged panel.

Fasten the inside and outside edges of the arm panels toward the back to the rear riser or tacking rails.

Fig. 34 shows other styles of curved and rounded arms. The important thing to remember is to make the seam lines as obscure as possible. The knife-edge arm style (Fig. 34A), for example, should have the inside muslin cover (represented by measurement A) tacked slightly below the outside edge. In Fig. 34B it would be best to cut a single piece to cover the entire arm. In Fig. 34C measurements A, B, and C should be separate pieces.

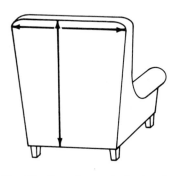

Fig. 35. Measuring a back that is wider at the top.

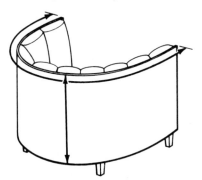

Fig. 36. Measuring a curved back.

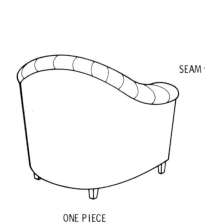

ONE PIECE

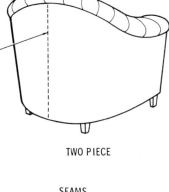

SEAM

TWO PIECE

Fig. 37. One, two, and three piece muslin back covers.

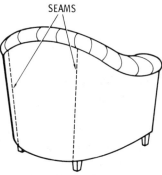

SEAMS

THREE PIECE

215

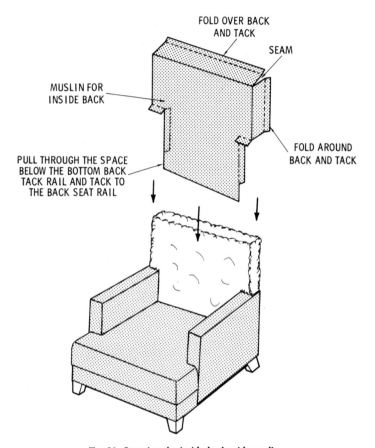

Fig. 38. Covering the inside back with muslin.

Wings present no special difficulty. Measure and cut the muslin so that the seam runs along the outside edge of the wing on chairs having muslin covers on both the inside and outside wing. If a muslin cover is used only on the inside wing, then cut it so that it extends around to the outside for tacking (Fig. 39).

Seat cushions are covered in Chapter Ten.

Whatever arm style you select, the frame must be constructed so that there are tack rails in the necessary locations (see Chapter Four: Frame Construction).

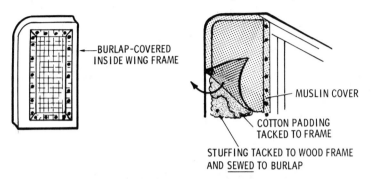

Fig. 39. Covering a wing with muslin.

MEASURING AND CUTTING THE MUSLIN FOR THE BACK

Both the inside and outside panels of the plain square back offer few problems. The same steps described for covering the seat are also applicable here. There are some backs that become wider at the top. These should be measured along the line of maximum width and height (Fig. 35).

Backs can also curve (see Fig. 36), sometimes to the extreme that the outside panels of the arms or sides are actually a continuation of the back itself.

If the latter is the case, the muslin cover could be one piece, two pieces, or three (Fig. 37).

The inside back can become complicated if piping or tufting is to be used (see Chapter Thirteen: Channels and Tufts). If the chair has a rectangular- or square-shaped back, there are several methods of measuring and constructing the muslin cover (Fig. 38). You may prefer to cut and sew four different pieces together (top, two sides, and the front). Another possibility is to cut the sides and front as one piece and sew a top piece to it. It really doesn't matter as long as you allow enough excess material (at least 1½ inches) for tacking and making seams.

CHAPTER 9

Pattern Layout

Pattern layout should be regarded as a very crucial stage in upholstering. Regardless of how skillfully you managed to construct your piece of furniture up to this point, the measuring and cutting of the fabric for the final cover will largely determine its appearance.

Most upholstery fabrics are sold in 54 inch widths, although 50 inch widths are also available. Material for slip covers is sold in a considerably greater variety of widths than upholstery fabric. However, never assume that you can use a slip cover fabric as a substitute for upholstery material. It does not have the strength or durability of the latter.

As you shall see, measuring for the final cover is far more complicated than simply taking the dimensions with a tape. After the measurements have been taken, they must be transferred to the length of upholstery fabric in such a way as to take into consideration the correct centering of any designs and the direction in which the fabric grain runs.

MEASUREMENTS

Fig. 1 indicates the approximate measurements for a number of different types of furniture. By comparing your piece of furniture with one of the outline drawings that most closely resembles it in style, you can arrive at a *rough* estimate of the length of material you will need. It is usually advisable to add a half yard to that measurement to be on the safe side.

Depending upon the furniture style, there will be a specific number of separate pieces to be cut from the length of fabric. These can be as few as a seat top and an inside and outside cover for the back to as many as 18-20 different types of cover pieces that can be encountered in upholstering (Fig. 2):

1. seat top (1)—Not illustrated
2. seat boxing (front and side) (1 to 4)
3. inside back (1)
4. outside back (1)—Not illustrated
5. back boxing (top and sides) (1 to 3)—Not illustrated
6. inside arm (2)
7. outside arm (2)
8. cushion top (1)
9. cushion bottom (1)—Not illustrated
10. cushion boxing (1 to 4)
11. arm top (2)—Not illustrated
12. front arm panel (2)
13. inside wing (2)
14. outside wing (2)
15. skirt or flounce (1 to 4)
16. welt

Pull strips are added to some of the above pieces. A pull strip is made from an inexpensive but strong material (e.g. denim) and sewn to the more expensive final cover. They can eliminate the use of expensive material in unexposed places. Additionally, the pull strip can be a stronger material and more susceptible to tacking at points of excessive strain. It is used to pull the final cover tight and into position in sections of the furniture that are awkward to manage. The pull strips are never exposed to view. Some of the final cover pieces to which pull strips are attached are illustrated in Fig. 3.

The procedure for measuring a piece of furniture is as follows:

1. Make a list of the final cover pieces to be measured. On your list allow a column for the name of the piece (e.g. "seat

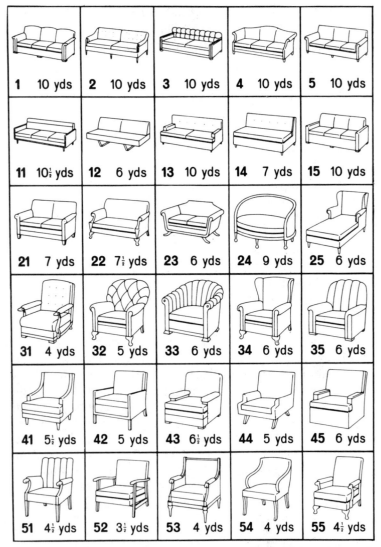

1 10 yds	**2** 10 yds	**3** 10 yds	**4** 10 yds	**5** 10 yds
11 10½ yds	**12** 6 yds	**13** 10 yds	**14** 7 yds	**15** 10 yds
21 7 yds	**22** 7⅓ yds	**23** 6 yds	**24** 9 yds	**25** 6 yds
31 4 yds	**32** 5 yds	**33** 6 yds	**34** 6 yds	**35** 6 yds
41 5½ yds	**42** 5 yds	**43** 6½ yds	**44** 5 yds	**45** 6 yds
51 4½ yds	**52** 3½ yds	**53** 4 yds	**54** 4 yds	**55** 4½ yds

Fig. 1. Fabric requirements for

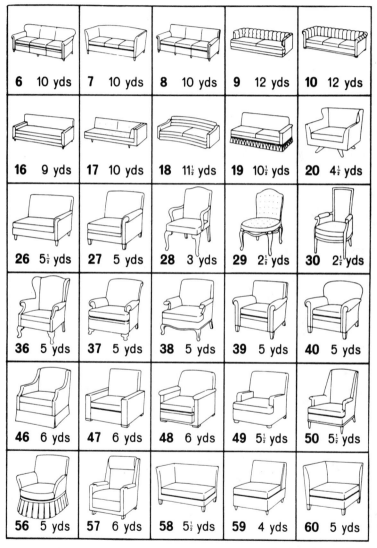

6 10 yds	**7** 10 yds	**8** 10 yds	**9** 12 yds	**10** 12 yds
16 9 yds	**17** 10 yds	**18** 11½ yds	**19** 10½ yds	**20** 4½ yds
26 5½ yds	**27** 5 yds	**28** 3 yds	**29** 2½ yds	**30** 2½ yds
36 5 yds	**37** 5 yds	**38** 5 yds	**39** 5 yds	**40** 5 yds
46 6 yds	**47** 6 yds	**48** 6 yds	**49** 5½ yds	**50** 5½ yds
56 5 yds	**57** 6 yds	**58** 5½ yds	**59** 4 yds	**60** 5 yds

Courtesy Uniroyal Corp.

various types of furniture.

PATTERN LAYOUT

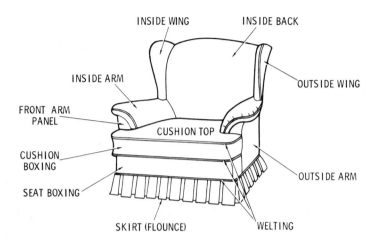

THERE ARE NOT MANY PIECES OF FURNITURE THAT WILL USE ALL SIXTEEN DIFFERENT
COVER PARTS. THIS CHAIR DOES NOT HAVE ARM TOPS (SEE NUMBER II IN CHART I)
AS YOU WOULD EXPECT TO FIND ON A LAWSON-TYPE CHAIR. THERE IS ALSO NO BACK
BOXING. THE OUTSIDE BACK, CUSHION BOTTOM, AND SEAT TOP CANNOT BE SEEN
WITH THE CHAIR IN THIS POSITION, BUT THEIR LOCATION SHOULD BE OBVIOUS.

Fig. 2. The names for the different parts of the cover.

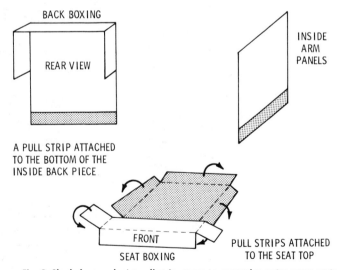

Fig. 3. Shaded areas depict pull strips sewn to expensive outer cover parts.

top," "inside back," etc.); the number of each piece required; the width measurements (including all allowances for seams tacking stretching, etc.); and the length (depth) measurements (including their allowances). See Table 1.

TABLE 1. List of Cover Measurements.

NAME OF THE COVER PIECE		NUMBER OF PIECES NEEDED	WIDTH	LENGTH
1	Seat Top	1		
2	Seat Boxing	1 to 4		
3	Inside Back	1		
4	Outside Back	1		
5	Back Boxing	1 to 3		
6	Inside Arm	2		
7	Outside Arm	2		
8	Cushion Top	1		
9	Cushion Bottom	1		
10	Cushion Boxing	1 to 4		
11	Arm Top	2		
12	Front Arm Panel	2		
13	Inside Wing	2		
14	Outside Wing	2		
15	Skirt (Flounce)	1 to 4		
16	Welting	Depends upon the number of seams to be covered		

TOTAL LENGTH
IN INCHES $\div 36 =$ TOTAL
YARDAGE
NEEDED

2. Measure the pieces in the order that you listed them. Lay the tape measure across the surface, pulling it as tight as you can *without depressing the surface.*
3. Take your *width* measurements first. These must be taken across the widest part of the surface. Make certain that you are measuring between the widest two points.

223

4. Add ½ to ¾ inch allowance for seams and tacking to exposed wood surfaces; 2 inches for attachment of stretchers or pullers; and 4 inches for pulling the fabric around frame edges and tacking.

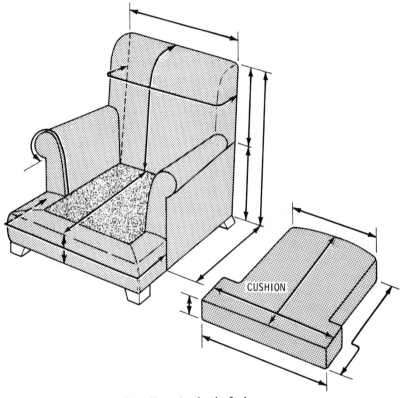

CUSHION

Fig. 4. Measuring for the final cover.

5. Fig. 4 illustrates the manner in which a number of various types of measurements are taken.

6. Transfer the measurements of each piece to a paper pattern. Mark the pattern so that the allowance is for each side.

7. Pin the paper patterns to the length of final cover fabric. Begin with the largest piece (or, in the case of the example, two that form the largest piece), proceed to the next largest

224

piece and so on. Place the pieces even with the left edge of the length of fabric. See Fig. 5.

Fig. 5. Cover patterns for chair of Table 1 pinned to fabric.

8. Lay out the welt strips across the width of the length of final cover fabric.

9. Special care must be taken to correctly center any design on the fabric. This is particularly true of stripes or patterns that repeat a floral design or some other motif.

10. The direction of the nap is also very important. On all pieces except the seat the nap should run downward (that is, in the direction of the floor). The seat should have the nap running toward the front.

After you have pinned each paper pattern to the final cover fabric, cut them out. Remove the paper patterns. You are now ready to begin sewing the final cover together and attaching it to your piece of furniture.

CHAPTER 10

Cushions

There are a variety of cushions used in upholstery, and they are best classified by their inner construction. The two basic categories are (1) stuffed cushions with springs and (2) stuffed cushions without springs. In the second category, we find cushions with side strips and those without (here the top is sewed directly to the bottom with a single strip of welting all around the cushion

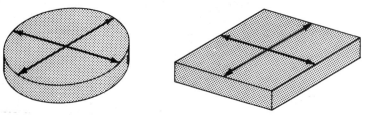

Fig. 1. Measurements for the top and bottom of a round and rectangular (square) cushion.

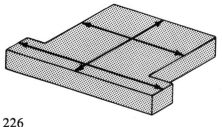

Fig. 2. Measurements for the top and bottom of a "T-shaped" cushion.

to conceal the seam). Cushions also come in a number of different shapes and sizes. The basic shape is the square or rectangular cushion, but there are also round cushions, triangular cushions, and, of course, the familiar T-shaped cushions used so frequently in over-stuffed furniture.

MEASUREMENTS

The measurements for the cushion must be taken over the widest and deepest portions of the seat area. The depth measurement will be from the farthest edge in the inside back to a corresponding point on the front. Of course, the tape must be kept exactly parallel to the side rail of the frame. Generally, a measurement extending between the insides of the two arms will produce the width measurement for the cushion. (Fig. 1). However, in the case of T-shaped cushions, a second measurement must be taken across the front of the frame between the two outside edges (Fig. 2). For all types of cushions there will be an additional ½ to ¾ inch allowance for seams when the pattern is cut.

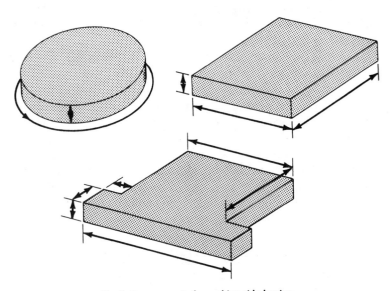

Fig. 3. Measurements for cushion side boxing.

The vertical width of the sides depends upon the thickness of the cushion. Once this is determined, place the end of the measuring tape in the middle of the back, and find the length measurement for a side strip that will fit all around the four sides of the cushion (Fig. 3). As was the case with the tops and bottoms, there will be an additional ½ to ¾ inch allowance for seams along the top and bottom edges of the side strip when the pattern is cut.

MAKING THE PATTERN

After having taken the depth and width measurements of the proposed top and bottom of the cushion, cut a paper pattern with at least a four-inch allowance around each edge for final adjustment. Place the pattern paper on the seat, take a marking pencil, and draw a line around the edges of the pattern corresponding to the upholstered curve of the inner arms and back. Now take a ruler and straighten the lines of the pattern so that the cushion sides will run in a straight line from corner to corner. An additional ½ to ¾ inch allowance must be made all around the edges for seams. This is the finished pattern for the tops and bottoms of both the casing and the outer upholstery cover. Trim away any excess paper beyond the outside edge of the seam allowance. The pattern is now ready for pinning to the material. If you prefer not using a paper pattern, cut out a piece of muslin (for a cushion casing) or a piece of the final cover fabric. Be sure to include a four inch allowance around each side for adjustments. Place this over the seat, mark the edges, and cut out both a top and a bottom for the cushion (Fig. 4).

Very little adjustment has to be made to the measurements of the side strip. Remember to add an additional ½ to ¾ inch allowance along the top and bottom edges for seams (and a like amount at the end of the side strip for a vertical seam on the back of the cushion) before cutting the pattern.

STUFFED CUSHIONS WITHOUT SPRINGS

Cushions that are stuffed with feathers, down, or animal hair should have an inner lining to prevent the stuffing from working

Courtesy Kwik-Bed Sofa Corp.

Fig. 4. (A.) Marking outline of cushion. (B.) Cutting the cushion top.

229

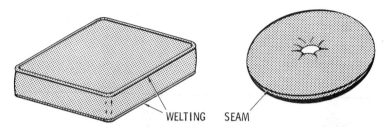

WELTING   SEAM

Fig. 5. Examples of cushion construction with and without side boxing.

its way through the outer upholstery fabric. In some respects this provides a function similar to that of the muslin cover described in Chapter Eight. That is, it contains the stuffing. It is wise to provide several compartments for the stuffing. This will prevent the stuffing from sliding from one end of the cushion to the other.

Stuffed cushions can be made with a side strip on all four sides or with the top sewed directly to the bottom. In the latter case a single seam runs completely around the cushion. This is concealed from view with a welting strip (Fig. 5).

The following outline covers the steps to be followed in constructing a springless, stuffed cushion.

1. Take the paper pattern for the top and bottom and place it on a heavy grade of muslin. Either pin the pattern to the material or carefully mark the edges of the pattern with a soft lead pencil. If the material color is dark, chalk is suitable for marking. Cut out the top and bottom and lay them aside for a moment.

2. Take the pattern for the side strips and place it on the muslin. Pin or mark the pattern on the material and cut out the side strip.

3. Sew the bottom of the casing to the front and sides of the side strip. Leave the back open. Now do the same with the top. The cushion will be filled with stuffing through the open back.

4. The stuffing should be inserted in the casing firmly, but not so that it is packed. The farthest corners (in this case the front corners) should be filled first. Fill outward from these

corners. If animal hair, down, or kapok are used, they must be separated so that there are no lumps when they are inserted into the casing.

5. In the type of cushion construction described in Steps One through Four there is the problem of the stuffing sliding from one end of the cushion to the other. This is particularly true if down or feathers are used. One consequence of this is that some stuffings will pack and form uncomfortable lumps. The stuffings can be kept from sliding by securing it in place with several stitches running through the top of the

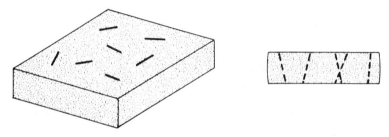

Fig. 6. Random stitches through the casing to keep stuffing in position.

casing (Fig. 6). Do not pull the stitches so tight that the surface of the cushion is depressed. Remember, these stitches are merely to hold the stuffing in position within the cushion casing.

6. Another method of preventing the stuffing from sliding is to divide the casing into several compartments. Divide the bottom cover into three equal sections. Use a soft lead pencil and mark the two lines dividing these three sections on the inside of the bottom cover (Fig. 7). Sew the side strips to the bottom all the way around the cushion, including the back.

7. The two inner partition walls dividing the interior of the casing into three compartments must have the same measurements as the side strip (except for length). For example, if the side strip is four inches wide with a ½ inch seam allowance on each edge, then the partitioning walls must be the same. Their length must be sufficient to reach across the interior of the casing with an additional allowance for

Cushions

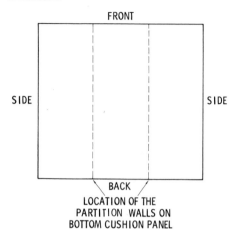

FRONT

SIDE

SIDE

BACK

LOCATION OF THE
PARTITION WALLS ON
BOTTOM CUSHION PANEL

Fig. 7. Marking the location
of the partition walls.

sewing to the inside at the front and back of the side walls of the cushion (Fig. 8).

8. Sew the top cover of the casing into position, leaving a gap at the back so that each of the three compartments can be filled (Fig. 9).

9. Fill the casing with stuffing, following the procedure detailed in Step Four. Having filled the casing, sew the remainder of the top closed.

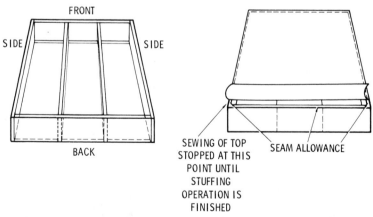

FRONT

SIDE

SIDE

BACK

SEWING OF TOP
STOPPED AT THIS
POINT UNTIL
STUFFING
OPERATION IS
FINISHED

SEAM ALLOWANCE

Fig. 8. Interior construction of a
partitioned casing.

Fig. 9. Stuffing a partitioned
casing.

10. We are now ready to construct the outer upholstery cover. The same pattern used to cut the casing can be used to cut the outer upholstery cover. Some precaution must be taken to center the design (stripes, checks, etc.). For example, stripes must be cut so that they run vertical to the bottom edge of the cushion (on the side strips) or parallel to the side edge (on the top and bottom cover) and not on a diagonal to them (Fig. 10). Stripes running from front to back

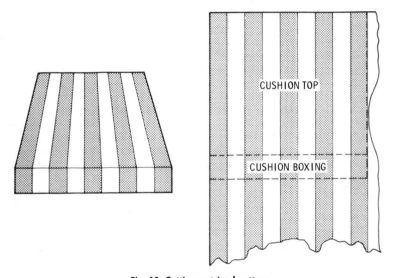

Fig. 10. Cutting a striped pattern.

on a cushion should be lined up to match the stripes on the inside back and bottom front of the chair or sofa. Failure to align them will reduce the neat appearance of the job. A major difference in constructing the outer upholstery cover is that the edges of the material will not be sewn directly together. Instead, welting will be inserted to conceal the seam. The seam itself will be blind sewn (Fig. 11). The only place where welting will not be used will be on the vertical seam on the side strip at the back of the cushion. The material pattern on the welting, particularly when stripes are

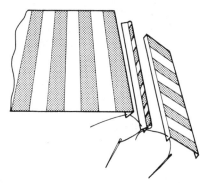

Fig. 11. Using welting on the edge of a cushion.

involved, is placed with the stripes running diagonally when assembling the welting.

STUFFED CUSHIONS WITH SPRINGS

The springs used in cushions are usually under 4 inches in height and diameter, which is smaller than those used in general upholstery work. In the case of springs used in cushions, a sturdy but compact unit is needed that will fit between the layers of stuffing and cotton on the inside.

Each row of cushion inner springs is individually encased in muslin. The number of rows that will fit the cushion in question is determined first. These rows are then sewed together to build a spring section of the desired size.

The following is an outline for constructing a stuffed cushion containing a spring unit.

1. Measure and cut the pattern in the same way as described at the beginning of this chapter. Take this pattern and cut a casing from a heavy grade of muslin. This same pattern can be used to cut the pieces for the outer upholstery cover.

2. Sew the side strip to the bottom of the casing. Position the seam of the side strip (the one joining the two ends of the side strip together) so that it is located on the back of the casing and sew it closed. This is, in a sense, a dry-run since the seam will not show regardless of where it is placed on

the casing. However, locating it on the back of the cushion is a must when the outer upholstery cover is made.

3. It is sometimes advisable to cover the inner spring unit with a layer of lightweight burlap. This will give added protection against the possibility of stuffing slipping out and working down through the springs (Fig. 12).

Courtesy Blocksom & Co.

Fig. 12. An innerspring unit covered with lightweight burlap.

4. Cover the bottom of the casing with a layer of cotton (Fig. 13).

5. Cover the cotton with a 1½ to 2 inch layer of stuffing. Spread the stuffing so that it is evenly distributed. Place the inner spring unit on top of this layer of stuffing (Fig. 13).

6. Spread a layer of stuffing across the top of the spring unit. Cover this with a layer of cotton. Cut a strip of cotton for the side strip and sew it into position (Fig. 14).

7. Sew the top of the casing to the side strips. The casing is now ready for the outer upholstery cover. The same patterns used to cut the casing can be used for the cover. The seams will be blind sewn and concealed by lengths of welting (Fig. 11).

8. Although the previous seven steps described the construction of a cushion with a muslin casing between the final cover and the cotton padding, it may be constructed without the casing. The layer of lightweight burlap around the springs is also optional (Fig. 15).

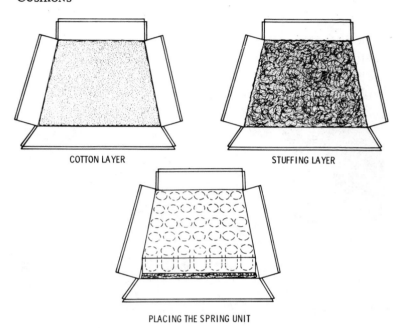

COTTON LAYER   STUFFING LAYER

PLACING THE SPRING UNIT

Fig. 13. Placing the cotton and stuffing base in a casing.

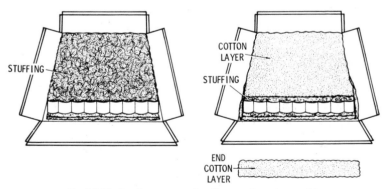

STUFFING

COTTON
LAYER

STUFFING

END
COTTON
LAYER

Fig. 14. Placing the cotton and stuffing top layer in a casing.

ZIPPERS

A zipper is sometimes used instead of sewing closed the back of the outer upholstery cover. This is placed in the middle of the side strip running across the back of the cushion. If the side strip

236

Courtesy Blocksom & Co.

Fig. 15. A spring cushion constructed without a casing.

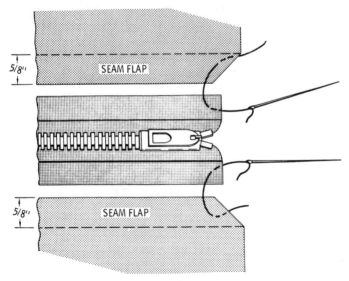

Fig. 16. Installing a zipper.

is 3 inches wide (on the finished cushion), cut *two* strips 1½ inches wide with an allowance of ⅝ inch (to be turned under along the center edge) plus ½ to ¾ inches on each outer edge for the seam allowance (Fig. 16). Sew the center edges and the zipper to-gether first. Note that the ⅝ inch turn-under along the center edge is sewn to the zipper material with a single stitch carried through the outer upholstery cover. The side strip with zipper is then sewed to the top and bottom covers with a welting strip to conceal the seam (Fig. 11). Since the back strip is a separate piece of material, vertical seams will connect it to the side strips at each corner. These seams do not have to be concealed with welting.

It is recommended to extend the zipper all the way across the back. This enables one to insert or remove the casing with less difficulty. There are variations in zipper openings on cushions. These range from only a partial opening on the back (e.g. about 2 inches short of each corner) to one which extends around the back for several inches (Fig. 17). Zippers can be purchased as units in a variety of lengths with instructions for installing them.

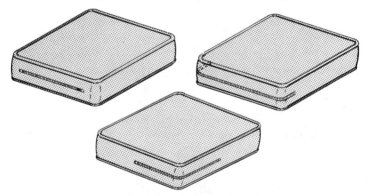

Fig. 17. Various zipper styles for cushions.

INSTALLING FINAL COVER (SPRING CUSHIONS)

Installing the assembled spring cushion into the final cover usually requires the use of cushion irons. Cushion irons compress the cushion so it can be placed inside the outer cover. Chapter Two gives a detailed account on how to use cushion irons or how to construct a home-made cardboard unit for temporary usage.

Fig. 18 shows the employment of a commercial unit. Fig. 18A depicts the top in the raised position. The top is lowered and the sides move toward each other. This action compresses the inner

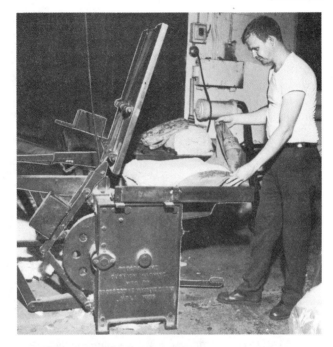

Courtesy Kwik-Bed Sofa Corp.

Fig. 18. Use of Commercial Cushion Machine.

cushion to a size smaller than the outer cover. As shown in Fig. 18B, the outer cover is placed over the compressing plates of the machine. A foot control then operates a back plate which moves toward the operator, pushing the inner cushion out of the compressing plates. This same action also pulls the outer cover off the machine. Once the stuffed cushion has cleared the machine, the rear zipper on the cover is closed and the cushion is finished.

Prior to inserting the inner spring unit on a "T" cushion, the "T" ends are hand-stuffed.

MORE ON CUSHIONS

It was mentioned in this chapter that cushions without inner spring units can keep the stuffing from sliding by stitching through the middle of the cushion. This can be carried through to the outer upholstery cover with a series of tufts (see Chapter Thirteen for details on constructing tufts).

Not only is it necessary to take care that the design on the outer upholstery cover is centered properly, but the same precaution should be extended to the pile. *Pile* fabrics (velvet, velveteen, corduroy, mohair, etc.) are so named because of the short hair-like filaments that cover the surface. When you run your hand across the pile it smoothes down or stands straight up (in much the same way that an animal's fur will) depending upon the direction in which you move your hand. The outer upholstery cover should be cut so that the pile smoothes down toward the floor on the side strips and toward the front on the top of the cushion. If you make a mistake and cut any of the pieces of the material so that the pile runs in a contrasting direction (for example, opposite directions on the joined ends of the pieces) then it will have the undesirable appearance of having two slightly different colors.

Cushions can be made to be reversible or non-reversible. Reversible cushions require equal attention in centering the design of both the top and bottom covers. Non-reversible cushions can use a plain, good quality material for the bottom cover. The material on the sides overlaps the bottom to conceal the plain fabric from view.

Instead of cutting a separate top and bottom cover, a single piece can be used. This must be cut long enough to extend from the back bottom edge of the cushion around the front to the back top edge. The interior construction remains the same, but instead of a flat piece of cotton over the stuffing in the front, a tightly rolled section of cotton can be used. This will give the front of the cushion a slightly rounded appearance. Welting is extended around the top and bottom edges of the sides and back.

Chapter Eleven gives a detailed description of the use of foam rubber in the construction of cushions.

Using Foam Padding

Foam padding is produced from either natural rubber or a synthetic plastic. It varies in density from very soft to very firm, depending upon the air content. The degree of softness or firmness is determined by how much weight is required to produce a depression of twenty-five percent. Thus, an extra soft density requires 5-10 lbs. pressure; whereas, a firm density needs 40 lbs. or more.

Foam rubber (the natural rubber derivative) is produced by whipping the latex mixture (composed of latex, gelling agents, and other ingredients) until a mixture of roughly 85% air to 15% rubber is attained. Flexible polyurethane foam (the plastic derivative) is produced by introducing a chemical activator into the

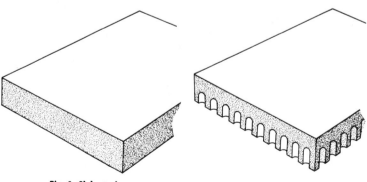

Fig. 1. Slab stock.   **Fig. 2. Cored stock.**

plastic base materials. Polyurethane foam is cheaper than foam rubber. It is also lighter. A square 22 inch by 4 inch piece of polyurethane foam weighs 1 lb. 4 oz. An identical piece of foam rubber, on the other hand, weighs 5 lbs. 3 oz. Foam rubber is considerably more expensive than polyurethane foam. Because of these weight and price factors, polyurethane foam is replacing foam rubber as an upholstering and cushion material.

THE MANUFACTURED PRODUCT

Foam rubber is manufactured in four forms: (1) slab stock, (2) cored stock, (3) molded cushion units, and (4) molded pillow units.

Slab stock (Fig. 1) is a thin pad ranging in thickness from ¼ inch to 2 inches (graduating by quarter inch sizes). It comes in a variety of widths and lengths depending upon the manufacturer.

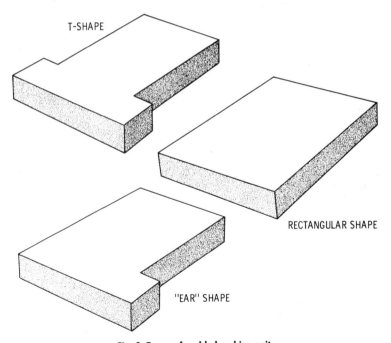

T-SHAPE

RECTANGULAR SHAPE

"EAR" SHAPE

Fig. 3. Types of molded cushion units.

Foam rubber slab stock is available in four densities: (1) very soft (5-10 lbs.); (2) soft (10-25 lbs.); (3) medium (25-40 lbs.); and (4) firm (40-60 lbs.).

Cored stock or cored utility stock (Fig. 2) contains numerous cores of a uniform size, shape, and distribution. These cores produce greater resiliency in the material which results in greater seating comfort. It ranges in thickness from ¾ to 4½ inches. The widths and lengths depend upon the manufacturer. It is available in the same densities as slab stock with an additional grade of extra firm (60-85 lbs.).

The molded cushion units (Fig. 3) are completely molded pieces of foam padding used in making cushions or bolsters. Square and rectangular cushion units are available in 12 × 12, 16 × 16, 16 × 18, 18 × 20, 18 × 22, 20 × 20, 20 × 22, 20 × 24, 22 × 22, 22 × 24, 22 × 32, and 22 × 36 inch sizes. T-shaped and L-shaped cushion units are also available. Bolster units can be found in wedge or round shapes.

Fig. 4. Molded pillow units.

The molded pillow units (Fig. 4) are manufactured in round or square shapes and are available in 12 × 12, 14 × 14, and 16 × 16 inch sizes.

Both cushion and pillow units are available in a variety of thicknesses.

Flexible polyurethane foam can be purchased in three forms: (1) slab stock or pad form, (2) molded cushion units, and (3) molded pillow units. The sizes offered are similar to those in foam rubber. However, it should be noted there is no cored stock in flexible polyurethane foam.

ADVANTAGES OF USING FOAM PADDING

There are many advantages to using foam rubber or flexible polyurethane foam in upholstering. Neither of the two will mildew (as other types of padding are prone to do), and they are non-allergenic. Although foam padding is slightly more expensive than other types, it is far easier to work with. It is lightweight, resilient, and washable. Foam padding gives a comfortable, uniform support by equalizing the pressure at the point of contact. When the pressure is removed, the foam padding immediately resumes its shape.

TOOLS AND SUPPLIES

A pair of heavy shears (at least six inches long) is recommended for cutting foam padding. The padding can be marked for the cuts on the smooth side with a marking pen and a straight edge. Soapstone—a powdery stone which takes its name from the soapy feel it imparts— is sprinkled across the surface of the working area to prevent the foam padding from sticking and gripping. It is also used to absorb the excess bonding cement along the edges of seams or dusted into the holes in cored stock to prevent the core walls from sticking together.

The manufacturer of the foam padding will also generally sell a bonding cement to use with his product. All of the mail-order houses sell a cement along with their foam padding. This bonding cement works on both polyurethane and foam rubber. It is used not only to bond seams together, but also to attach the tacking (or reinforcement) tape and to cement the padding to the base. Tapes can be purchased in a number of widths depending upon the requirements of the particular piece of work.

LAYING OUT AND CUTTING FOAM PADDING

Foam padding is very resilient. The padding gives quite easily under pressure but immediately springs back to its original shape once the pressure is released. Therefore, in order for the upholstery covers to form a smooth, snug fit, the foam padding must be

245

cut slightly larger than the measurements required for the pattern. The excess, or allowance, is determined by the size of the padding and its firmness. However, this is not true for fully molded reversible cushions, pillows, or bolsters because an allowance has already been included in their measurements before they were cut.

Firm padding requires a smaller allowance than softer types. Larger pieces of padding require greater allowances than smaller ones. Anything under 6 inches in width or length should receive an allowance of ¼ inch. Up to one foot, the allowance should be at least one-half inch. Above one foot, the allowance increases a quarter inch to one half inch for each foot. (Refer to Table I.)

Table 1. Allowances for Measurements in Excess of One Foot

Measurement	Allowance
12-23″	1″
24-35″	1¼″
36-47″	1½″
48-59″	1¾″
60-71″	2″
72-83″	2¼″

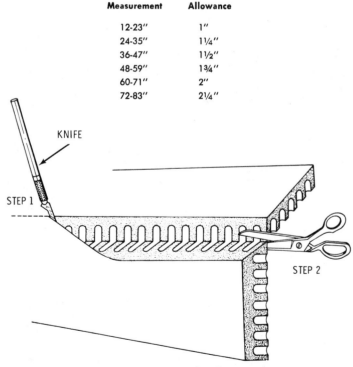

KNIFE

STEP 1

STEP 2

Fig. 5. Cutting cored stock.

All thicknesses of slab stock can be cut with heavy shears. This holds true for cored stock up to 2 inches thick. Thicker cored stock should be cut twice—once along the top and once along the bottom. The top cut is made first across the smooth (closed) surface. This cut must be deep enough to separate each core at the top. The second cut is made from the bottom (the open cores) for the purpose of separating the core walls. Either heavy shears or a sharp knife can be used to make the two cuts (Fig. 5).

REVERSIBLE OR LOOSE CUSHIONS

Both foam rubber (cored stock) and polyurethane foam can be purchased in the form of T-shaped, L-shaped, square-shaped, and rectangular-shaped cushions to be used as reversible or loose cushions on a piece of furniture. These cushions are manufactured in a variety of sizes so it is not too difficult to find the right size for your needs. There is sometimes a slight crown on these cushions, but it is not a very high one. A higher crown can be constructed by gluing together two pieces of crowned cored foam rubber. The procedure is as follows:

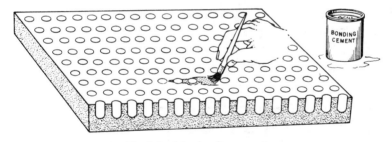

Fig. 6. Applying bonding cement.

1. Assuming that you have selected two crown cored sections of equal measurements, position them together so that the core openings meet one another. After you are certain that the two pieces match in their dimensions, apply the bonding cement to their surfaces (Fig. 6). Place them on a flat surface with the core openings facing up. Brush the bonding cement on the surface and allow it to dry until it becomes tacky.

247

2. As soon as the cement has become tacky, place the two halves together. Make certain that they are both aligned correctly. Hold them in this position for about a minute or two. Let them dry for two hours (Fig. 7).

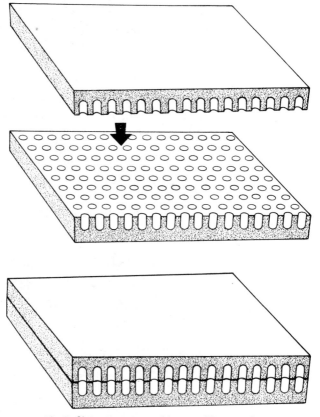

Fig. 7. Gluing two pieces of foam padding together.

3. The crown can be made higher by bevelling the open core bottoms and inserting a few glued layers of thin slab stock before cementing the two halves together (Fig. 8). The total amount of the material removed from the top and bottom when bevelling should be less than the total thickness of the slab insert. The greater the difference, the greater the arch.

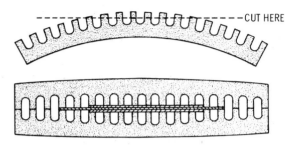

Fig. 8. Inserting thin slab stock to create a crown.

4. The edges of the cushion can be given a rounded contour by cementing a piece of slab foam padding on each side of the cushion. This slab foam padding should be 1 inch thick with a width 1½ to 2 inches less than the center crown of the cushion. Its length should be the same dimensions as the cushion side to which it is glued. Cement the slab to the edge of the cushion using tape for additional joint strength as illustrated in Fig. 9. This tape can be purchased along with the bonding cement. The combined unit is then cut for whatever contour is desired.

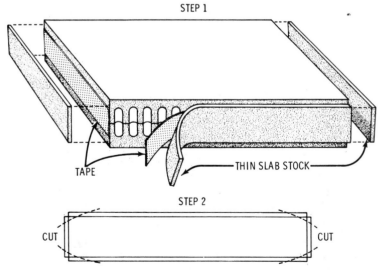

Fig. 9. Cementing foam slabs to sides of a cushion.

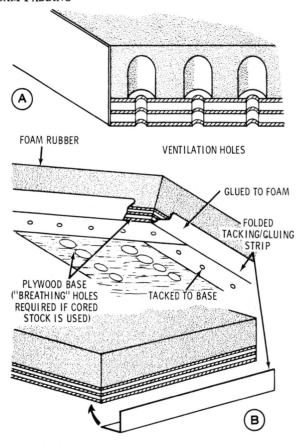

Fig. 10. Foam padding used over a solid base.

ATTACHING FOAM PADDING

Foam padding can be attached to either an open or a closed base. Open bases employ springs or webbing or both. In either case, the very nature of this type construction provides ample ventilation when using foam padding. However, closed bases of metal, wood, or plastic should have holes drilled through them at regularly-spaced intervals to provide the necessary ventilation (Fig. 10). Tape can be glued to the sides and folded under the bottom for tacking to securely hold the foam in place.

If springs are used as a base, they should be covered with burlap which is stitched to the coil tops. The foam padding is then placed over the burlap and may be covered with a layer of muslin (Fig. 11).

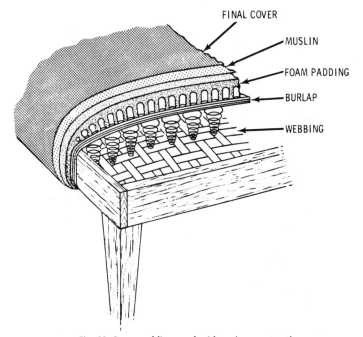

FINAL COVER

MUSLIN

FOAM PADDING

BURLAP

WEBBING

Fig. 11. Foam padding used with spring construction.

FORMING EDGES

The advantage of working with foam padding is the ease with which edges can be made. Three of the more common types of edges are: (1) the square or straight edge, (2) the feathered or contoured edge, and (3) the cushion edge (Fig. 12).

The square or straight edge is cut so that there is a ¼ to ½ inch overhang around the edges of the base. This is the upholstery allowance. Attach the tape to the sides of the foam padding and bend the excess tape around to the bottom of the base. DO NOT pull it taut or it will distort the contour of the square edge. Tack the tape to the bottom of the base. The edge will not be

251

exactly vertical because of the upholstery allowance (the top of the pad still extends beyond the base). Once the cover is placed over the padding this overhang will be eliminated (Fig. 13).

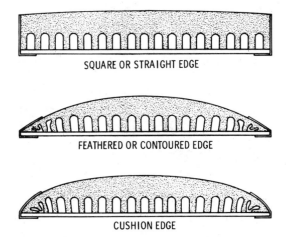

SQUARE OR STRAIGHT EDGE

FEATHERED OR CONTOURED EDGE

CUSHION EDGE

Fig. 12. Three types of edges used with foam padding.

To form the cushion edge, cut the foam for a ⅞ inch overhang. The tape is cemented one inch in on the upper edge of the foam padding and allowed to dry. Then, it is pulled down so that the upper outside edge is even with the top of the base. Carry the excess tape around to the bottom of the base and tack it into place. This operation will cause the core walls near the outside of the padding to collapse and be forced in toward the center of the padding. This is important to the formation of the cushion edge (therefore, do not cement the bottom of the padding to the base) (Fig. 14).

The feathered or contoured edge is distinguished from the cushion edge in that there is a more gradual curvature to the edge. The latter is formed by compressing (tucking under) the cores. The overhang allowance for the foam pad is the same as that for the cushion edge. However, in this case the lower outside edge is bevelled. The amount of bevelling determines the degree of curvature for the feathered edge. The tape is applied as described for the cushion edge. (Fig. 15).

252

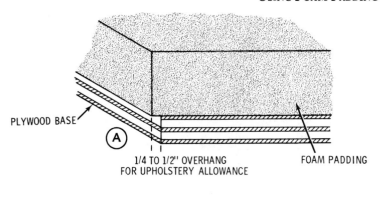

PLYWOOD BASE

(A)

1/4 TO 1/2" OVERHANG
FOR UPHOLSTERY ALLOWANCE

FOAM PADDING

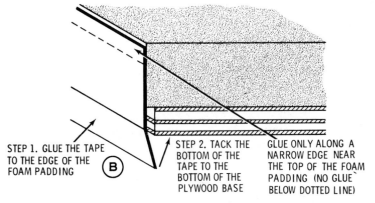

STEP 1. GLUE THE TAPE
TO THE EDGE OF THE
FOAM PADDING

(B)

STEP 2. TACK THE
BOTTOM OF THE
TAPE TO THE
BOTTOM OF THE
PLYWOOD BASE

GLUE ONLY ALONG A
NARROW EDGE NEAR
THE TOP OF THE FOAM
PADDING (NO GLUE
BELOW DOTTED LINE)

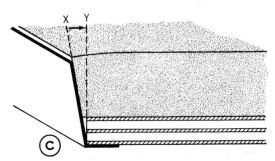

X   Y

(C)

PULLING THE FINAL COVER TAUT WILL COMPRESS THE FOAM PADDING
FORCE THE EDGES INTO A VERTICAL POSITION (X TO Y). AND
THIS, IN TURN, WILL CREATE A FIRMER, MORE COMPACT SHAPE.

Fig. 13. Forming the square edge.

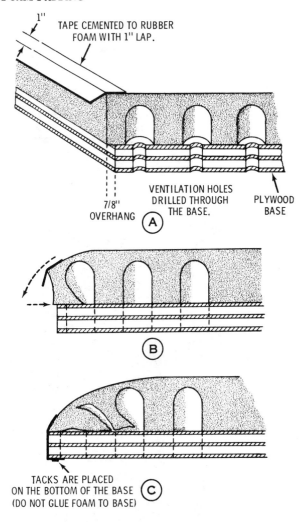

Fig. 14. Forming the cushion edge.

CROWNS, SADDLE SEATS, AND SLIP SEATS

Both the cushioned and feathered edges produce slight crowns. However, higher crowns—especially near the very center of the seat—can be constructed by inserting sections of slab stock beneath

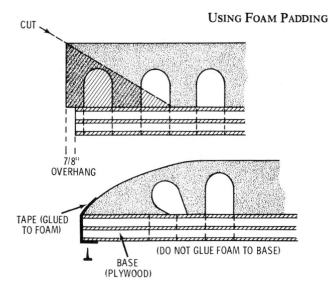

CUT

7/8"
OVERHANG

TAPE (GLUED
TO FOAM)

(DO NOT GLUE FOAM TO BASE)

BASE
(PLYWOOD)

Fig. 15. Forming the feathered or contoured edge.

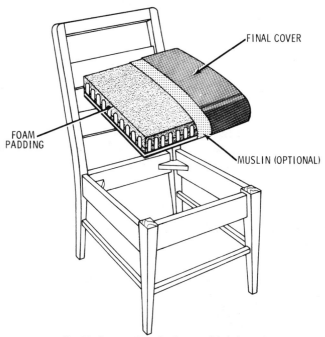

FINAL COVER

FOAM
PADDING

MUSLIN (OPTIONAL)

Fig. 16. Construction of a foam-padded slip seat.

255

the main padding. The height of the crown depends upon the number and thickness of slab stock sections inserted.

The opposite of the crown is the contoured depression found in saddle seats or seats molded to fit the shape of the human body. It is best to cut the wood base to the desired shape and cover it with a thin layer of slab stock foam padding.

Slab stock is also used in the construction of slip seats. The padding is about ¾ to 1 inch thick and is cut to include a ¼ to ½ inch upholstery allowance (Fig. 16).

BACKS

Backs can be constructed from either solid slab or cored stock. The base for the back can be either closed or open. Again, remember to provide the necessary ventilation holes in a closed base. Because backs receive less pressure than seats, foam padding of a softer density is generally used in their construction. Methods of back construction are the same as those of seat construction.

ARMS

Arms, particularly the inside arm sections of overstuffed furniture, use either solid slab or cored stock. Again, because the pressure is not as great against this surface, a softer-density padding is usually used (Fig. 17).

Note that stuffing can also be placed between the foam padding and the top of the arm rail for greater resiliency.

PIPES AND TUFTS

Using foam padding makes the construction of pipes (channels) and tufts much easier than is the case with loose stuffing. This is because the foam padding can be cut to the desired shape. Each section is then of a uniform size and in a single piece. See Fig. 18 for the steps in using foam padding in the construction of channels (pipes) and Fig. 19 for tufts. The formed channel slabs are inserted into pockets in the final cover. See the next chapter for more details.

256

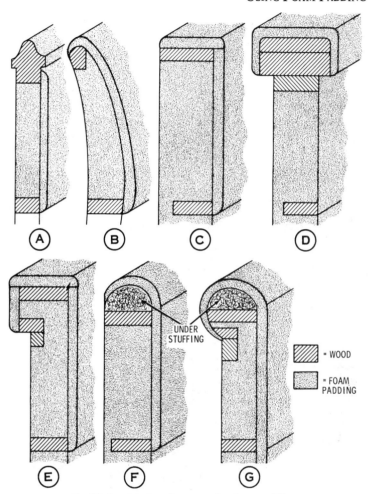

Fig. 17. Construction of an arm using foam padding.

THE UPHOLSTERY COVER

The upholstery cover is attached over foam padding in exactly the same way it is attached over loose stuffing (see Chapter Twelve: The Final Cover). A muslin cover is generally not necessary over foam padding though its use does reduce any possible friction between the padding and outer cover.

257

Using Foam Padding

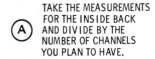

TAKE THE MEASUREMENTS FOR THE INSIDE BACK AND DIVIDE BY THE NUMBER OF CHANNELS YOU PLAN TO HAVE.

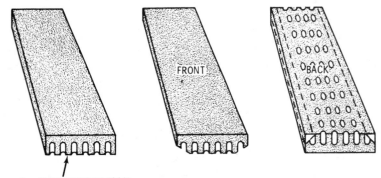

1. CUT A PIECE OF FOAM PADDING (CORED STOCK) FOR EACH CHANNEL, ADDING ABOUT 1/4 INCH ALLOWANCE FOR EXTRA FIRMNESS.

2. CUT A BEVEL ALONG THE BACK EDGE OF THE CHANNEL.

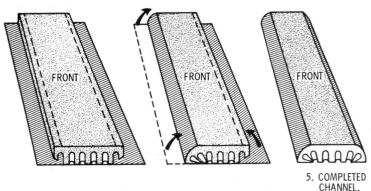

3. GLUE A MUSLIN BACKING TO THE BACK OF THE CHANNEL. GIVE ENOUGH ALLOWANCE FOR THE MUSLIN TO EXTEND 1 INCH INSIDE THE FRONT.

4. PUSH DOWN AGAINST THE EDGES SO THAT THE BEVEL TOUCHES THE MUSLIN. PULL THE MUSLIN AROUND AND GLUE IT TO THE FOAM PADDING.

5. COMPLETED CHANNEL.

Fig. 18. Constructing channels with foam.

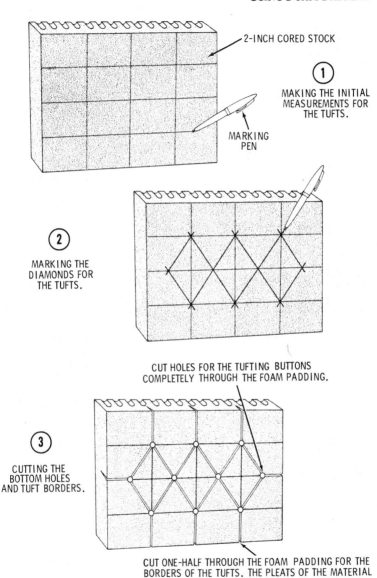

2-INCH CORED STOCK

1 MAKING THE INITIAL MEASUREMENTS FOR THE TUFTS.

MARKING PEN

2 MARKING THE DIAMONDS FOR THE TUFTS.

CUT HOLES FOR THE TUFTING BUTTONS COMPLETELY THROUGH THE FOAM PADDING.

3 CUTTING THE BOTTOM HOLES AND TUFT BORDERS.

CUT ONE-HALF THROUGH THE FOAM PADDING FOR THE BORDERS OF THE TUFTS. THE PLEATS OF THE MATERIAL FORMING THE TUFTS WILL PULL DOWN INTO THESE SLOTS WHEN THE BUTTONS ARE ATTACHED.

Fig. 19. Constructing tufts with foam.

259

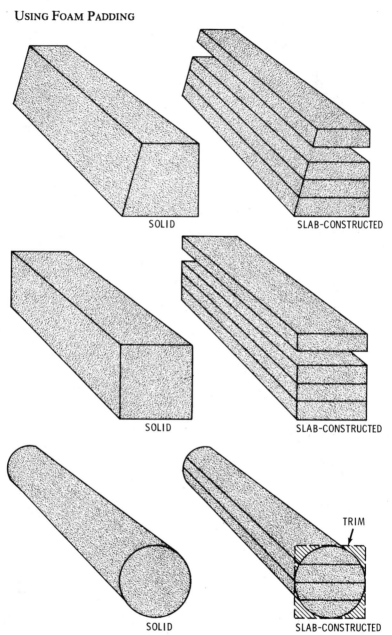

SOLID
SLAB-CONSTRUCTED

SOLID
SLAB-CONSTRUCTED

TRIM

SOLID
SLAB-CONSTRUCTED

Fig. 20. Varieties of foam bolsters.

BOLSTERS

Bolsters are long pillows or cushions that extend the width of a couch or bed. They are loose—that is, they are not permanently attached to the furniture—and they are covered with an upholstery fabric. The fabric of the bolster can be either sewed permanently closed or can be made removable by placing a zipper along one side. Bolsters are found in a variety of sizes and shapes including wedge-shaped, round-shaped, and square-shaped (Fig. 20).

The shape of a bolster can be changed by cementing other pieces of foam padding to it or by cutting away unwanted material.

Foam padding can be purchased in pre-molded shapes for the construction of bolsters. These are generally either wedge-shaped or roll-shaped. As was the case with reversible (or loose) cushions and pillows, pre-molded bolsters already have the upholstery allowance included in their measurements.

A muslin cover is not required between the bolster's upholstery cover and the foam padding.

CHAPTER 12

The Final Cover

In Chapter Nine we were introduced to a number of different patterns for measuring and cutting the final cover. This chapter is concerned with describing the methods of sewing the cover together, and the types of decoration and trim used to enhance the final product.

NEEDLES, THREADS, AND THIMBLES

The different types of needles used in upholstering were described in the second chapter. Some additional comments seem appropriate at this point. Needles will last longer if you buy good quality steel ones and take care of them properly. Protect needles from rusting by keeping them covered when not using them. Try to avoid hitting wood sections of the frame when sewing to protect the points from dulling.

Thimbles should be used whenever possible. Thimbles are especially useful when pressure is required to push the needle through thick materials. There are arguments pro and con for using either the steel or plastic thimble. The author is a partisan of neither, but he does urge you to purchase a thimble that fits properly (and *use* it).

Both nylon and flax stitching twines are used for hand sewing, but are usually limited to sections of the furniture not exposed to view (springs to webbing, burlap to springs, etc.). Sometimes these twines are coated with a wax finish.

Blind stitching is one of the few places in which the nylon or flax stitching twine may be used on the final cover. Regular sewing thread is used for all other exposed seams. The weight of the thread will depend upon the weight of the fabric.

SEAMS AND STITCHES

Seams are the edges of the material that have been joined together with stitches. There are many types of seams, but not all are suitable for upholstery work. A few are mentioned in this chapter only as examples for you to consider. Elsewhere in this book the use of the words "seam" or "stitch" has been purposely left unspecified. This is due to the fact that different upholstery fabrics have differing characteristics (weight, weave, etc.). Consequently, the type of seam or stitch that you use will depend upon the characteristics of the fabric with which you are working. By way of example, a plain stitch can be used with lighter weight fabrics, whereas, a welt stitch is more suitable for the heavier ones.

Before we begin a discussion of stitches, it might be wise to mention a few words about the basting process. *Basting* is a method of temporarily attaching two pieces of fabric together. It is temporary so that the worker can determine fit, design-centering, and other necessary adjustments before the pieces of material are permanently attached. Basting can be done with pins or a loose, widely spaced stitch. Once all adjustments have been made, a permanent stitch is run parallel to the basting stitches or pins. Then the pins or basting stitches are removed.

Care should be taken not to run a permanent stitch across a basting stitch. This makes it very difficult to remove the basting stitch.

The terms *right side* and *wrong side* are often encountered in descriptions of seam construction (Fig. 1A). These refer to the finished and unfinished sides of the fabric. The right side (or finished side) is the surface side, and the one that the manufacturer intended to be exposed to view. The *seam flap* (Fig. 1D) is the small portion of material that extends beyond the seam stitches.

The *plain seam* illustrated in Fig. 1 is the easiest seam to construct. It consists of a single, straight stitch. Note in Fig. 1A that

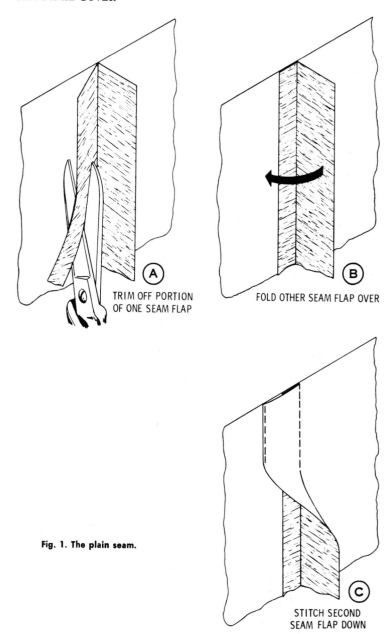

A — TRIM OFF PORTION OF ONE SEAM FLAP

B — FOLD OTHER SEAM FLAP OVER

C — STITCH SECOND SEAM FLAP DOWN

Fig. 1. The plain seam.

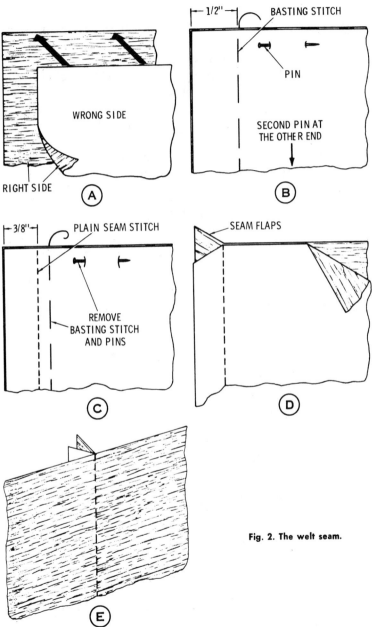

Fig. 2. The welt seam.

the *right sides* (the shaded portions in the line drawing) of the two pieces of material are placed facing each other before the stitch is run.

The *right sides* of the material are also placed together for the construction of the *welt seam* (Fig. 2). Until Fig. 2A, the procedure for forming a welt seam is identical for that of the plain seam. Note, however, that in steps A, B, and C the "welt" is formed on the *wrong side* (unfinished side) of the material.

There are many books on sewing that will give detailed descriptions of the above-mentioned seams as well as other types (French seam, flat-fell seam, finished edges, etc.) suitable for use in upholstering.

WELTS

Welts are long, fabric-covered cords used to conceal seams and to decorate edges (Fig. 3). They are attached by inserting and sew-

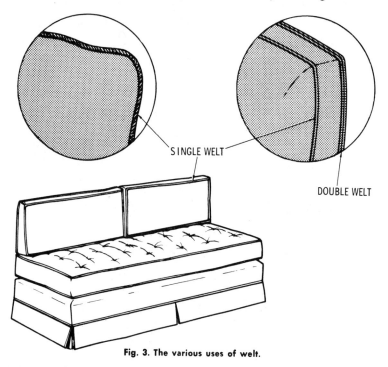

SINGLE WELT

DOUBLE WELT

Fig. 3. The various uses of welt.

ing the welt flaps between the final cover pieces. Because of this, they are discussed before any detailed description of sewing the final cover together is given.

Welts can be purchased ready-made or you can make them yourself. The ready-made welts are manufactured in a great variety of colors from a wide selection of materials. They are easy for the beginner to use and give his work a neat, professional touch. However, if you wish to match the welting fabric with that of the final cover, then you will have to make your own welts.

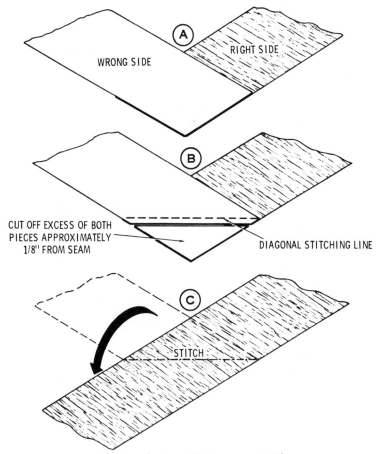

Fig. 4. Lengthening welt strip cover material.

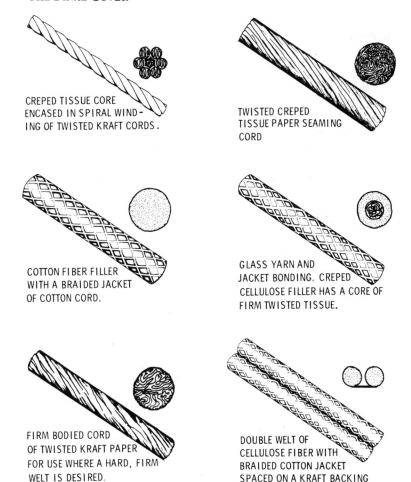

CREPED TISSUE CORE
ENCASED IN SPIRAL WIND-
ING OF TWISTED KRAFT CORDS.

TWISTED CREPED
TISSUE PAPER SEAMING
CORD

COTTON FIBER FILLER
WITH A BRAIDED JACKET
OF COTTON CORD.

GLASS YARN AND
JACKET BONDING. CREPED
CELLULOSE FILLER HAS A CORE OF
FIRM TWISTED TISSUE.

FIRM BODIED CORD
OF TWISTED KRAFT PAPER
FOR USE WHERE A HARD, FIRM
WELT IS DESIRED.

DOUBLE WELT OF
CELLULOSE FIBER WITH
BRAIDED COTTON JACKET
SPACED ON A KRAFT BACKING
STRIP.

Courtesy Sackner Products, Inc.

Fig. 5. Different types of welt cord used in upholstering.

The procedure for making welts is as follows:

1. The welt should be cut from the same material as the final cover. In doing so, the design and material characteristics should be taken into consideration. The material should be cut so that the design (e.g. stripes) runs diagonally on

each piece to eliminate matching problems. Such material characteristics as nap (found in velvet and similar fabrics) must be cut so that each welt piece has the nap running in the same direction as the larger material pieces whenever possible.

2. Cut sufficient 1½ to 2 inch wide strips of fabric to provide all the welt lengths you will require. Be certain that your estimate is correct. If you are caught short, it may be very difficult to find more of the same material.

3. If it is necessary to sew several pieces of fabric together for the welt, then join two pieces at a 90° angle and stitch a diagonal seam across the fabric. Trim off the excess and open the two pieces so that they extend as a continuation of one another (Fig. 4).

4. Welt *cords* can be purchased in rolls (up to 500 yards) and in a number of thicknesses. The most common sizes range

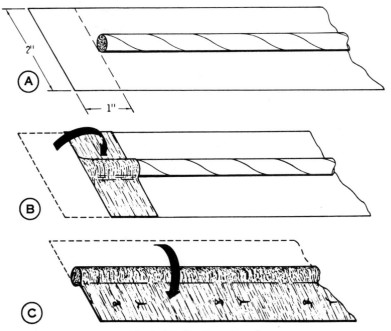

2"

1"

Fig. 6. Covering the welt cord.

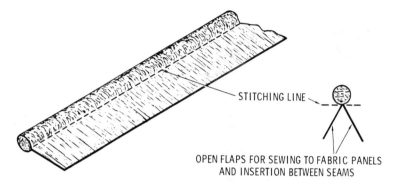

STITCHING LINE

OPEN FLAPS FOR SEWING TO FABRIC PANELS
AND INSERTION BETWEEN SEAMS

Fig. 7. Stitching the welt.

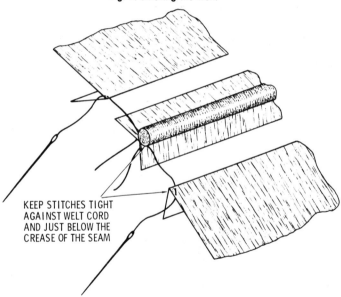

KEEP STITCHES TIGHT
AGAINST WELT CORD
AND JUST BELOW THE
CREASE OF THE SEAM

Fig. 8. Attaching welt to two different pieces of fabric.

between $\frac{1}{8}$ and $\frac{3}{16}$ inch. Welt cord is made from several different materials depending largely upon the stiffness desired. See Fig. 5.

5. Lay the welt cord along the exact center of the welting material. Fold the end over at about 1 inch. Fold the welting

material over the welt cord so that the edges are even. Pin
the two flaps together so that the material does not slip when
it is run through the sewing machine (Fig. 6).

6. Attach a welting (cording) foot to your sewing machine and
   run a stitch along the fabric as close as possible to the
   welt cord. Keep the seam straight. Remove the pins (Fig. 7).

7. Fig. 8 illustrates the method of attaching the completed
   welt to a section of the final cover.

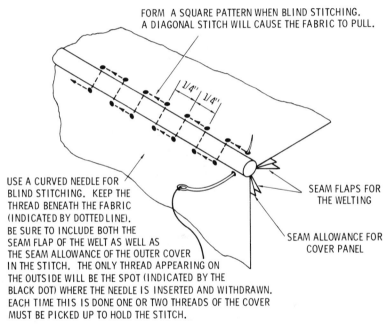

FORM A SQUARE PATTERN WHEN BLIND STITCHING.
A DIAGONAL STITCH WILL CAUSE THE FABRIC TO PULL.

1/4" 1/4"

USE A CURVED NEEDLE FOR
BLIND STITCHING. KEEP THE
THREAD BENEATH THE FABRIC
(INDICATED BY DOTTED LINE).
BE SURE TO INCLUDE BOTH THE
SEAM FLAP OF THE WELT AS WELL AS
THE SEAM ALLOWANCE OF THE OUTER COVER
IN THE STITCH. THE ONLY THREAD APPEARING ON
THE OUTSIDE WILL BE THE SPOT (INDICATED BY THE
BLACK DOT) WHERE THE NEEDLE IS INSERTED AND WITHDRAWN.
EACH TIME THIS IS DONE ONE OR TWO THREADS OF THE COVER
MUST BE PICKED UP TO HOLD THE STITCH.

SEAM FLAPS FOR
THE WELTING

SEAM ALLOWANCE FOR
COVER PANEL

Fig. 9. Blind stitching.

BLIND SEWING OR STITCHING

A blind stitch is so named because it is sewn or stitched in such
a way that it is concealed from the eyes of the viewer. Blind sewing
is frequently used to attach padded panels and the outside portions
(back, wing, arms) of the final cover. The seam is completely
hidden from view.

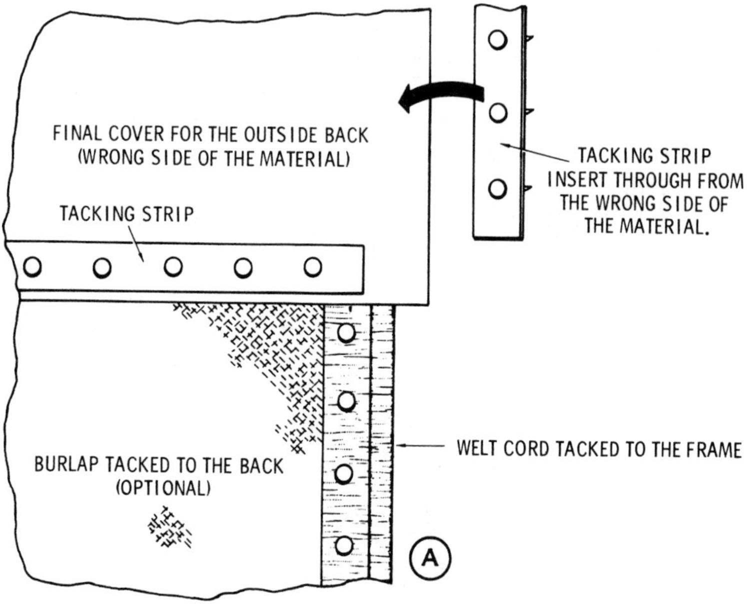

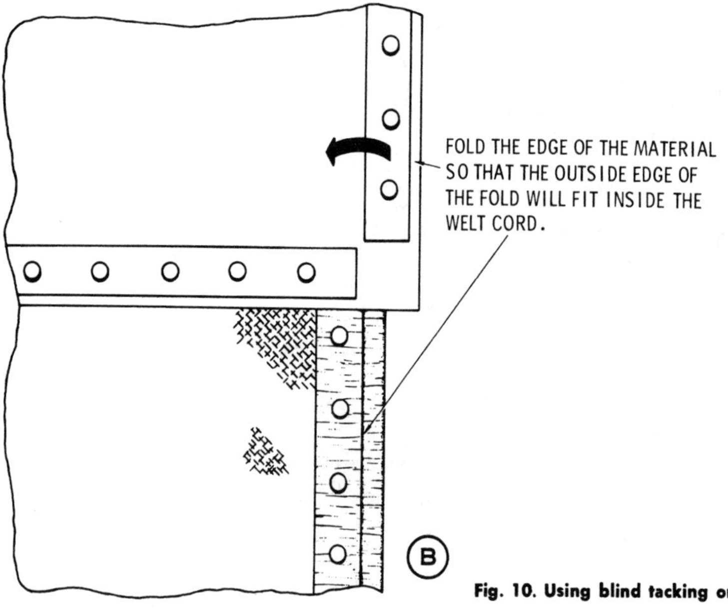

The Final Cover

FINAL COVER FOR THE OUTSIDE BACK
(WRONG SIDE OF THE MATERIAL)

TACKING STRIP

TACKING STRIP
INSERT THROUGH FROM
THE WRONG SIDE OF
THE MATERIAL.

BURLAP TACKED TO THE BACK
(OPTIONAL)

WELT CORD TACKED TO THE FRAME

(A)

FOLD THE EDGE OF THE MATERIAL
SO THAT THE OUTSIDE EDGE OF
THE FOLD WILL FIT INSIDE THE
WELT CORD.

(B)

Fig. 10. Using blind tacking on

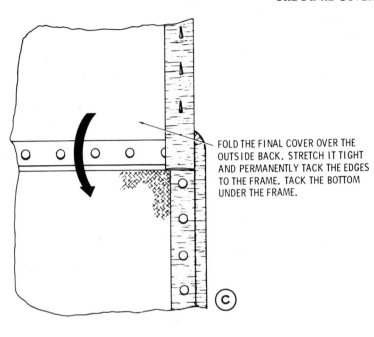

FOLD THE FINAL COVER OVER THE
OUTSIDE BACK. STRETCH IT TIGHT
AND PERMANENTLY TACK THE EDGES
TO THE FRAME. TACK THE BOTTOM
UNDER THE FRAME.

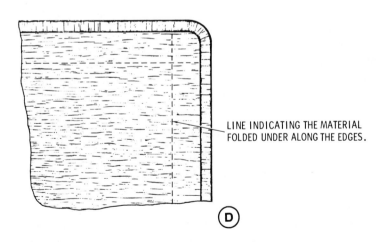

LINE INDICATING THE MATERIAL
FOLDED UNDER ALONG THE EDGES.

the outside back cover.

Three things should be remembered when using a blind stitch:

1. Keep the thread beneath the top of the fabric. Try to keep the stitching line straight without deviating above or below an imaginary line.
2. Pull the thread tight each time the needle is pulled through the fabric. Do *not* pull the thread *too* tight. This will cause the fabric to bunch.
3. Knot your thread at the beginning and end of your blind stitch.

Fig. 9 illustrates in detail the procedure for blind sewing.

BLIND TACKING

Here, too, the upholsterer wishes to conceal an operation from view. Blind tacking is usually used along areas close to an available section of wood, Fig. 10.

SEWING THE FINAL COVER

In Chapter Nine a method for laying out the pattern of a final cover was described in some detail. As was mentioned before, this pattern varies according to the type of furniture being covered. However, at the very minimum, you should at least have pieces of fabric for the seat, the inside back, and the outside back. Additional pieces will depend upon the style of the furniture.

Procedures for sewing the final cover follow in the sequence that the work should be done.

THE SEAT

The seat is usually covered first, and the procedure for covering it varies according to the style. Sometimes there is a little confusion about what precisely is meant by the term "seat." It is not always that portion of the furniture on which one sits. On upholstered chairs that have loose cushions, the seat is that portion of the chair on which the cushion rests. It also may include the front panel of the frame and portions of the sides extending back to the

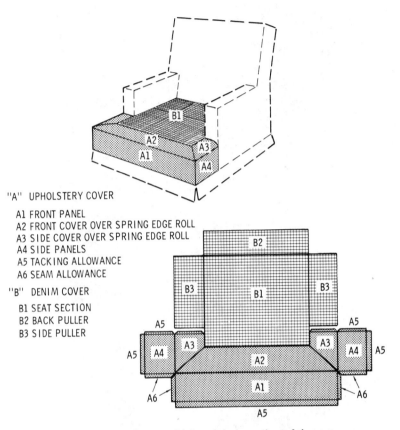

"A" UPHOLSTERY COVER

A1 FRONT PANEL
A2 FRONT COVER OVER SPRING EDGE ROLL
A3 SIDE COVER OVER SPRING EDGE ROLL
A4 SIDE PANELS
A5 TACKING ALLOWANCE
A6 SEAM ALLOWANCE

"B" DENIM COVER

B1 SEAT SECTION
B2 BACK PULLER
B3 SIDE PULLER

Fig. 11. Joining the cover fabric and denim sections of the seat.

arm posts. This basically describes a chair designed for a loose T-cushion.

The procedure for attaching the seat and front panel is illustrated with the same chair used to describe a number of other upholstering procedures in earlier chapters. The steps are as follows:

1. Most of the fabric covering the seat will be a denim or some other cheaper but strong fabric. Since this will be beneath the cushion and not exposed to view, there is no need to use the more expensive final cover fabric for this area. However,

275

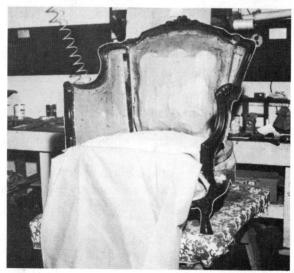

Courtesy Kwik-Bed Sofa Corp.

Fig. 12. Installing the seat cover.

Courtesy   Kwik-Bed Sofa Corp.

Fig. 13. Fastening the front panel of the seat cover.

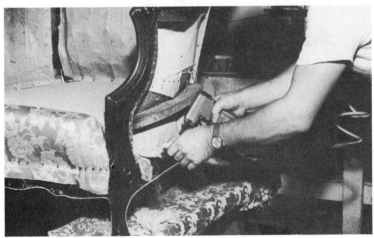

Courtesy   Kwik-Bed Sofa Corp.

Fig. 14. Fastening the seat cover side.

277

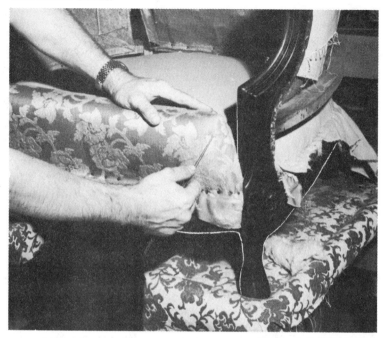

Courtesy Kwik-Bed Sofa Corp.

Fig. 15. Regulating the front panel corners.

Courtesy Kwik-Bed Sofa Corp.

Fig. 16. Back edge of the seat cover fastened in position.

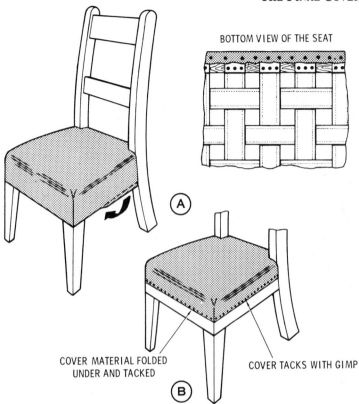

BOTTOM VIEW OF THE SEAT

COVER MATERIAL FOLDED
UNDER AND TACKED

COVER TACKS WITH GIMP

Fig. 17. Two methods of covering the side rails.

this is sewed to the portions of the more expensive material that covers the front area of the seat and the front panel. Sections of the cheaper material to be used as pullers are sewed to the sides and back of the seat material (Fig. 11).

2. It is assumed the front of the seat has been covered with a layer of cotton padding or whatever under layers you have chosen for the job. Place the upholstery material over the cotton padding and tack it to the frame. The seat area should also have a layer of stuffing and an upper layer of cotton padding (Fig. 12).

3. Pull the seat cover down through the frame between the tacking rails and the tops of the seat rails. Finish tacking

279

The Final Cover

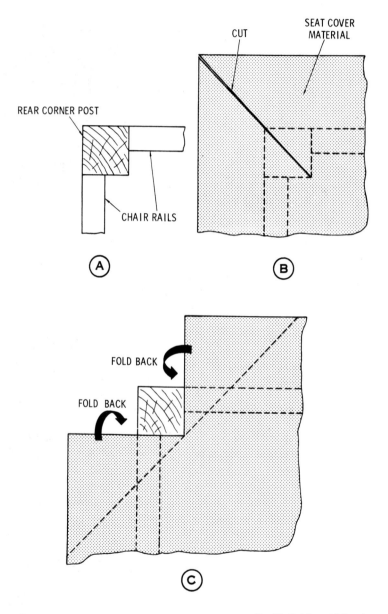

Fig. 18. Cutting and forming

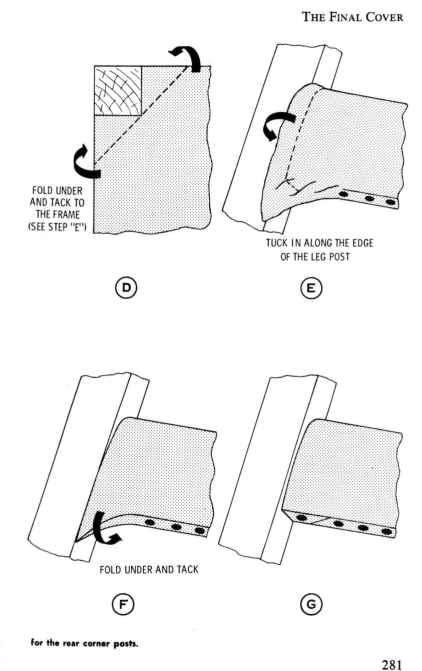

A

B CUT HERE

C LD BACK TO HE EDGE OF HE LEG POST

D TUCK IN / FOLD UNDER AND TACK

E

Fig. 20. Fitting the final cover at a corner leg post—method #1.

D FOLD UNDER AND TACK TO THE FRAME (SEE STEP "E")

E TUCK IN ALONG THE EDGE OF THE LEG POST

F FOLD UNDER AND TACK

G

for the rear corner posts.

the upholstery cover over the front of the chair frame (**Fig. 13**).

4. Tack the sides of the seat cover to the outside seat rail (**Fig. 14**), and use a regulator to adjust the padding in the front panel (**Fig. 15**).
5. Pull the seat cover through the back and tack it to the outside back seat rail (**Fig. 16**). Trim off all the excess.

An open-type seat is one which is not closed in by upholstered arms or a back. Essentially, it is open to view from all sides. Therefore, it does not have pullers attached to the seat cover fabric. The fabric may be pulled down and tacked to the bottom of the frame or to a point mid-way down on the side of the seat rail. The occasional chair, dining room chair, and kitchen chair are examples of open-type seat construction.

The procedure for covering the seat varies according to the style. Consequently, the following outline should be altered where necessary to fit the requirements of the particular piece of furniture being covered.

1. Do you plan to expose to view all or a portion of the seat rail? If none is to be exposed, then the fabric must be carried down and around the bottom of the seat rail. If you intend to expose some portion of the wood, fold the cover under at least ½ inch before tacking (Fig. 17).
2. Slip-tack the final cover down on the back seat rails smoothing out any wrinkles in the material as you proceed from the center toward the corners. Stop about 2-3 inches before reaching the back posts.
3. Pull the fabric toward the front seat rail. Do not pull the fabric so tight that you risk depressing the springs. You are only interested in achieving a tight, smooth fit. Slip-tack the fabric to the front seat rail in the manner described in Step Two.
4. Pull the fabric to each side rail and slip-tack the cover in place. Again, follow the instructions described in Step Two.
5. At each rear post, cut the fabric to fit the post. Fold under the excess, and attach it to the frame by slip-tacking (Fig. 18).

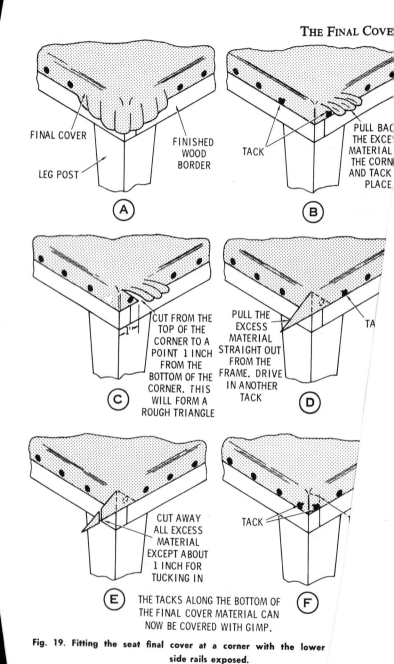

(A) FINAL COVER — FINISHED WOOD BORDER — LEG POST

(B) TACK — PULL BAC THE EXCE MATERIAL THE CORN AND TACK PLACE

(C) CUT FROM THE TOP OF THE CORNER TO A POINT 1 INCH FROM THE BOTTOM OF THE CORNER. THIS WILL FORM A ROUGH TRIANGLE

(D) PULL THE EXCESS MATERIAL STRAIGHT OUT FROM THE FRAME. DRIVE IN ANOTHER TACK — TA

(E) CUT AWAY ALL EXCESS MATERIAL EXCEPT ABOUT 1 INCH FOR TUCKING IN

(F) TACK — THE TACKS ALONG THE BOTTOM OF THE FINAL COVER MATERIAL CAN NOW BE COVERED WITH GIMP.

Fig. 19. Fitting the seat final cover at a corner with the lower side rails exposed.

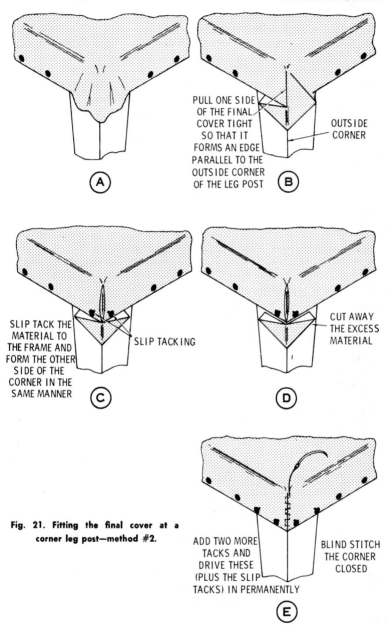

A

B

PULL ONE SIDE OF THE FINAL COVER TIGHT SO THAT IT FORMS AN EDGE PARALLEL TO THE OUTSIDE CORNER OF THE LEG POST

OUTSIDE CORNER

C

SLIP TACK THE MATERIAL TO THE FRAME AND FORM THE OTHER SIDE OF THE CORNER IN THE SAME MANNER

SLIP TACKING

D

CUT AWAY THE EXCESS MATERIAL

E

Fig. 21. Fitting the final cover at a corner leg post—method #2.

ADD TWO MORE TACKS AND DRIVE THESE (PLUS THE SLIP TACKS) IN PERMANENTLY

BLIND STITCH THE CORNER CLOSED

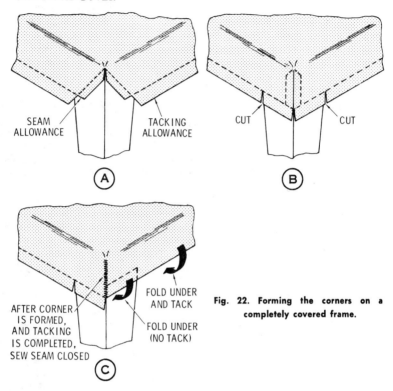

Fig. 22. Forming the corners on a completely covered frame.

6. The front corners of the seat can be finished in a number of ways depending upon the type of chair (particularly whether the bottom of the frame rail is partially or completely covered by the final cover) (Figs. 19 thru 22).

7. If you are now satisfied that the cover is smooth and tight (without unnecessarily depressing the springs), drive in the tacks and sew any finishing seams desired.

If the chair you are working on has uncovered arms, allowance must be made for the arm posts. See Fig. 23 for hints in fitting the material around the post. Some arm posts' outside edge may be flush with the outside edge of the side rail, while on other chairs the arm post may be fastened with screws that may be removed, thus freeing the arm post from the side rail during the upholstering

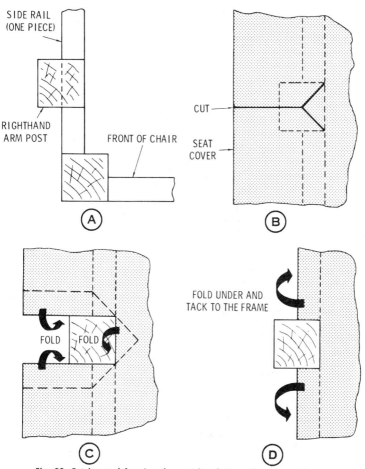

SIDE RAIL
(ONE PIECE)

RIGHTHAND
ARM POST

FRONT OF CHAIR

CUT

SEAT
COVER

Ⓐ

Ⓑ

FOLD UNDER AND
TACK TO THE FRAME

FOLD | FOLD

Ⓒ

Ⓓ

Fig. 23. Cutting and forming the seat for chairs with uncovered arms.

procedure. Examine your chair carefully and plan your actions accordingly.

UPHOLSTERED ARMS

The inside arm covers are usually installed on a closed type frame after the seat is finished. Often the top of the inside arm cover may be cut and attached so that the tacking or sewing is

287

done along an *outside* edge. Thus, with this type of arm, both the arm top and the inside arm cover are cut as one piece. However, it should be pointed out that this is only one of several arm styles encountered in upholstering (Fig. 24).

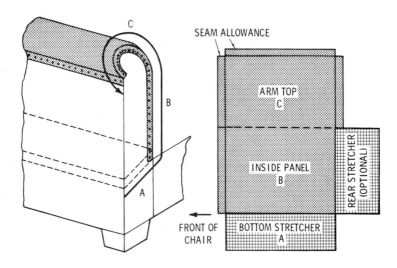

Fig. 24. An inside arm cover that also covers the top of the arm and attaches on the outside.

If there is to be a padded panel on the front of the arm, then the one to two inch overlap of the material must be fitted around the front of the arm and permanently tacked to the frame. It should be noted the front edge of the arm is fastened a little differently for the muslin cover. For the final cover the material is not cut around the rolled edge. Instead, a drawstring is fashioned as illustrated in Fig. 25. Pull the drawstring and shape uniform pleats. After the pleats are formed, they are tacked as shown. If, on the other hand, there is to be no padded panel, the material must be pulled around the front of the arm, folded under ½ to ¾ inch and tacked to the outside edge of the frame.

The procedure for attaching the inside arm cover to a closed-type frame is illustrated with the same chair used in Figs. 12 through 16. The arms of this particular chair were built so that

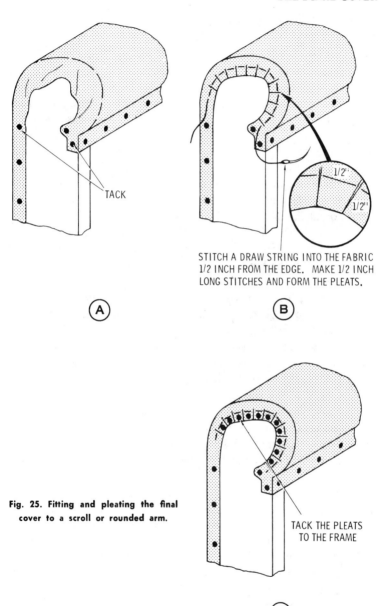

TACK

STITCH A DRAW STRING INTO THE FABRIC
1/2 INCH FROM THE EDGE. MAKE 1/2 INCH
LONG STITCHES AND FORM THE PLEATS.

(A)

(B)

Fig. 25. Fitting and pleating the final cover to a scroll or rounded arm.

TACK THE PLEATS
TO THE FRAME

(C)

289

an exposed wood surface extends from the front leg posts all along the top of the chair frame. This finished wood surface functions as a border, separating the outside and inside arm panels.

The procedure for attaching such an inside arm cover is as follows:

1. Position the cotton padding on the burlap covering the inside arm. No stuffing is used between the burlap and the cotton padding on this particular chair. The cotton padding was fastened to the frame with staples. Place the staples well below the finished wood border (Fig. 26).

2. Place the inside arm material over the area to be covered (Fig. 27). On this particular chair, the upholsterer has chosen to cut the arm piece slightly oversize and will trim away the excess. This is frequently done where a pattern may be difficult to cut for an exact fit. Note the cheaper material sewed to the bottom and rear edges of the inside arm cover for pulling and tucking.

3. The top of the inside arm cover is tacked to the frame at the edge of the exposed finished wood border (Fig. 28). Note that the excess material, which will be trimmed off, overlaps the top of the arm. An alternate, but more difficult, procedure would have been to cut the cover to the exact size (plus allowances), fold under the tacking allowance, and tack it to the frame.

4. Tuck the back edge of the inside arm material in between the inside arm and inside back.

5. Work the stretcher sewn to the bottom of the inside arm panel down around the edge of the seat and out over the side tacking rail.

6. Pull the back edge taut that was tucked through in Step 4. Smooth out any wrinkles and tack it down to the rear back post or tacking rail (this will depend upon the chair's construction).

7. Pull the bottom tacking strip taut (Fig. 29) and fasten it to the side seat rail (Fig. 30).

8. Trim away the excess material used as a puller (Fig. 31).

9. Trim away the excess material that overlaps the top of the arm (Fig. 32).

The outside arm covers present no particular difficulties.

In Fig. 33 the upholsterer is covering the outside arm with a layer of stuffing. This, in turn, is covered with a half thickness of cotton padding (Fig. 34). All excess of the cotton padding is trimmed away. Next, the upholstery cover is placed over the cotton padding, tacked (or stapled) into position, and the excess trimmed away (Fig. 35). Note in Fig. 35 that the outside arm cover extends around to the back of the chair, and is tacked to the rear leg post.

THE UPHOLSTERED BACK

Backs, like seats, can be either open or closed. The closed back is the more complicated of the two types to construct, and will be considered first.

The inside cover of the closed back offers certain special problems not found in the open back. It is quite apparent that the material cannot be stretched around and attached to the back of

Courtesy Kwik-Bed Sofa Corp.

Fig. 26. Applying cotton padding to inside arm.

Fig. 27. Tacking the top of the inside arm panel.

Courtesy Kwik-Bed Sofa Corp.

Fig. 28. Bottom and rear tacking strips on inside arm panel
tucked through the frame.

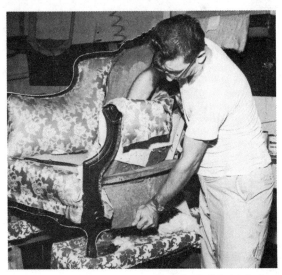

Courtesy Kwik-Bed Sofa Corp.

Fig. 29. Pulling the inside arm panel taut.

293

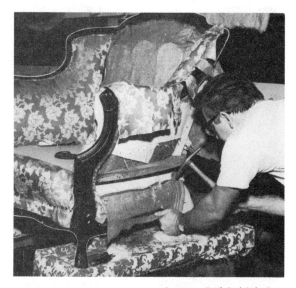

Courtesy Kwik-Bed Sofa Corp.
Fig. 30. Tacking the bottom edge of the inside arm panel.

Courtesy Kwik-Bed Sofa Corp.
Fig. 31. Trimming off the excess material of the lower inside arm tacking strip.

Courtesy   Kwik-Bed Sofa Corp.

Fig. 32. Trimming off excess material of the upper inside arm panel.

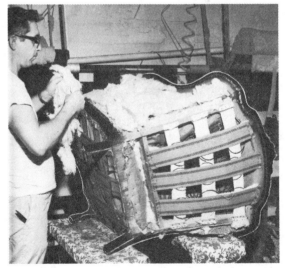

Courtesy   Kwik-Bed Sofa Corp.

Fig. 33. Applying stuffing to outside arm.

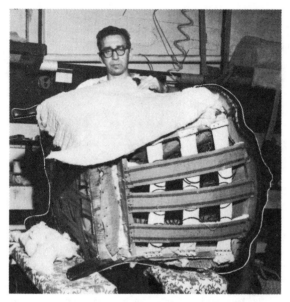

Fig. 34. Applying thin cotton layer to outside arm.

the frame if the arms are closed too. A stretcher or puller can be added to the bottom of the cover material to conserve expensive cover fabric since it will be positioned so that it is hidden from view.

The procedure for attaching the inside cover to a closed back is illustrated with the same chair used elsewhere in this chapter to describe other upholstering procedures. The steps in the procedure are as follows:

1. Position any stuffing and cotton padding over the burlap on the inside back (Fig. 36).
2. Place the inside cover over the cotton padding and slip-tack the cover across the top of the frame. Tack from the center out to the sides of the frame, smoothing out all wrinkles as you proceed (Fig. 37).
3. Pull the bottom and side stretchers (or pullers) between the tacking rails and the frame to the outside back. Pull them

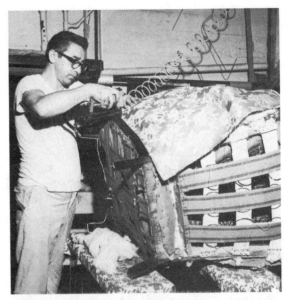

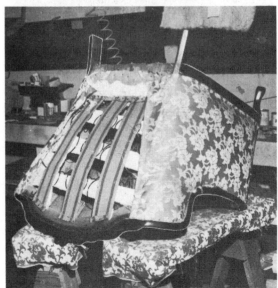

Courtesy Kwik-Bed Sofa Corp.

Fig. 35. Installing outside arm panel.

297

Courtesy *Kwik-Bed Sofa Corp.*
Fig. 36. Appying cotton layer to inside back.

Courtesy *Kwik-Bed Sofa Corp.*
Fig. 37. Installing inside back cover.

Courtesy Kwik-Bed Sofa Corp.

Fig. 38. Tacking strips pulled through for inside back cover prior to tacking.

Courtesy Kwik-Bed Sofa Corp.

Fig. 39. Cotton padding installed for outside back.

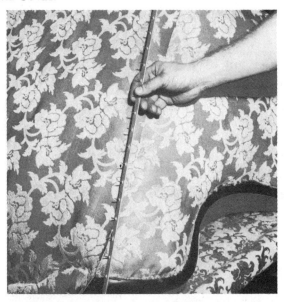

Courtesy Kwik-Bed Sofa Corp.

Fig. 40. Applying blind-tacking strip on outside back cover.

tight enough so that the inside cover is tight and smooth. Tack them to the frame, and trim away the excess material (Fig. 38).

4. The outside back is a single panel tacked over the back of the frame. On this particular chair, the outside back is first covered with cotton padding (Fig. 39). The top of the final cover panel is then tacked to the frame just below the exposed, finished wood border. The back cover is then pulled taut and tacked underneath to the bottom of the seat frame. The sides are blind-tacked to the frame (Fig. 40) along the leg post.

5. Trim off any excess material across the top outside portion of the chair.

The construction of the open back (Fig. 41) is far less complicated than the closed one. The inside of the back should be covered first. Since this is the side most often exposed to view, certain precautions should be taken to insure a smooth, tight fit.

Fig. 41. Chairs with open backs.

301

The Final Cover

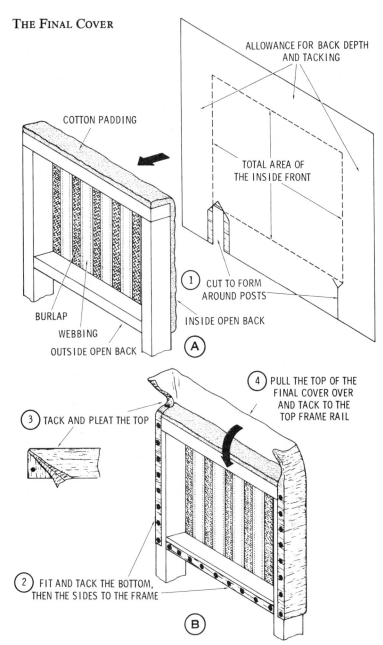

ALLOWANCE FOR BACK DEPTH AND TACKING

TOTAL AREA OF THE INSIDE FRONT

COTTON PADDING

① CUT TO FORM AROUND POSTS

INSIDE OPEN BACK

BURLAP

WEBBING

OUTSIDE OPEN BACK

Ⓐ

④ PULL THE TOP OF THE FINAL COVER OVER AND TACK TO THE TOP FRAME RAIL

③ TACK AND PLEAT THE TOP

② FIT AND TACK THE BOTTOM, THEN THE SIDES TO THE FRAME

Ⓑ

Fig. 42. Fitting the inside cover for an open-back chair.

302

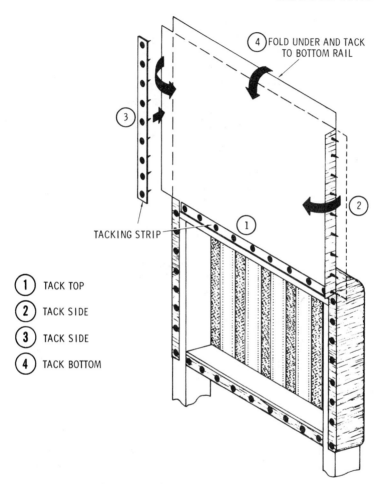

Fig. 43. Tacking the outside back cover of an open type chair.

The inside covers for open backs are cut so that there is enough fabric to tack to the chair frame. No puller or stretcher piece needs to be added to the cover fabric.

The procedure for attaching the final cover to an open back is as follows:

1. Slip-tack the inside back cover into position. Work from the center toward each corner smoothing out the wrinkles

303

as you proceed. Do not tack the material near the frame posts or corners. Be certain that you have correctly centered the material. This holds true not only for the material itself, but especially for any design or pattern on the fabric.

2. Cut the material so that if it will fit around the frame posts. Fold the material where you have made the cut and slip-tack it into position. Pull the material toward the post as you tack it to remove any wrinkles.

3. Corners may require folds or pleats in the material to obtain a proper fit (Fig. 42).

4. If you are satisfied that the cover is positioned correctly, drive the tacks in permanently.

5. The cover piece for the outside of the open back is now ready to be attached. Begin at the top. Center the material (equal overlap on both sides). Turn 1 inch of the material under along the top and fasten it using a tacking strip. Work from the center toward each side smoothing out all wrinkles as you proceed (Fig. 43).

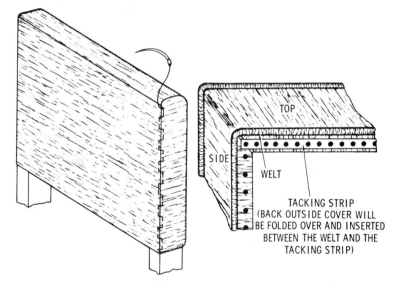

Fig. 44. Blind stitching the side corners.

Fig. 45. Attaching a welt to an outside back.

6. Pull the outside piece tight and slip tack it to the bottom of the back horizontal rail. Use only two or three evenly-spaced tacks in the *center* of the material. The sides of the outside cover will have to be attached first before the bottom can be permanently tacked into position. The sides may be blind-tacked also.

7. If you choose not to blind-tack the sides, then turn under 1 inch of material along the sides. Temporarily pin each side of the outside back cover. Begin at the top and work to-

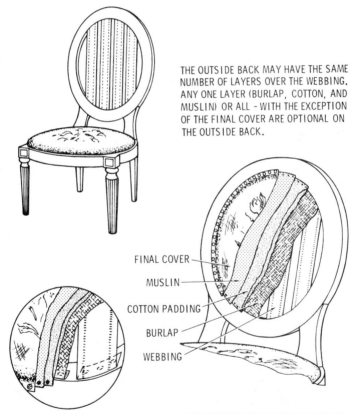

THE OUTSIDE BACK MAY HAVE THE SAME NUMBER OF LAYERS OVER THE WEBBING. ANY ONE LAYER (BURLAP, COTTON, AND MUSLIN) OR ALL - WITH THE EXCEPTION OF THE FINAL COVER ARE OPTIONAL ON THE OUTSIDE BACK.

FINAL COVER
MUSLIN
COTTON PADDING
BURLAP
WEBBING

THE WEBBING AND BURLAP ARE ATTACHED TO THE INSIDE RIM OF THE BACK RAILS. THE COTTON, MUSLIN AND FINAL COVER ARE ATTACHED TO THE OUTSIDE SURFACE OF THE BACK RAIL.

Fig. 46. Upholstering an irregularly shaped back.

ward the bottom, smoothing out all wrinkles as you proceed. Pull the material tight as you do so. Using a 4-inch curved needle, sew the side edges of the outside back cover to the sides of the back cover (Fig. 44). Permanently tack the bottom edge of the outside back cover to the bottom of the horizontal back rail.

8. With the same needle, sew the top seam of the back together (including the corner pleats or folds).

If you intend to use welting, this must be attached before Step Five above. Tack the welt strip into position along the top of the back and down the sides (place the tacks in the flap of the welting strip). Cut into the welt strip to form the

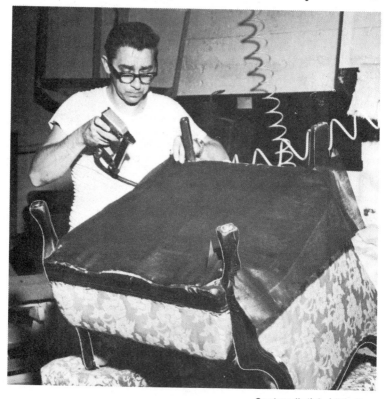

Courtesy Kwik-Bed Sofa Corp.

Fig. 47. Installing the cambric dust cover.

corners (Fig. 45). Now, proceed to Step Five, but make certain that the flap of the welt strip is beneath the outside back cover and the tacking strip.

Irregular backs (curved tops, shields, etc.) can be covered by cutting a back cover piece to the size of the area to be covered, allowing about ½ to ¾ inch extra material for folding under. Fold the material under and tack as close to the edge as possible with metaline nails (Fig. 46).

APPLYING THE CAMBRIC

The "cambric" is also referred to as the "dust cover." Some upholsterers prefer to attach the dust cover after any skirts are attached; others leave such skirts to the very last.

The dust cover is an inexpensive fabric that has been made dustproof as a result of a sizing or glazing treatment. It is designed to catch particles of stuffing and dust that fall from within the chair. The cambric used in making dust covers is usually black.

Measure the bottom of the piece of furniture from the outside edge of the frame. Add 1 inch for fold-under and tacking. Turn the piece of furniture upside down. Begin at the *center* of the bottom of the back seat rail. Lay the cambric so that the glazed surface faces outward, fold the edge under 1 inch, and slip tack the material to the frame. Move toward the corners, but stop at least 2 to 3 inches from them. The cambric will have to be cut and folded to fit around the leg posts. Pull the cambric to the bottom of the front seat rail and repeat the procedure. Now do the same with the sides. Is the surface of the material smooth and tight? If so, drive the tacks in permanently. Cut the corners for fitting around the leg posts, fold them, and tack them to the frame (Fig. 47).

STUFFED PANELS

Some sections of furniture are covered with stuffed panels or stuffed trim. These panels consist of a base (usually a thin piece of plywood) cut to the shape of the area to be covered. The base

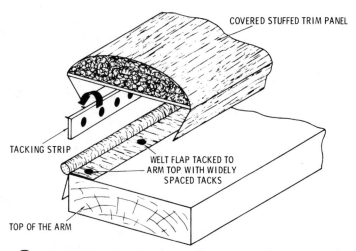

COVERED STUFFED TRIM PANEL

TACKING STRIP

WELT FLAP TACKED TO
ARM TOP WITH WIDELY
SPACED TACKS

TOP OF THE ARM

1) BEGIN BY TACKING A LENGTH OF WELTING TO THE EDGE OF THE ARM TOP.
BLIND TACK ONE SIDE OF THE STUFFED TRIM TO THE ARM TOP.

(A1)

2) USING A BLIND TACKING STRIP, ATTACH
THE EDGE OF THE STUFFED TRIM DIRECTLY
OVER THE WELTING.

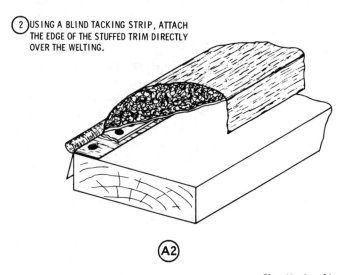

(A2)

Fig. 48. Attaching a

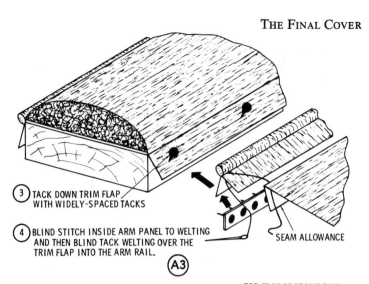

③ TACK DOWN TRIM FLAP
WITH WIDELY-SPACED TACKS

④ BLIND STITCH INSIDE ARM PANEL TO WELTING
AND THEN BLIND TACK WELTING OVER THE
TRIM FLAP INTO THE ARM RAIL.

SEAM ALLOWANCE

A3

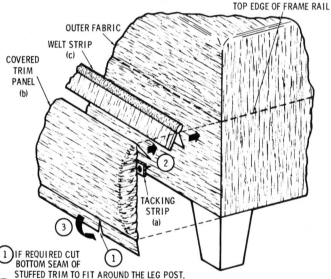

TOP EDGE OF FRAME RAIL

OUTER FABRIC

WELT STRIP
(c)

COVERED
TRIM
PANEL
(b)

TACKING
STRIP
(a)

① IF REQUIRED CUT
BOTTOM SEAM OF
STUFFED TRIM TO FIT AROUND THE LEG POST.

② BLIND TACK THE TOP SEAM OF THE STUFFED TRIM TO THE CHAIR FRAME. BLIND TACK
THE TRIM SO THAT THE TACKS DRIVE THROUGH FIRST THE TACKING STRIP (a);
THEN THE SEAM OF THE STUFFED TRIM (b); NEXT THROUGH BOTH FLAPS OF THE WELT (c);
AND FINALLY THROUGH THE FABRIC INTO THE FRAME WOOD.

③ TACK THE BOTTOM SEAM OF THE STUFFED TRIM UNDERNEATH THE BOTTOM EDGE OF
THE CHAIR FRAME.

B

bottom band of stuffed trim.

is covered with the same fabric used for the final cover. Welt is used around the edges as a trim. The stuffed panel may be glued, or tacked and sewed to the wood surface (Fig 48).

Ready-made panels are also available in many shapes and from a variety of materials. These would be of particular value where quantities of a given style are anticipated such as by a furniture manufacturer or a large-scale re-upholstering operation (Fig. 49).

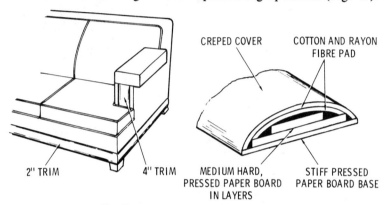

2" TRIM   4" TRIM

CREPED COVER   COTTON AND RAYON FIBRE PAD

MEDIUM HARD, PRESSED PAPER BOARD IN LAYERS   STIFF PRESSED PAPER BOARD BASE

Fig. 49. Examples of commercial trim (Stafirm®).

GIMP AND GIMP TACKS

Gimp is a strip (about ½ inch wide) of decorative trim used to cover edges that border on exposed wood surfaces. Its primary purpose is to cover the tacks used to attach the final cover.

Gimp is manufactured in a number of colors and designs, as well as a variety of materials (cotton, silk, rayon, leather, and plastic).

Gimp is usually glued into position. Gimp tacks (2 to 8 oz. tacks with small heads) hold it in place until the glue dries. The tacks can be covered with decorative nails. However, this is only one of four basic methods of attaching gimp. These four methods can be summarized as follows:

1. Glue and slip-tack the gimp strip in position, and remove the tacks when the glue has dried.
2. Glue the gimp strip to the surface using gimp tacks to hold it in position. Cover the gimp tacks with decorative nails.

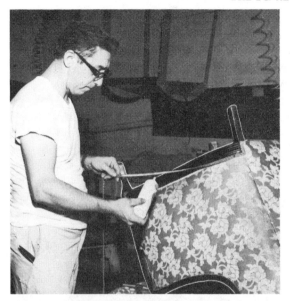

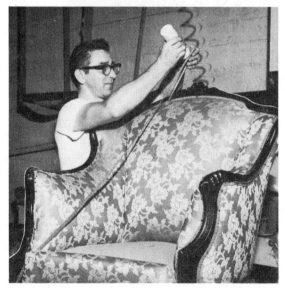

Courtesy   Kwik-Bed Sofa Corp.

Fig. 50. Gimp strip being glued into position (temporarily held with tacks until dry).

311

3. Use glue and gimp tacks.
4. Use glue and metaline (decorative) nails.

As you can see, you have considerable freedom in the procedure you use to attach the gimp strip. Use a miter pleat when extending gimp strips around particularly sharp corners. Finally, you should take care not to stretch the gimp strip (Figs. 50 and 51).

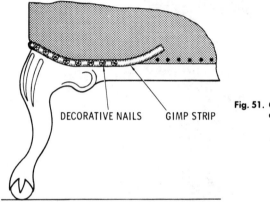

DECORATIVE NAILS   GIMP STRIP

Fig. 51. Gimp strip held with decorative nails.

DECORATIVE NAILS

Decorative nails (Fig. 52) are manufactured in a wide variety of colors, designs, and sizes. They can also be ordered to specification for a particular job. As their name suggests, these nails are used to give an additional decorative touch. They are often used as a border along the edges of the final cover. They are also used when it is not desired or is impossible to conceal a tacking operation.

METALINE NAILS

Metaline nails (Fig. 53) are generally used for fastening plastic or leather final covers to furniture, although they are employed in other ways as well. Essentially, the metaline nail is an enamel-coated, round-head tack, commonly called "upholsterer's tacks." Note in the figure two of the example nails have flared or flattened

312

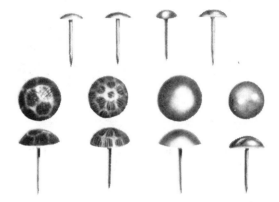

Courtesy Handy Button Machine Co.

Fig. 52. Decorative nails.

Courtesy Handy Button Machine Co.

Fig. 53. Metaline nails.

edges. These are primarily used on plastics and light fabrics to prevent cutting of the material.

SKIRT FASTENERS

One alternative to stitching a skirt to the bottom of the chair is to tack it in place with decorative nails. Special fasteners are also manufactured for just this purpose (Fig. 54).

FRINGES AND EDGINGS

Brush fringe (or edging) is used as a seam trim. It usually is made from rayon or cotton and sold by the yard. Brush fringe

313

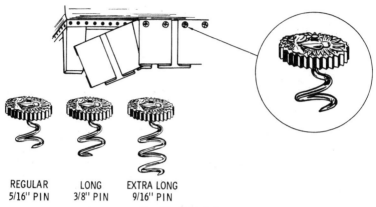

REGULAR
5/16'' PIN

LONG
3/8'' PIN

EXTRA LONG
9/16'' PIN

Fig. 54. Skirt fasteners.

is used in place of welt when a more decorative effect is desired (Fig. 55).

Boucle edging serves the same purpose as brush fringe. It is made from rayon, silk, or nylon and is generally considered to be of a higher quality than brush fringe (Fig. 56).

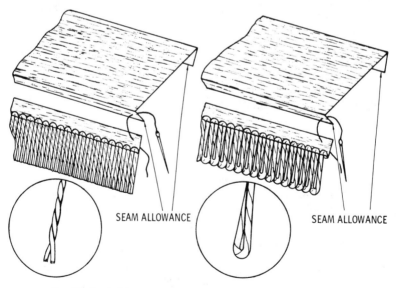

SEAM ALLOWANCE

SEAM ALLOWANCE

Fig. 55. Brush fringe.

Fig. 56. Boucle edging.

Bullion fringe serves a purpose similar to that of the skirt (or flounce) and yet it resembles a brush or boucle edging. The bullion fringe is attached to the bottom of the furniture frame and extends downward to within ½ inch of the floor. It, too, is made from rayon, silk, or nylon, and is usually available in rolls with widths of 3 to 6 inches (Fig. 57).

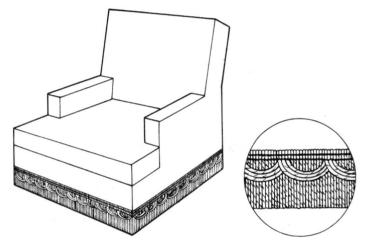

Fig. 57. Bullion fringe.

SKIRTS OR FLOUNCES

Skirts or flounces are strips of material (identical to that of the final cover) attached on all four sides of the piece of furniture. The skirt hangs down to within ½ inch of the floor hiding the legs from view (Fig. 58).

STYLES

Skirts or flounces are strips of material made in a variety of styles. The three most common styles are: (1) the shirred or gathered skirt; (2) the pleated skirt; and (3) the straight or plain skirt.

THE GATHERED OR SHIRRED SKIRT

The shirred skirt (or gathered skirt) contains a drawstring which is installed in the upper hem of the skirt. This drawstring is used

315

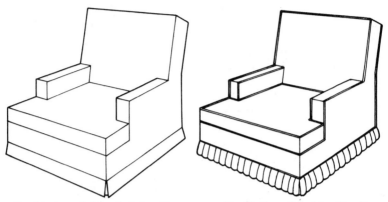

Fig. 58. An upholstered chair with a
plain skirt.

Fig. 59. The gathered (or shirred)
skirt.

to form the "gathers." See Fig. 59 for an example of the shirred skirt.

The procedure for making a shirred skirt is as follows:

1. Determine the measurements. Since the skirt should hang ½ inch above the floor and should extend ½ inch above the bottom edge of the furniture frame, the net result is that the skirt's height is the same as the distance from the floor to the bottom of the frame. In addition, allowances must be made for hems: ½ inch for the bottom hem and 1½ inch for the top hem. Stated another way, the distance from the floor to the frame plus two inches equals the total width of the material before sewing. See Fig. 60.

2. Although it is possible to sew several lengths of material together to make the skirt, it is always preferable to use one continuous length. However, in the case of sofas or similar large pieces, such action may not be practical so splicing may be necessary. Be sure to match any pattern and weave so they all run in the same direction.

    To determine the total length of the skirt, experiment with a scrap of material. Arrange the material into the size gathers you desire. Do this until a gathered length of 12 inches is completed. Mark the 12 inch point with a pin.

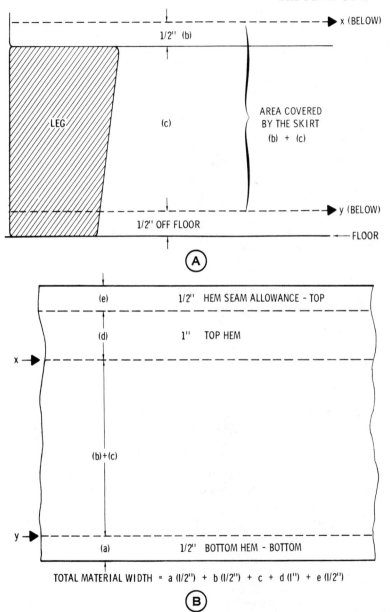

Fig. 60. Measuring for the width of the skirt.

317

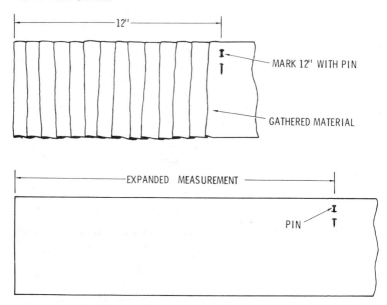

Fig. 61. Determining the length of a gathered skirt.

Now release the gathers and measure the length of the material from the starting point to the pin. See Fig. 61. The difference between 12 inches and the new location of the pin is that amount of material which must be added for every foot of circumference of the chair or sofa. As an example let us assume the pin moved 5 inches (or, it required 5 inches of material to form the gathers for one foot of skirt), and the measured circumference of the chair to be fitted for the skirt is 12 feet. The gathering allowance would be 60 inches or 5 inches for each foot (5 × 12 = 60). The 60 inches (or 5 ft.) would be added to the 12 feet of circumference which would give a grand total of 17 feet of skirt material before it is gathered.

If the fabric of the skirt is not a heavy one, it might be wise to back the skirt with a length of muslin.

3. Insert a drawstring through the upper hem (Fig. 62) that is strong enough not to break when pulled but small enough not to show through the hem.

318

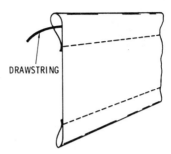

Fig. 62. Installing a permanent drawstring.

DRAWSTRING

4. Take a steam iron and press out all the wrinkles in the skirt. Now, pull the drawstring until the material is gathered for the desired effect. If desired, run a permanent stitch about one inch from the top edge of the skirt to hold the gathers in place. Additionally, a length of welt may be sewn along the top edge of the skirt after the gathers have been formed. A welt can provide a means of attaching the skirt.
5. The skirt should be attached so the seam joining both ends of the material is centered at the back of the piece of furniture.

The skirt may be fastened by several methods. One means is by the special fasteners shown earlier in Fig. 54. Other means may be decorative nails or by hand-sewing directly to the cover. One of the more common means is by use of a tacking strip as illustrated in Fig. 63.

Fig. 63. Attaching the skirt with a blind-tacking strip.

TACKING STRIP

THE PLEATED SKIRT

Pleated skirts are of two basic types: (1) the box pleat and (2) the kick pleat (Fig. 64). The box pleat has two variations depending upon whether the pleats are side-by-side or spaced some distance apart (Fig. 65).

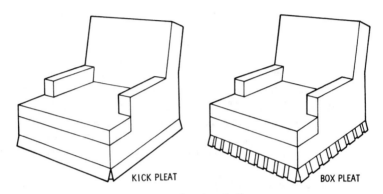

KICK PLEAT BOX PLEAT

Fig. 64. The pleated skirt.

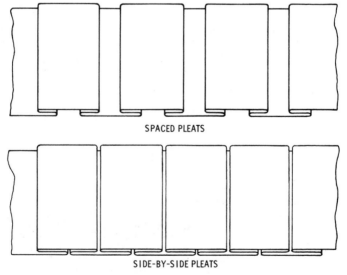

SPACED PLEATS

SIDE-BY-SIDE PLEATS

Fig. 65. Two styles of box pleats.

320

The methods for taking measurements for the shirred skirt (described in Steps One and Two) also apply to the pleated skirt except for one aspect of the length. As can be seen in Fig. 65, pleats result in an overlap of fabric which requires the use of extra material. In addition, the pleats must be carefully spaced. It is essential that they be positioned an equal distance from each corner of the piece of furniture. Furthermore, they must be exactly the same distance apart. In view of all this, for the beginner it is suggested a paper pattern be made. Once you have incorporated the desired number of pleats with their correct positioning onto the paper pattern, you may extend the paper pattern to its original length and cut your fabric. Pin the pleats in the fabric strips according to the measurements used in the paper pattern. Stitch the pleats and press the entire skirt with a steam iron (Fig. 66). Welting and attachment follow the procedures described in Steps Three through Five of the shirred (gathered) skirt.

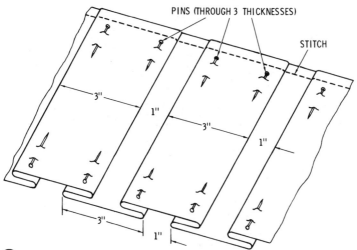

① FOLD THE MATERIAL FOR THE DESIRED PLEAT SIZE.

② PIN THE PLEATS SO THAT THEY WILL NOT LOSE THEIR SHAPE.

③ RUN A PERMANENT STITCH ALONG THE TOP EDGE.

Fig. 66. Constructing spaced, box pleats.

321

THE STRAIGHT OR PLAIN SKIRT

This is an extremely easy skirt to make. Follow the procedures described for a shirred or pleated skirt. The distinguishing feature of the straight skirt is that it is joined at the corners with welt. This welt cord also sometimes borders the bottom edge (Fig. 67).

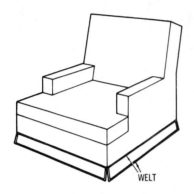

Fig. 67. A plain skirt with welt trim.

WELT

BUTTONS

A wide variety of finished buttons can be purchased for use in upholstering, or you can finish your own. These buttons are used primarily as a form of decoration, although in some instances they prevent the upholstery stuffing from slipping out of position (this is particularly true in the case of tufting).

Buttons can be covered in the home. This may be done either by hand or with a button-making machine. Button-making machines usually have detailed instructions for their use.

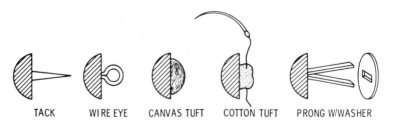

TACK   WIRE EYE   CANVAS TUFT   COTTON TUFT   PRONG W/WASHER

Fig. 68. Types of button attachment.

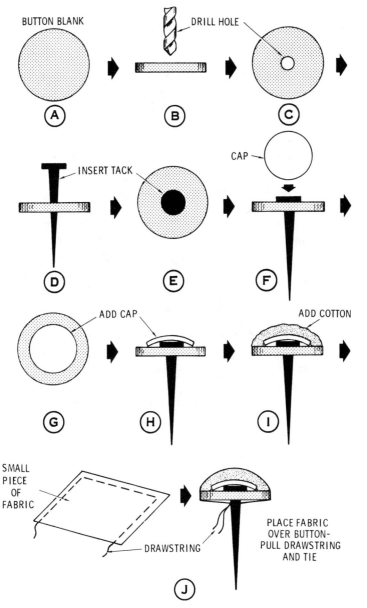

Fig. 69. One method of making a button.

There are basically four types of buttons, each type being classified by its method of attachment. The four methods of attachment are: (1) tack, (2) a tuft of material sewn to the cover, (3) a wire loop, and (4) metal prongs or clinch (Fig. 68).

Covering buttons is not as difficult as it might first appear. Each button contains a base which provides the shape for the button and a means of attaching it to the piece of furniture. This base is usuaally ½ to ¾ inches across, circular, and made from heavy-duty cardboard, thin plywood, plastic, or metal. A hole should be punched or drilled through the base. The tack, metal prongs, loop, or tuft of material is inserted through the hole. A cap is glued over the opening. Cotton is glued on the cap and the cover material is applied over the cotton. Sew a draw-string (actually a length of thread) into the fabric of the button cover about ½ to ⅝ inches beyond the edge of the button before attaching it to the button (Fig. 69). The button illustrated utilizes a tack—others can be constructed using the other fastening methods shown in Fig. 68.

Now the buttons must be attached to the piece of furniture. Determine the spacing of the buttons first. Measure out the position of each tack (or loop, etc.) and mark the cover lightly with a piece of chalk. Place a piece of cardboard over the fabric-covered heads of tack buttons before driving them into the wood. Do not strike them too hard.

Buttons used in tufting are tied to the webbing or burlap underlayers. See Chapter Thirteen for a detailed description of this upholstering process.

CHAPTER 13

Channels and Tufts

Channels and tufts are two upholstery forms that require special attention. This is because the procedure for their construction is more complicated than other forms. I would recommend that the beginner use muslin or some other inexpensive material to practice constructing tufts and channels before atttempting to use the more expensive final cover fabrics. I would also recommend using a plain fabric for the final cover. Prints and designs tend to become distorted when the material is pulled to form the channel or tuft. In addition, it can be a formidable task to center or match these designs.

Channels are also referred to as *pipes* or *flutes*. The most common style for channels is a vertical, straight up-and-down arrangement (Fig. 1). Variations of this style include the fan-back

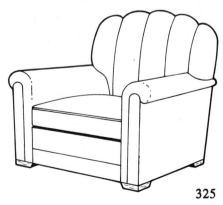

Fig. 1. A chair with vertical channels.

325

Fig. 2. Fan-back and curve-back styles.

and curved-back styles (Fig. 2). There are also examples of furniture in which the channels are arranged horizontally. In this case the channels are carried down to include the seat (Fig. 3). This is unusual since channels are generally found in only backs and the insides of arms.

THE PROCEDURE FOR CONSTRUCTING CHANNELS

Some upholsterers construct their channels by working directly on the surface of the inside back. Others find it more convenient to construct channels as separate units and then attach them to the inside back. The latter method is probably more convenient,

326

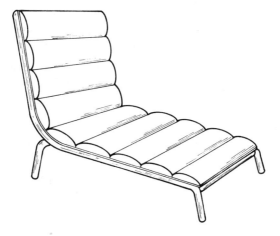

Fig. 3. Horizontal channels.

because it gives the upholsterer access to both ends of the channel when stuffing it. When working directly on the inside back surface, the channel covering material (both the muslin and the final cover fabric) may be individually cut and resewn, or used as one uncut piece.

The following is an outline for constructing channels as a separate unit for a chair.

1. The first step is to determine the width and depth of each channel, and the number of channels to be used. Divide the total width of the inside back by the total number of channels you plan to use. This will give you the width of each channel. Try to make the size of the channels in proportion to the overall size of the chair (or sofa). Basically, narrow channels tend to give an impression of additional height; whereas, wider ones emphasize width. The chair back illustrated in Fig. 4 is approximately 32 inches across. This width can be divided into eight 4-inch wide channels. My choice of the number and size of the channels was purely arbitrary. I felt that eight channels of this size provided the right number and size for the area to be covered.

327

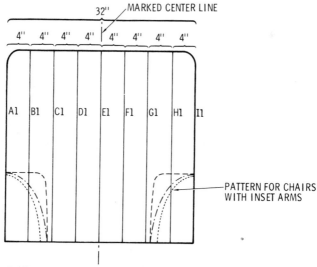

Fig. 4. Marking center line and channel edges on muslin (even number of channels).

The burlap on the inside back of the chair may be covered with a layer of muslin which, in turn, has been stitched to the burlap. Using a soft lead pencil, mark the exact center of the inside back (Fig. 4). Mark the same center line on the top of the back seat rail. The stretcher on the final cover will be pulled down to this rail and tacked to it.

Starting with a new piece of muslin, slightly larger than the chair back, lay it out flat and commence your channel pattern. First locate your center line from top to bottom.

If you have decided to use an even number of channels, then mark off the other channels with full measurements (the total width of the channel) from the center line. In Fig. 4 four channels were marked off on either side of the center line (lines B1, C1, D1, F1, G1, and H1). If you have decided to use an odd number of channels, the center line divides the centermost channel exactly down the middle. Mark off this center channel with a one half measurement (one half the total width of the channel) from both sides of the center line. Mark off the rest of

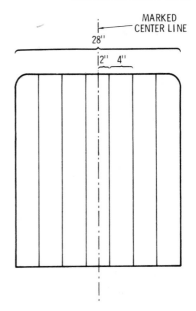

MARKED
CENTER LINE

28"

|2" 4"

Fig. 5. Marking center line and channel
edges on muslin (odd number of
channels).

the channels using full measurements from each edge of
the center channel (Fig. 5).

After the pattern is marked on the muslin, cut away
any excess material beyond the outer limits of the pattern.

2. The depth of a channel is also arbitrarily determined. Take
a strip of heavy paper and bend it to assume the desired
curved shape of the channel. Cut off the end of the strip
until you have arrived at the depth you want. When this
is flattened out, it will also provide the width dimension
of each channel to be used when computing the total width
of the final cover (Fig. 6).

3. Measuring and cutting the final cover: Mark the final cover
fabric on the *wrong side* of the material. Using our eight
4-inch channel chair as an example, you will need a width
of at least 60 inches. This includes six inches (width) for
each of the eight channels, and an extra six inches added
to each of the end channels for a tacking or sewing allowance. Some types of furniture may require that this be increased. Others, particularly those with finished wood

329

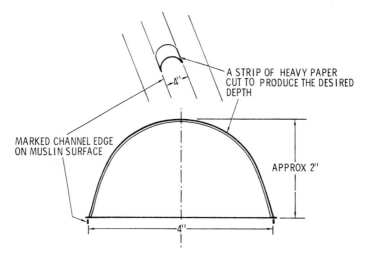

A STRIP OF HEAVY PAPER
CUT TO PRODUCE THE DESIRED
DEPTH

MARKED CHANNEL EDGE
ON MUSLIN SURFACE

APPROX 2"

-4"-

Fig. 6. Determining the depth of a channel.

borders separating the final cover on the inside and outside backs, require only enough material to fold under and
tack in place. (Fig. 11 shows examples of this type chair.)
A method of determining the exact amount of the allowance is described further on in Step 11. The chair in our
example measures 30 inches from the top of the back to the
top of the seat. Add four inches at the bottom for a seam
allowance to be sewed to a stretcher, and four inches at
the top for closing the channels and attaching to the frame
(Fig. 7). Note that the final-cover channels are two inches
wider than those marked on the muslin. The extra width
includes the depth allowance. In other words, to go across
the four-inch channel width in an arc, it requires an additional two inches or a total of six inches of material for
each channel.

4. Sew lines B2-H2 on the wrong side of the final cover
   material to lines B1-H1 marked on the muslin (Fig. 4).
   Stitch them so that B2 is stitched to B1, C2 to C1, and
   so on. Do not sew the tops or bottoms of the channels
   closed. Additionally, do not sew lines A2 to A1 or lines
   I2 to I1. These will be sewn after the channels are stuffed,

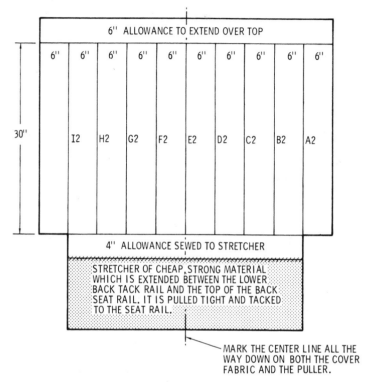

6" ALLOWANCE TO EXTEND OVER TOP

6" | 6" | 6" | 6" | 6" | 6" | 6" | 6" | 6" | 6"

30"

I2 | H2 | G2 | F2 | E2 | D2 | C2 | B2 | A2

4" ALLOWANCE SEWED TO STRETCHER

STRETCHER OF CHEAP, STRONG MATERIAL WHICH IS EXTENDED BETWEEN THE LOWER BACK TACK RAIL AND THE TOP OF THE BACK SEAT RAIL. IT IS PULLED TIGHT AND TACKED TO THE SEAT RAIL.

MARK THE CENTER LINE ALL THE WAY DOWN ON BOTH THE COVER FABRIC AND THE PULLER.

Fig. 7. Marking the channel pattern on the wrong side of final cover fabric.

and the channel unit is attached to the inside back. The thread used for this stitching preferably should match the color of the final cover. Additionally, stitching must be done with the outer cover facing up (and lying over the muslin).

5. The channels may be stuffed with foam padding (see Chapter 11), cotton felt padding, or a number of loose stuffings. The last named is the most difficult procedure and should be avoided by the beginner.

Cotton felt padding is available in a variety of thicknesses. For channels it should be thin enough so that it can be formed into rolls and stuffed into the pockets which were created when the final cover was sewn to the muslin

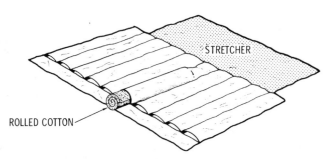

Fig. 8. Cotton padding rolled and stuffed into a channel.

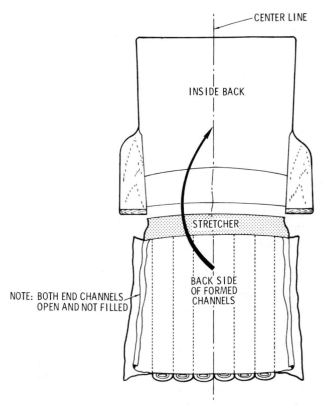

Fig. 9. Attaching channel unit to inside back so center lines coincide.

base. See Fig. 8. The rolls should be longer than the length of the channel. Excess can always be trimmed away.

6. Fill the first three channels on either side of the center line. Do not fill the outside channels until after the unit has been attached to the inside back.

7. Place the channel unit on the inside back so that the center lines marked on both coincide with one another. In other words, the center line on the channel unit must be placed so that it is directly over the center line of the inside back (Fig. 9).

8. Push the stretcher down between the bottom of the inside back and the back of the seat. Tack it to the back seat rail. Make certain that the center line marked on the stretcher coincides with the center line marked on the back seat rail. Be careful that you do not pull the channels down too far (Fig. 10).

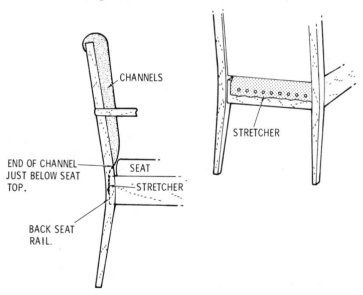

Fig. 10. Tacking the stretcher to the back seat rail.

9. The attachment of the top depends upon its style. The channel tops may extend over the top and taper to the

333

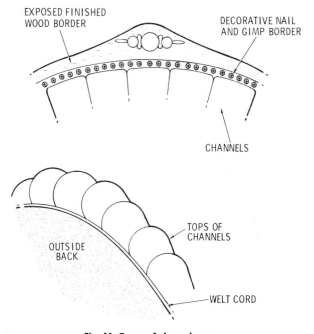

EXPOSED FINISHED WOOD BORDER

DECORATIVE NAIL AND GIMP BORDER

CHANNELS

TOPS OF CHANNELS

OUTSIDE BACK

WELT CORD

Fig. 11. Types of channel tops.

outside back or they may end and be attached before reaching the top of the chair (Fig. 11).

10. Slip-tack the top of the center of the channel unit (marked by the center line) to the top back rail. Pull the cover tight before tacking. Proceed from the center line toward each of the sides of the chair (or sofa). Smooth out the material as you do so. Examine what you have just done. If the channels seem to be centered correctly, then permanently tack them in place. If the channels taper over the top of the outside back, then the outside back panel will cover the tacking line. As the channel tapers, the amount of stuffing will by necessity have to decrease. Pleat the excess material in the channel cover before tacking or stitching it down (Fig. 12).

11. The channels on each extreme end of the channel unit must now be stuffed and attached to the frame. An addi-

DOUBLE PLEAT UNDER THE CENTER CHANNEL.
ALL THE REST HAVE A SINGLE PLEAT ON THE
SIDE OF THE CHANNEL CLOSEST TO THE LEG
POSTS.

Fig. 12. Attaching the tops of the channels.

tional 6 inch allowance was added to each end channel
(lines A2 and I2 in Fig. 7) for tacking or stitching. Some
styles of chairs (or sofas) require a greater allowance than
6 inches, while others may require less. To determine the
approximate amount, measure from the last marked channel edge on the inside back of the chair (lines B1 and H1
in Fig. 4) to the point where the final cover for the channels will be attached. Add (for this particular chair) 2
inches for a depth allowance and 6 inches for a stitching or
tacking allowance. The end channels should be stuffed with
the same material used in the others.

The top outside edge of the chair should be folded to
form a pleat and tacked to the frame. This pleat is formed
so that the pleat is toward the outside (Fig. 13).

The preceding description of channel construction dealt with
those constructed from a single piece of fabric. An alternative form
of construction is to cut out each channel cover separately and
re-sew them. This is a recommended procedure when channels
taper to smaller dimensions at their bottom. Fig. 14 illustrates a
typical pattern for laying out individual channel covers. Fig. 15
illustrates the method used in joining these channel covers together,
of attaching them to the inside back surface, and in stuffing the
individual channels.

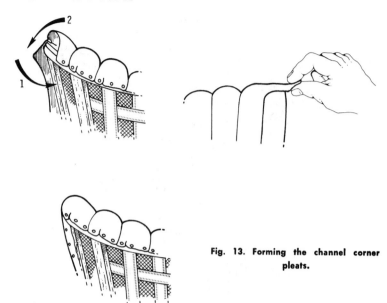

Fig. 13. Forming the channel corner
pleats.

Draw strings (or twines) are sometimes sewed into the seam allowance of the channels on the wrong side of the fabric *after* the seams of the channels have been joined together. These strings extend far enough beyond the tops of the channels to be attached to the outside surface of the top back rail (Fig. 16). Draw strings aid in centering each channel and should be attached *before* the material of the top of the channel is tacked to the frame.

TUFTS

Tufts represent another form of upholstering which, like channels, give a decorative touch to a piece of furniture. Furniture that has been tufted has a quilted effect. Tufts share with channels a more difficult construction procedure that the average upholstery forms, and for that reason they receive special attention in this chapter. Unlike channels which may be constructed as separate units or directly on the inside back, tufts must be constructed directly on the back. As is the case with channels, the stuffing in

336

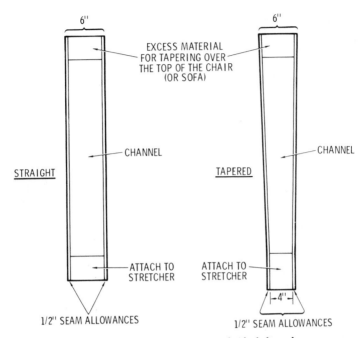

Fig. 14. Pattern layout for cutting individual channels.

tufts is not sewed down. Here, again, the construction of the tuft itself is considered sufficient to hold the stuffing in position. Unlike channels, tufts are found almost as commonly in seats as they are in backs and arms.

PROCEDURE FOR CONSTRUCTING TUFTS

The shape of the tuft is determined by the location of the buttons. If the tufting buttons are so arranged that there is an equal number in each row, then the tufts will be square-shaped (Fig. 17). If, on the other hand, rows with an even number of buttons alternate with those having an odd number, then the tufts will have a diamond shape (Fig. 18). Generally the height of a tuft will be greater than its width. There are also combinations of these patterns. Fig. 19 shows a sofa having an equal number of buttons in the top two rows, but staggered ones in the bottom row.

337

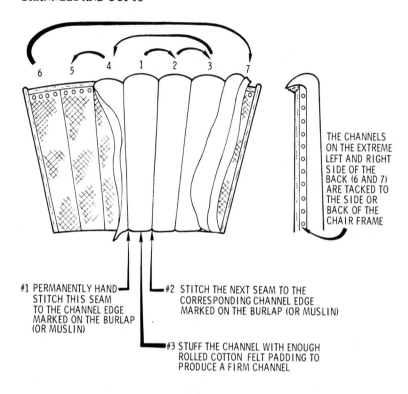

THE CHANNELS
ON THE EXTREME
LEFT AND RIGHT
SIDE OF THE
BACK (6 AND 7)
ARE TACKED TO
THE SIDE OR
BACK OF THE
CHAIR FRAME

#1 PERMANENTLY HAND
STITCH THIS SEAM
TO THE CHANNEL EDGE
MARKED ON THE BURLAP
(OR MUSLIN)

#2 STITCH THE NEXT SEAM TO THE
CORRESPONDING CHANNEL EDGE
MARKED ON THE BURLAP (OR MUSLIN)

#3 STUFF THE CHANNEL WITH ENOUGH
ROLLED COTTON FELT PADDING TO
PRODUCE A FIRM CHANNEL

#4 FORM AND STUFF THE CHANNELS 2-5

#5 FORM AND STUFF THE END CHANNELS
6 AND 7.

Fig. 15. Attaching channels directly to the inside back surface.

The procedure for constructing tufts is as follows:

1. The first step is to determine the measurements of each
tuft and the number of tufts to be used. Equally important
is the pattern in which they will be arranged. Use a marking pencil or soft lead pencil to mark the position of the
tufting buttons on the burlap (or muslin) underlayer. Find
the exact center by drawing lines from the middle of each
side and the middle of the top all the way across the sur-

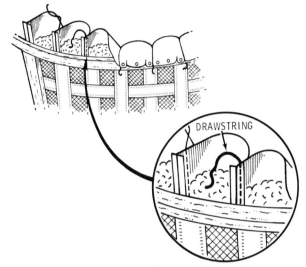

Fig. 16. The drawstring.

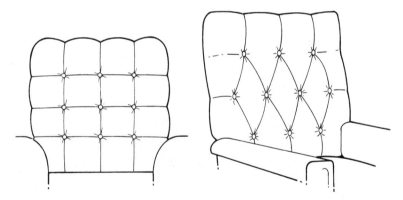

Fig. 17. A chair with square-shaped tufts.

Fig. 18. A chair with diamond-shaped tufts.

face of the inside back. These lines will intersect at the center. This intersect point will act as the exact center of the central tuft (Fig. 20).

2. Decide upon the measurements for your tufts. I would recommend making these higher than they are wide.

339

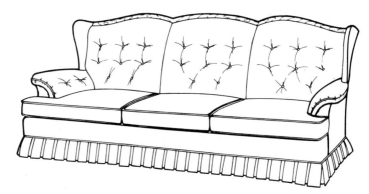

Fig. 19. A sofa with a different tufting pattern.

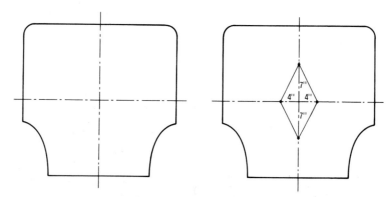

Fig. 20. Locating the center of the back for the center-most tuft.

Fig. 21. Marking the button location on the outer boundaries of the tuft.

3. Measure off half the width of the central tuft to either side of the intersect point. Do the same with the height (Fig. 21). The dimensions shown are only representative.

4. Now that the central tuft has been located, we can determine the positions of the remainder of the tufts. These are established by measuring the *full* width or *full* height distances from any of the four points of the centrally located tuft. Each new row of tufts is marked off in a similar manner (using the tuft in the preceding row as a reference point) (Fig. 22).

340

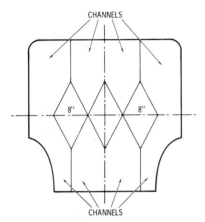

Fig. 22. Marking locations for other tufts.

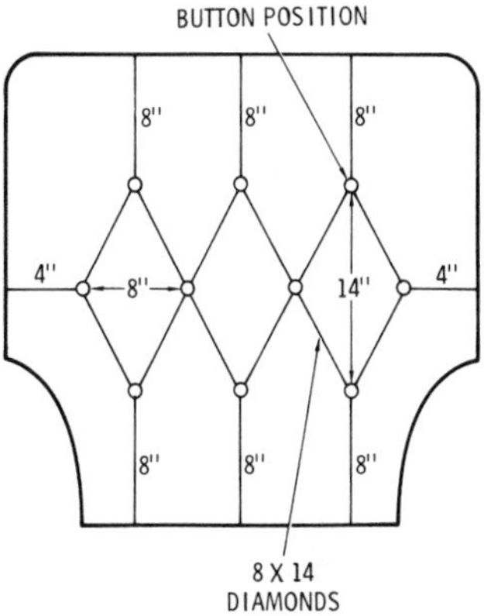

Fig. 23. The minimal distance of the tufting buttons from the chair edge.

5. Continue to mark the positions of all the tufts until the entire piece of burlap or muslin is marked off. The last rows of tufting buttons (both horizontal and vertical rows) must be *at least* one half the width or height of a tuft from the edge of the furniture frame (Fig. 23). If there is to be no exposed wood border around the tufted portion, then an additional allowance must be made on the outer cover material for overlapping the sides and back and tacking to the frame. How much this allowance will be depends upon the measurements of the chair.

6. The next step is to determine the depth of the tufts. As in the case with channels, the tufts are marked off on the wrong side of the final cover material and must be larger than those marked off on the material covering the inside back. Again, this extra allowance provides for the stuffing that will fill the tufts. The greater the allowance, the deeper the tufts. A 2-inch allowance for stuffing is given for the example tufts in Fig. 24.

7. The positions for the tufting buttons are marked off on the wrong side of the outer upholstery cover to correspond with those already marked off on the burlap or muslin covering the inside back.

341

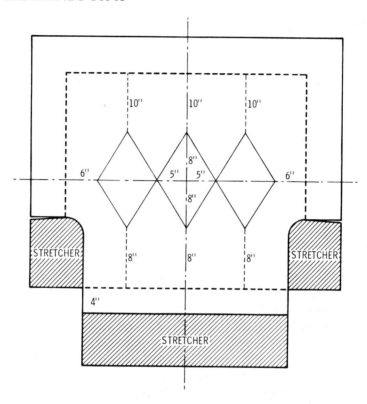

Fig. 24. Final cover tufting measurements.

8. If the tufts are to be cut out and resewn (rather common practice with such materials as vinyl), you must also allow for a ½ to ¾ inch seam allowance on each side of the tuft (Fig. 25).

9. You may find that the material you are using is not wide enough for the width of the chair back. This will be automatically true of sofas. A method for adding more material is illustrated in Fig. 26. By cutting the material to follow the edge of the tuft (rather than using a vertical cut that would cross a tuft), the resulting seam is hidden from view.

10. If the tufts are not cut and resewed and these tufts are especially large or deep, then it may be necessary to pleat

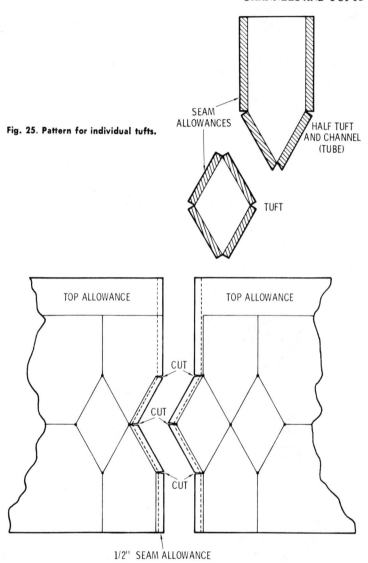

Fig. 25. Pattern for individual tufts.

SEAM ALLOWANCES

HALF TUFT AND CHANNEL (TUBE)

TUFT

TOP ALLOWANCE

TOP ALLOWANCE

CUT

CUT

CUT

1/2" SEAM ALLOWANCE

Fig. 26. Adding additional materials.

the excess material between the tufting buttons. These pleats (or folds) are made on the inside of the tuft (Fig. 27).

343

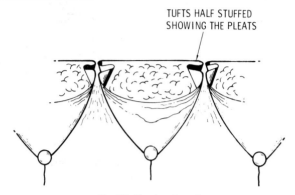

TUFTS HALF STUFFED
SHOWING THE PLEATS

Fig. 27. Pleating the tufts.

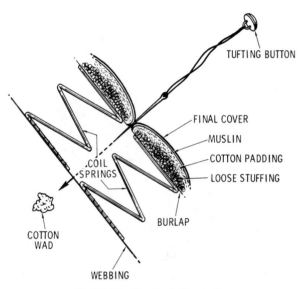

TUFTING BUTTON

FINAL COVER

MUSLIN

COTTON PADDING

LOOSE STUFFING

COIL SPRINGS

BURLAP

COTTON WAD

WEBBING

Fig. 28. Attaching the tufting button.

11. Take a length of stitching twine, attach it to one of the tufting buttons, attach the other end to an upholstery needle, and insert it through the center-most button mark on the bottom row of the outer upholstery cover (remember you will be piercing the cover from the outside through the button mark on the inside). Insert and pull the stitching

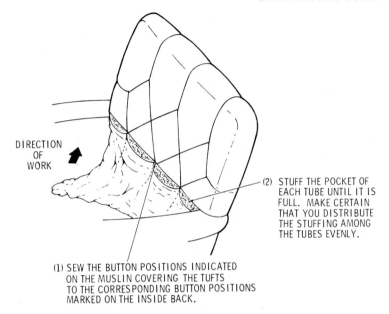

DIRECTION
OF
WORK

(2) STUFF THE POCKET OF
EACH TUBE UNTIL IT IS
FULL. MAKE CERTAIN
THAT YOU DISTRIBUTE
THE STUFFING AMONG
THE TUBES EVENLY.

(1) SEW THE BUTTON POSITIONS INDICATED
ON THE MUSLIN COVERING THE TUFTS
TO THE CORRESPONDING BUTTON POSITIONS
MARKED ON THE INSIDE BACK.

Fig. 29. Stuffing the tufts.

twine through the burlap and webbing. Tie the twine in back of the webbing, using a button or piece of cotton to prevent it from cutting through the webbing and slipping back through. Before tying the knot in the stitching twine, make certain that the button on the face of the outer cover has been pulled as close to the inside back surface as the material will allow (Fig. 28) without depressing the springs.

12. Moving either to the right or left of the center button position, sew the rest of the button positions marked on the muslin covering the tufts to the corresponding positions marked on the material of the inside back. The button positions on this bottom row form the tops of the half-tufts whose bottoms are channels or tubes that end on the seat. Take pieces of cotton cut to the size of these bottom half-tufts or channels and insert them. Next, insert the hair or moss stuffing between the cotton and the inside back surface. Make certain that the stuffing is distributed evenly

345

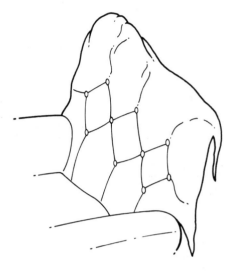

Fig. 30. Finishing the tufts.

and firmly. Now tack the bottom of the cover material to the back of the seat rail (Fig. 29).

13. Attach each row of buttons and fill the tufts in the same manner as described in Steps Eleven and Twelve (Fig. 30).

14. The sides and top of the back are similar to the bottom in that they end in half-tufts or channels. These must be stuffed in the same manner as the rest of the tufts. However, in this case, the cover must be pulled around to the back of the frame and tacked (Figs. 11 and 12). Care must be taken to exert uniform tension when pulling the cover. Work with the top first and then with the sides. The procedure here is the same as that outlined in Steps Eight through Eleven for the channels.

The preceding detailed the construction of triangular or diamond tufts. Square or rectangular tufts require only slight modifications of these steps. The procedure for using a muslin layer is similar to that described in the construction of channels.

The use of foam padding in the construction of tufts is described in Chapter Eleven: Using Foam Padding.

CHAPTER 14

Padded Seats
and Slip Seats

Much of the emphasis in this book up to this point has been placed on upholstery construction of either the overstuffed or tight-spring variety. Overstuffed construction is usually characterized by the use of two sets of springs (in the seat and back) and several layers of stuffing and upholstery material. The result is a piece of furniture with far greater seating comfort than other types. It is also generally much heavier and more expensive. Tight-spring construction, on the other hand, is characterized by having only one set of springs (in the seat) and a padded back. It is lighter and generally less expensive than the overstuffed type.

The padded seat is a third type of furniture construction. Its principal characteristic is that it uses no springs at all.

Padded seats can have either closed seat bases (a solid piece of wood) or open ones. Both the open and closed seat bases can be permanently attached or so constructed that they are removable. The removable seat base (also known as a "slip seat") can be removed by loosening the screws or fasteners holding it to the frame. Chairs having padded seats may also have padded backs which may be removable.

If an open frame is used for the seat base, the opening must be covered with webbing and burlap.

Both the closed (solid wood base) and open bases on slip seats should have the upper outside edge of the wood chamfered. The chamfered edge gives a smoother surface against the pull of the fabric (Fig. 1). Chamfered edges are also frequently found on the outside edge of closed seats on padded chairs. These are non-removable seat bases.

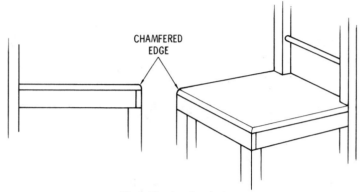

CHAMFERED
EDGE

Fig. 1. The chamfered edge

CLOSED SEAT BASE (Non-Removable)

In order to upholster a chair with a non-removable closed seat base (that is, a solid piece of wood used as the seat base), the following procedure should be followed:

1. If the seat is to be reupholstered, then remove the old upholstery. Check the outside top edge of the seat base. It may be necessary to round the edges (Fig. 2). The amount of rounding should be approximately one-quarter of the thickness of the seat base and should be done to the front and both sides.
2. Since the closed seat construction has a solid wood base, there will be no need for springs, webbing, or an initial layer of heavy grade burlap.
3. The seat can be padded with three kinds of stuffing: (1) loose (animal hair, moss, etc.), (2) cotton, or (3) some form of foam padding. The third type of stuffing is described in detail in Chapter Eleven: Using Foam Padding.

4. If you choose to use a loose stuffing, you must attach an edge roll around the edges of the seat base. The primary purpose of the edge roll in this construction is to prevent the stuffing from slipping down over the edges of the frame. Read the appropriate section in Chapter Eight and follow the instructions for attaching an edge roll (Fig. 3).

5. Loose stuffing may be added in two layers. The first or lower layer is distributed so that it is level with the top of the edge roll. Spread it evenly, removing all lumps as you do so. Do *not* pack it down (Fig. 4.).

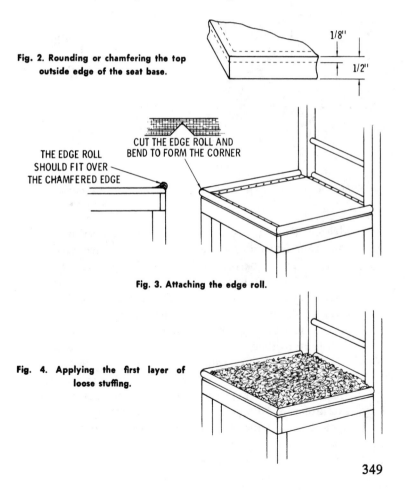

Fig. 2. Rounding or chamfering the top outside edge of the seat base.

1/8"

1/2"

CUT THE EDGE ROLL AND BEND TO FORM THE CORNER

THE EDGE ROLL SHOULD FIT OVER THE CHAMFERED EDGE

Fig. 3. Attaching the edge roll.

Fig. 4. Applying the first layer of loose stuffing.

349

6. The second or upper layer of stuffing should be so distributed that once it is compressed by the covering material the edges of the seat will be firm (you do not want lumps or depressions here) and there will be a crown in the middle (Fig. 5).
7. Cover the stuffing with a cotton pad (Fig. 6), which extends over the edge roll.

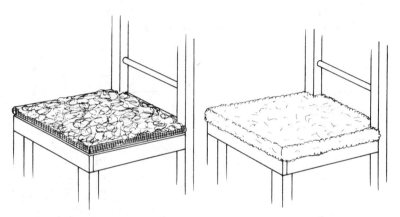

Fig. 5. Applying the second layer of loose stuffing.

Fig. 6. Applying the cotton padding over the stuffing.

8. Measure and cut a piece of muslin to fit over the cotton and around to the underneath edge of the side rails by at least ¾ inch. Tack the muslin to the frame (Fig. 7).

Another method is to place the muslin over the loose stuffing. Allow it to extend around to the bottom and tack it down. Place the cotton over the muslin cover. This will be held in place by the outer cover (Fig. 8).

A third method is to measure and cut a light-weight burlap to fit over the loose stuffing, allowing it to extend around the bottom for tacking. Place the cotton over the burlap. Measure and cut a piece of muslin to fit over the cotton and around the bottom of the seat. Tack the muslin to the frame bottom (Fig. 9). The muslin will be covered by the final cover.

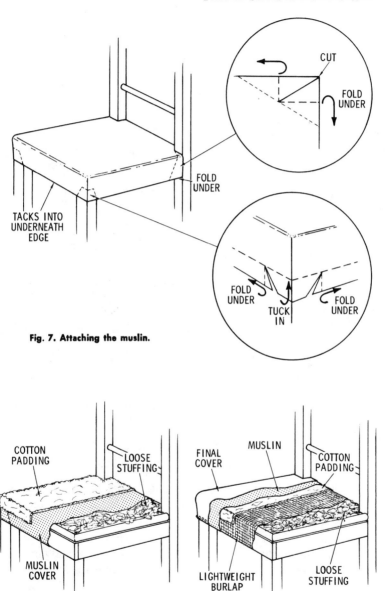

CUT

FOLD
UNDER

FOLD
UNDER

TACKS INTO
UNDERNEATH
EDGE

FOLD
UNDER

TUCK
IN

FOLD
UNDER

Fig. 7. Attaching the muslin.

COTTON
PADDING

LOOSE
STUFFING

MUSLIN
COVER

Fig. 8. Cotton over muslin over loose stuffing.

FINAL
COVER

MUSLIN

COTTON
PADDING

LIGHTWEIGHT
BURLAP

LOOSE
STUFFING

Fig. 9. Muslin over cotton padding over burlap over loose stuffing.

351

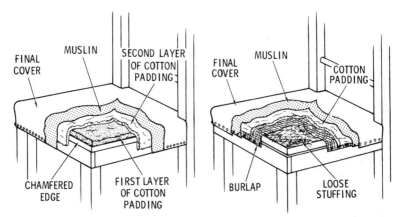

Fig. 10. Using cotton padding in place of loose stuffing.

Fig. 11. Tacking at mid-point on the seat rail.

Still another method is to avoid using loose stuffing altogether. In its place, two layers of cotton felt padding are used. The lower layer is cut smaller than the upper layer and extends to (but does not overlap) the chamfered edge (Fig. 10). Foam padding is also used to replace loose stuffing. This is described in greater detail in Chapter Eleven.

9. The burlap and muslin layers do not need to be carried around to the bottom of the frame. Since the side rails of the frame are wide enough, both layers of material can be tacked at mid-point (Fig. 11).

CLOSED SEAT BASE (Removable)

1. Remove the seat from the chair. These seats are usually attached with screws through the bottom of the frame. If the seat is to be re-upholstered, then remove the old upholstery (Fig. 12).

2. The arrangement of the layers of upholstery stuffing and material is a matter of personal choice and can be one of the methods just described for the non-removable closed seat base. The major factor is the degree of softness desired. See Fig. 13.

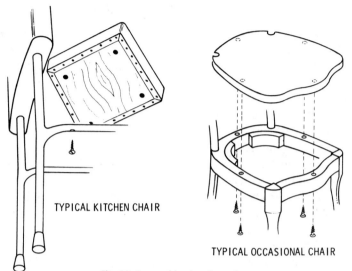

TYPICAL KITCHEN CHAIR

TYPICAL OCCASIONAL CHAIR

Fig. 12. Removable closed seat bases.

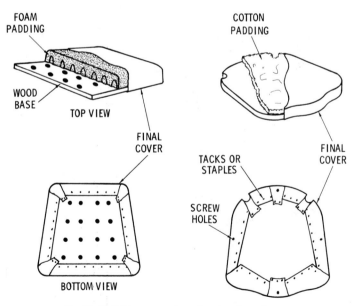

FOAM
PADDING

COTTON
PADDING

WOOD
BASE

TOP VIEW

FINAL
COVER

FINAL
COVER

TACKS OR
STAPLES

SCREW
HOLES

BOTTOM VIEW

Fig. 13. Upholstery procedures for closed seat bases.

OPEN SEAT BASE (Non-Removable)

The lightweight frame construction of this type chair is similar to that found in the tight-spring type. The principal difference between the two is that the former does not use a spring base (Fig. 14). These non-spring, padded chairs are found in bedrooms, in dining rooms (as the more expensive dining room furniture), and in other scattered locations around the house. Because of their lightweight, they are easy to move. Their padding gives better than average comfort.

Most of the information concerning the construction of furniture with non-removable open seat bases has already been covered in detail in other chapters. An important fact to remember is that the webbing is attached to the *top* of the seat rail in this type of construction. Fig. 15 illustrates the various steps in the construction of furniture with non-removable open seat bases. The layers shown in the illustration depict those materials generally employed in chairs of this type of construction. Variations of additional layers can be added to increase the comfort of the chair. For example, a layer of foam rubber could be inserted in the layers to enhance the comfort of the chair.

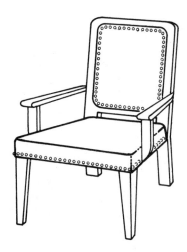

Fig. 14. Padded chair with non-removable open seat base.

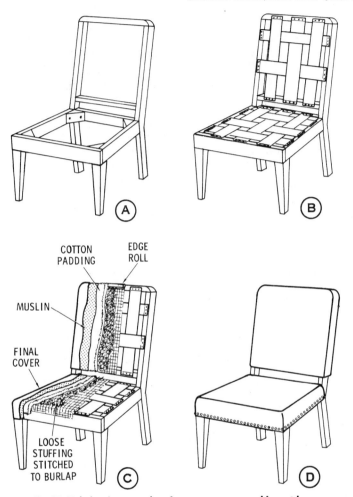

Fig. 15. Upholstering procedure for open, non-removable seat base.

OPEN SEAT BASE (Removable)

A removable seat (slip seat) can also have an open seat base. The opening must be covered with webbing before the burlap layer is attached.

The procedure for constructing a removable seat with an open seat base is as follows:

355

1. Attach the webbing to the *top* of the seat base. Fig. 16 illustrates the method of attaching webbing to a removable open seat base. More detail on attaching webbing is given in Chapter Six.

2. Measure and cut a piece of heavy grade burlap to fit over the webbing. Do not extend the burlap so that it overlaps the edges of the open seat base. Fold the burlap back and tack it down on the upper surface. A tacking strip may be used to give additional strength (Fig. 17). This strip may be open- or blind-tacked although the latter is stronger.

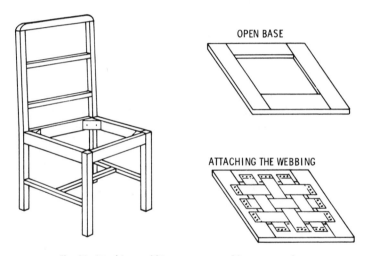

OPEN BASE

ATTACHING THE WEBBING

Fig. 16. Attaching webbing on a removable open seat base.

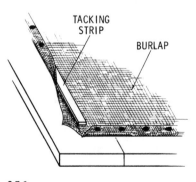

TACKING STRIP

BURLAP

Fig. 17. Attaching a burlap panel with tacking strips over webbing.

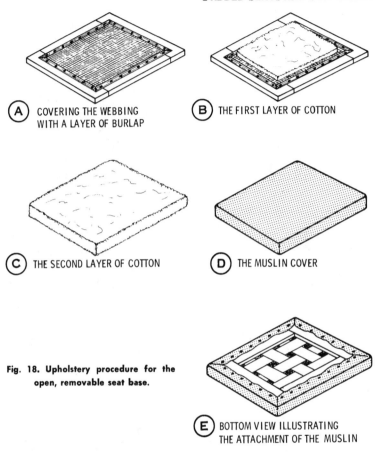

(A) COVERING THE WEBBING WITH A LAYER OF BURLAP

(B) THE FIRST LAYER OF COTTON

(C) THE SECOND LAYER OF COTTON

(D) THE MUSLIN COVER

Fig. 18. Upholstery procedure for the open, removable seat base.

(E) BOTTOM VIEW ILLUSTRATING THE ATTACHMENT OF THE MUSLIN

The rest of the construction is illustrated in Fig. 18. Basically, this follows the procedure described for the construction of a removable closed seat base.

Note that the second layer of cotton (Fig. 18C) extends around to the bottom outside edge of the seat base. However, it does not extend underneath the bottom of the seat base. Only the muslin (Figs. 18D and 18E) and the final cover extend underneath where they are tacked in place. The final cover is attached in the same way as the muslin except that greater care is taken when making corners.

357

CHAPTER 15

Upholstery Fabrics

It is not always easy to determine what is specifically an upholstery fabric and what is not. Many fabrics serve more than one
purpose, being acceptable as material for upholstery as well as
valances and drapes. Monk's cloth, Grenfell cloth, brocatelle (or
brocatel), corduroy, and satin are examples of fabrics serving at
least a dual role.

Upholstery fabrics are generally sold in 50 and 54 inch widths,
and should not be confused with slip-covering fabrics which are
not as strong nor as durable. It is not wise to upholster a chair with
slip-covering fabric despite its cheaper price. The material will
simply not last as long as upholstery fabrics.

FABRIC TERMINOLOGY

There is a basic terminology used in reference to fabrics and
fabric weaves that should be explained before we proceed any
further. The most important at this point are *warp, filling,* and
selvage.

Warp or *warp yarn* refers to the yarns in a fabric which run
parallel to the selvage. The *selvage* is the term used to describe the
border woven along the edge of a length of fabric to prevent un-
raveling. The *filling* or *filling yarn* is woven across the width of
the fabric (in other words, horizontally).

The weave of a fabric is determined by the pattern in which the
filling yarns and warp yarns are interwoven.

The terms *nap* and *pile* are frequently encountered in descriptions of fabrics and should not be confused. They are not synonymous, but refer to two different characteristics of fabrics. Nap refers to the fuzzy surface created by raising (usually by brushing) the fibres of the fabric. Pile, on the other hand, refers to a surface consisting of loops of yarn sewed to a ground or background material.

CLASSIFICATION OF UPHOLSTERY FABRICS

Upholstery fabrics are produced in a wide variety of weaves and patterns. In addition, new ones are frequently introduced by manufacturers. These factors plus the wirespread use of both trade names and generic names for the fabrics makes the task of classification very difficult.

The two principal methods of classifying fabrics are by (1) weave and pattern, and (2) origin (animal, vegetable, etc.). The second classification is particularly important in terms of cleaning a fabric or removing spots and stains. Some fabrics react unfavorably to certain cleaners and cleaning methods. This can be avoided if the origin of the fabric is known beforehand.

The three basic weaves in upholstery fabrics are:

1. *plain weave* (also referred to as *tabby weave* and *taffeta weave),*
2. *twill weave,* and
3. *satin weave.*

Plain weave is characterized by an over-and-under weaving of the filling yarn with the warp yarn. This is on a one for one basis; that is, the filling yarn will pass under the first warp yarn, over the next, under the third, and so on. Two variations of plain weave are (1) *basket weave* (plaid, monk's cloth) and (2) *rib weave* (bengaline).

A *twill weave* is characterized by a diagonal pattern created by weaving the warp yarn under one and across two filling yarns, repeating this pattern through the length of the material. This pattern is staggered in each row to create the diagonal effect.

359

Twill is the strongest of the basic weaves. Examples of twill weave are (1) denim and (2) khaki.

A *satin weave* is characterized by weaving in which the warp yarns are passed over the filling yarns (or vice-versa) at widely spaced regular or irregular intervals. This is the weakest of the three basic weaves. Examples of a satin weave are (1) damask and (2) sateen.

Sometimes the *pile weave* is added to the above three to make a fourth basic weave. However, a pile weave is a more complex form than any of the three basic weaves. It is created by weaving the filling and warp yarns into a ground (background) material. the pile itself consists of the individual loops of a third yarn extending above the ground surface. Thus, a pile weave creates a textured surface which stands in contrast to the flat surfaces of the plain, twill, and satin weaves. Examples of pile weaves are (1) plush, (2) velvet, and (3) velveteen.

A *Jacquard weave* refers to any fabric woven on a loom equipped with a Jacquard device. Such looms are capable of producing the elaborate designs which characterize the Jacquard weave. This device was introduced by Joseph Marie Jacquard in 1805 and functioned as an automatic selective shedding mechanism. Examples of fabrics woven with this device are (1) brocade, (2) matelasse, (3) tapestry, and (4) damask.

FABRIC PROCESSES

There are a number of special processes that are designed to improve some or several characteristics of a fabric. Some of these processes are (1) sizing, (2) bleaching, (3) singeing and mercerization, (4) calendering, (5) Sanforizing, (6) beetling, and (7) weighting (loading).

Sizing can be temporary (starch) or permanent (a chemical additive). In either case, the purpose of sizing is to add stiffness, strength, and weight to a fabric. Because sizing results in the filling of openings in the fabric, it also increases the surface smoothness. Sized fabrics are used primarily in curtains and are of little concern to the upholsterer.

Bleaching a fabric to create a lighter effect can be done after first neutralizing the materials with a weak sulfuric acid solution. There are several household bleaches that are suitable for bleaching fabrics.

Singeing is a process of removing fibres and fuzz from fabric yarns (or threads) by passing them quickly over a gas flame or heated rollers.

Singeing results in fabrics with very smooth surfaces, but without the weight produced by sizing them. In the *mercerization* process, the fabric is placed in a caustic soda solution after it has been signed. This increases both the strength and luster of the material and increases its affinity for dyes.

Calendering refers to the pressing of fabric between heated rollers to temporarily increase the luster. After a period of time, the luster diminishes.

Sanforizing is a patented process of treating fabrics so that shrinkage is reduced to a guaranteed rate of one per cent or less.

Beetling refers to the flattening of such fabrics as cotton or linen to give a compact appearance or add a lustrous finish.

Weighing (*loading*) is a process if adding metallic substances to the fabric to increase its weight (sizing is another form of weighting). Silk is frequently weighted in order to increase its weight.

BASIC FIBRES

One point of confusion about fabrics (which adds to the problem of classifying them) is the question of determining the origin of their fibres. For example, satin can be made from either silk or rayon fibres, or a combination of silk and cotton fibres. Plush can be made from rayon, silk, or mohair fibres, and cretonne can trace the origin of its fibres to linen, cotton, or rayon. These are not isolated examples.

All upholstery fabrics are made from one or a combination of five basic fibres. Two of these basic fibres are derived from vegetable sources (cotton and linen); two from animal sources (wool and silk); and one is synthetic in origin. The synthetic (or manmade) fibres were until recently represented exclusively by rayon. However, developments in chemistry in the past few decades has resulted in the addition of several more synthetic fibres. Synthetic fibres have either a cellulose origin (rayon and acetate) or are a result of the polymerization process (nylon, acrylic, Saran). Thus, the basic fibres found singularly or in combination in upholstery fabrics can be listed as follows:

1. Vegetable origin
   (a) cotton
   (b) linen
2. Animal origin
   (a) wool
   (b) silk
3. Synthetic source
   (a) cellulose base
      (i) rayon
      (ii) acetate
   (b) polymer base
      (i) nylon
      (ii) acrylic
      (iii) Saran

The synthetic fibres listed here are the most commonly known and are by no means intended to represent a complete list.

UPHOLSTERY FABRICS

The following is a representative list of upholstery fabrics. It, too, should not be considered a complete listing.

armure. A fabric characterized by small, woven designs on a rep base. It is a twilled fabric made most commonly from cotton, but also from silk, wool, rayon, or a mixture of materials.

Beauvais. A tapestry fabric used in upholstering.

Bengaline. An imitation of the distinctive Bengal silk made from cotton, wool, rayon, or silk. Its appearance is similar to ordinary rep or poplin with cords extending either crosswise or lengthwise.

brocade. Brocade has an embossed (raised) effect with usually a figure or flower pattern. The raised pattern is generally in color or texture contrast with the background. Brocade can be made from silk, wool, or cotton.

brocatelle (brocatel). Brocatelle is a coarser and heavier variety of brocade. The relief is generally higher. A good quality brocatelle

Fig. 1. Brocatelle.

fabric is made from a mixture of rayon (55%) and cotton (45%) fibres (Fig. 1).

burlap. Burlap is a coarse, cheap material produced from jute and used for covering springs and other internal aspects of furniture construction.

cambric. A thin, closely woven fabric used as a dust cover for the bottom of furniture. The exposed side is glazed.

chintz. A cotton (lightweight) or rayon fabric having small, gay designs printed on its surface. It may be either glazed or unglazed.

corduroy. A cotton or rayon velvet with a cut pile in a ridge or cord effect.

crash. A term characterizing upholstery fabrics with a coarse, uneven texture resulting from weaving uneven yarns. It can be made from rayon, linen, cotton, or combinations of these.

cretonne. A printed fabric very similar to chintz except that the design patterns are larger. Cretonne is made from cotton, rayon, or linen.

damask. Damask is a flat fabric without the relief of brocade. However, unlike brocade it is reversible. Damask is made from cotton, rayon, silk, wool, and linen, not to mention various fibre

Fig. 2. Damask.

combinations. A 100% rayon damask has a smooth silk-like texture and sheen (Fig. 2).

denim. Denim is generally a twill weave fabric produced from cotton. It is classed and sold by the weight. Unlike most fabrics, it can be used for both upholstering and slip covering.

faille. A fabric similar to rep or poplin in rib variations of plain weave running fillingwise. Faille is made of rayon, cotton, or silk.

Frieze is a durable pile fabric made from cut or uncut loops. It is produced from mohair, silk, rayon, cotton, or various combinations of these. Different effects can be achieved by contrasting yarn colors or the lengths of the loops (cut or uncut).

Grenfell cloth. Grenfell cloth is a very closely woven fabric with excellent water repellent characteristics.

hair cloth (or horsehair). A fabric made from either cotton or linen warps with horsehair filling threads.

Herculon is a trade name that indicates a fabric is made from 100% Herculon olefin fibre. This is a synethetic fibre with stain and soil resistant powers well beyond those provided by *Zepel* or *Scotchgard* fabric protectors. The latter two are surface coatings; whereas, *Herculon* is the fibre itself and consequently carries

Fig. 3. Herculon.

Fig. 4. Linen print.

365

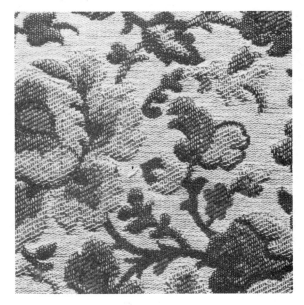

Fig. 5. Matelasse.

its protection all through the fabric. *Herculon* olefin fibres produce a rough, tweed-like fabric (Fig. 3).

imitation leather. Imitation (artificial) leather is an inexpensive substitute made from a chemical coating on a cotton base. The coating is embossed to simulate genuine leather. One of the more common types of imitation leather is a vinyl plastic (see Chapter Sixteen).

jaspe. A term of French origin indicating a fabric which has colored stripes or streaks. The effect is created by weaving into the fabric warp yarns of varying shades of the same color.

linen. Linen fibers are usually combined with a 40% mixture of cotton to produce a light, closely woven fabric. Linen can have the appearance of a brocatelle fabric's raised surface (Fig. 4).

matelasse. Matelasse is made from cotton, rayon, silk, and combinations of fabrics and gives the appearance of a quilted surface. (Fig. 5).

metal cloth. Metal cloth is any fabric having metal threads (usually silver, gold, or copper) sewn into the material.

mohair. Mohair is a pile fabric very similar to frieze, having both cut and uncut loops. The backing is generally wool or cotton with the

Fig. 6. Nylon.

Fig. 7. Tapestry.

367

Fig. 8. Needlepoint tapestry.

pile made from Angora hairs. Embossing and printing are only two of several processes that result in a wide variety of mohair styles. Mohair is one of the more durable of the pile fabrics.

moire. A lightweight and fragile ribbed fabric of rayon or silk.

monk's cloth. Monk's cloth is a rough cotton material characterized by extreme durability. Sometimes jute or hemp is interwoven in the fabric.

muslin. Muslin is a lightweight fabric produced from cotton. It is promarily used beneath more expensive fabrics in upholstered furniture.

nylon. Nylon is a synthetic polymer fibre capable of being produced in many forms. A 100% nylon fabric is strong, lightweight, and retains its shape well (Fig. 6).

poplin. Similar to rep, but slightly lighter in weight, poplin is made from cotton.

plush. Plush is a pile fabric made from mohair or silk. The pile is deeper than velvet.

radnor. Radnor is a fabric which uses a closely woven background on which are superimposed various small surface designs.

rep. Rep is a heavy cord fabric made from wool, silk, or combina-

Fig. 9. Tweed.

tions of yarns. It is sometimes used as a background for a Jacquard figure (see *armure*).

satin. Satin is a fabric noted for its smooth, lustrous surface, and characterized by a broken twill weave. It is made from silk threads, rayon, or combinations of silk and cotton.

taffeta. A ribbed (fillingwise), quilted, or embroidered fabric made of silk or rayon.

tapestry. Tapestry is a heavy, durable fabric produced on a loom equipped with a Jacquard device (and, consequently, erroneously referred to as a "Jacquard" loom). Patterns are woven into the material which results in a ribbed surface and a reversible fabric. (Figs. 7 and 8).

tweed. Tweed is a term used to refer to a number of rough-textured fabrics sharing color-and-weave characteristics similar to those found in clothing tweed. However, upholstery tweed is heavier in both texture and weight. (Fig. 9).

velveteen (or *fustian*). A closely woven, short pile, cotton fabric designed to imitate silk velvet.

velvet. Velvet is another term used to describe a specific set of fabric characteristics. In this case it is used to describe fabrics having a

Fig. 10. Plain velvet.

Fig. 11. Crushed velvet.

short, thick, warp pile (excluding *plush*). Some forms of velvet are made with a cotton backing and a silk or rayon pile. (Figs. 10 and 11). *velour.* A short, thick, warp pile fabric. It is heavier than velvet and made from cotton, rayon, linen, or silk.

LEATHER

The preparation of an animal hide for use as upholstery leather is a complicated procedure. To make a long story short, the hide (usually steer hide) is split into four or five layers after the tanning process has been completed. Each layer (or split) provides a characteristic grade of leather. Upholstery leathers are taken from the first and second splits.

One of the major advantages of upholstery leather is that it is extremely easy to maintain. Usually little more than wiping the surface with soap and water is necessary to keep it clean. It is far more expensive than the imitation leathers, but it compensates for this by being much more durable. When the surface of an imitation leather receives a deep scratch, the backing is exposed to view. This is not the case with genuine leather.

PLASTIC FABRICS

Plastic fabrics are described in detail in Chapter Sixteen.

FABRIC FINISHES

Fabrics can be treated with special finishes to make them resistant to staining and soiling. These finishes (which are almost always applied by the manufacturer) appear under such trade names as *Scotchgard, Zelan, Syl-mer,* and *Zapel.* They are invisible to the naked eye, and do not change the feel or appearance of the fabric in any way.

SELECTING AN UPHOLSTERY FABRIC

The problem of determining whether or not a fabric has the qualities you want is not an easy one to solve. However, it can be narrowed down to two basic areas: (1) its wearability and (2) the decorative aspects.

The wearability of a fabric can be determined in a number of ways. one method is to pull the fabric lengthwise and crosswise and release it. The yarns that shift out of place and stay there are a poor quality fabric, and those that return to their original position are of good quality for upholstery work.

Remember, it is not always the type of fibre used as it is the heaviness of the material and the closeness and tightness of the weave. Generally speaking a tightly woven fabric will wear better than the looser weaves.

A method for testing color steadfastness and reactions to cleaning are discussed in Chapter Seventeen.

The colors, patterns, and textures you select will be determined by your personal tastes. Table 1 gives you a general guide for coordinating fabrics, colors and furniture styles.

Table 1. Color and Fabric Coordination Chart.

PERIOD STYLE	FABRIC	DRAPERIES COLORS	DESIGN	UPHOLSTERY FABRICS
EARLY ENGLISH TUDOR JACOBEAN CHARLES II	Crewel embroideries, Hand blocked linen, Silk & worsted damask, Velvet, Brocade	Full bodied crimson green and yellow	Large bold patterns: tree branch, fruits, flowers, oak leaf, animals, heraldic designs	Tapestry Leather Needlework Velvet Brocade
ANGLO-DUTCH WILLIAM & MARY QUEEN ANNE	Crewel embroideries, Hand blocked linen, Silk & worsted damask, Velvet Brocade, India prints	Full bodied crimson green and yellow	Large bold patterns: tree branch, fruits, flowers, oak leaf, animals, heraldic designs	Tapestry Leather Needlework Velvet Brocade
EARLY GEORGIAN CHIPPENDALE	Crewel embroideries, Hand blocked linen, Silk & worsted damask, Velvet Brocade, India prints	Full bodied crimson green and yellow	Jacobean motifs Also classic medallions and garlands	Tapestry Leather Needlework Velvet Brocade
LATE GEORGIAN ADAM HEPPLEWHITE SHERATON	Brocades. Damask, Chintz, Taffeta, Satins, Toile de Jouy	Delicate subdued hues of rose, yellow, mauve, green and gray	Classic designs, small in scale: garlands, urns, floral, animals, etc.	Damask, Brocade, Velor, Satin, Petit Point, Leather in libraries
LOUIS XVI	Silks, Satin Damask, Crewel work ask, Taffeta, Muslins, Brocade, Toile de Jouy	Delicate powder blue, oyster white, pearl, rose, pale greens, mauve, yellow	Stripes sprinkled with ribbons, flowers, medallions, lyres and other classic motifs	Petit Point, Satin Moire, Velours, Chintz, Damask, Brocade, Tapestry

Table 1. Color and Fabric Coordination Chart (Cont'd.)

PERIOD STYLE	FABRIC	DRAPERIES COLORS	DESIGN	UPHOLSTERY FABRICS
SPANISH RENAISSANCE	Velvet, Damask, India prints, Printed and emb. linen	Rich vigorous colors; red, green and gold	Bold patterns in classic and heraldic designs, also arabesques	Leather Tapestry Velvet Linen Brocatelle
EARLY COLONIAL	Crewel embroideries, Hand blocked linen, Silk & worsted damask, Velvet, Brocade	Full bodied crimson green and yellow	Large bold patterns: tree branch, fruits, flowers, oak leaf, animals, heraldic	Tapestry Leather Needlework Velvet Brocade
LATE COLONIAL	Toile de Jouy, Damask, Chintz, Organdy, Cretonne	All colors, but more subdued than in early period	Scenic Birds Animals Floral	Haircloth Mohair Rep Linen Chintz Velours
MODERN	Textured and novelty weaves. All fabrics	All colors. Bright to pastel.	Solid colors Modern Designs Stripes	All Fabrics Novelty weaves Plastics
FRENCH PROVINCIAL	Chintz Cretonne Blocked linen Velvet	Subdued colors. Pastel shades.	Screen Prints Block print	Solid colors Textured weaves Tapestry
VICTORIAN	Velvet. Brocades Damask	Turkey Red. Other rich colors.	Solid colors Formal Patterns	Haircloth Needlework

Upholstering With Plastics

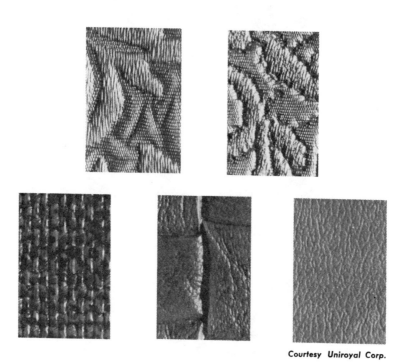

Fig. 1. Examples of "Naugahyde"® textured patterns.

Fig. 2. A typical "Koroseal"® finish.

Courtesy B. F. Goodrich Co.

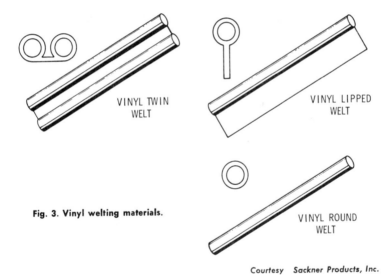

VINYL TWIN
WELT

VINYL LIPPED
WELT

Fig. 3. Vinyl welting materials.

VINYL ROUND
WELT

Courtesy Sackner Products, Inc.

Vinyl plastic fabrics offer a wide range of colors and styles for upholstering. Vinyl plastic fabrics also show considerable differences in quality. The cheapest grades are sheet plastic without any backing for support. Better grades will have a knitted or woven backing for added durability. This fabric backing is permanently fused to the vinyl plastic. Some plastic vinyls (the

375

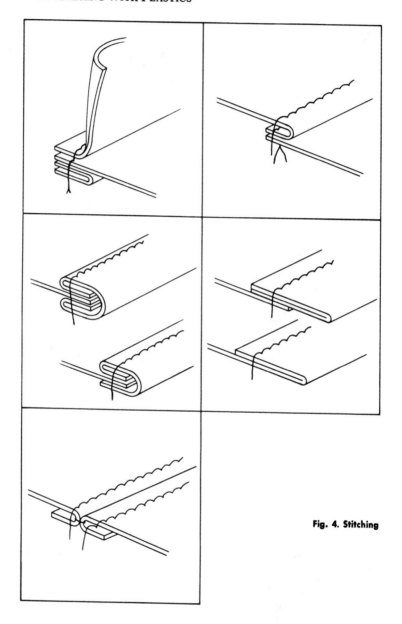

Fig. 4. Stitching

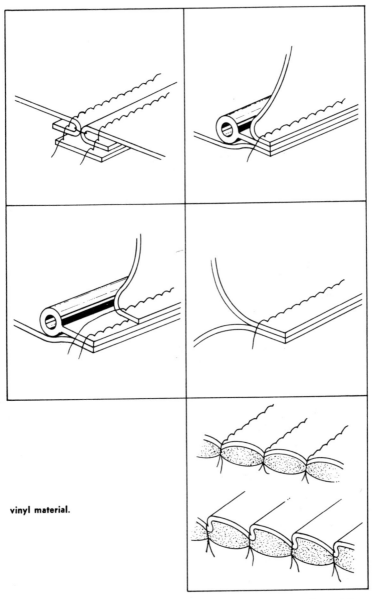

vinyl material.

so-called "expanded vinyls") are manufactured with thousands of tiny air cells that provide extra softness and comfort.

Naugahyde®, a leading trade name of Uniroyal Corporation, is a vinyl plastic produced in over 500 colors, textures, and patterns (Fig. 1).

Koroseal®, another expanded vinyl upholstery material manufactured by The B. F. Goodrich Company, is also available in a wide range of colors (Fig. 2). Various types of vinyl welt are also manufactured for use with these materials (Fig. 3).

Vinyl plastics are derived from synthetic resins which are mixed with a number of substances selected for particular characteristics needed in the end-product, and subjected to high temperature and pressure. The surfaces of the vinyl plastic sheets are then imprinted with the desired color, pattern, and style. Vinyl plastic fabrics are usually sold in 54 inch wide rolls.

Plastic vinyl fabrics are durable and easy to keep clean. Ordinary soap and water is all you need to keep them clean under normal conditions.

Suggestions for upholstering with a plastic vinyl fabric are as follows:

1. Determine the amount of fabric yardage needed for the job. Rough yardage estimates are given for a number of different furniture styles in Chapter Nine.

2. Use standard upholstery shears for cutting plastic vinyl fabrics. It cuts easily with a sharp, clean edge. Allow about 1 inch for fitting and handling. Make all corner cuts with a rounded corner line

3. Plastic vinyls with fabric backing can be tacked or styled to the frame in the same manner as other fabrics. Since there is enough elasticity in the material, it can be pulled tight without straining it.

4. A heat lamp can be used to heat the plastic vinyl in order to increase its elasticity. This is particularly useful in fitting the material around corners or rounded surfaces without wrinkles.

5. Cardboard tacking strips are used for "blind tacking" when upholstering with vinyl plastic fabrics in the same manner as with other upholstery fabrics.

6. Plastic vinyls are sewn in the same manner as other fabrics. It is suggested that you use a strong upholstery thread and take a larger stitch (7 to 8 stitches per inch).

7. Seams and other joining operations suggested by Uniroyal are illustrated in Fig. 4.

8. Channel backs and tufted backs are constructed in the same manner as those using non-plastic vinyl fabrics (see Chapter Thirteen).

9. The bottom edge can be finished by carrying the plastic vinyl fabric under the frame and tacking it in place. A cambric dust cover is used to cover the bottom. Rather than carry the fabric under the frame, you might want to use a single or double welting along the bottom edge.

10. Cushions are constructed in the same manner as those using non-plastic vinyl fabrics (see Chapter Ten).

Nylon thread is recommended by the manufacturers for use with vinyl plastics, although the author prefers a heavy cotton thread. The nylon thread has a tendency to cut the vinyl plastic fabric.

CHAPTER 17

Furniture Care

Cleaning upholstery from time-to-time will prolong its life and add to its appearance. The type of cleaning given it will naturally depend upon the type of upholstery. Plastics and vinyls should be occasionally wiped with a mild soap and warm water. Be sure to use a soft cloth for wiping. Upholstery fabrics require a little more time and effort. They should be kept relatively dust-free with frequent vacuuming. Most vacuum cleaners have attachments that are designed to make cleaning upholstery more convenient. Wood surfaces should be dusted and polished or waxed. This not only protects them, but enhances their appearance.

Upholstery shampoos can be purchased in the store or made at home. The best shampoos produce a thick, soapless lather. Add two to three tablespoons of borax to a solution of soap and water. The soap in this solution should consist of pure, white flakes (having none of those "super-power" additives). Add about six teaspoons of soap flakes to a pint of boiling water.

Many people are so nervous about new or favorite pieces of furniture that they cover them with slipcovers. Some slipcovers are made from a clear plastic through which one can still see the original cover fabric. However, most slipcovers are made from a material that completely hides the one beneath. This is perfectly reasonable if the original cover is damaged or faded. It is carrying caution to the extreme if the only reason for using a slipcover is to protect a favorite fabric. Slipcovers are also used to change the decor of a room. If the fabric on a particular piece of furniture clashes with others in the room, it can be covered with a slipcover made from a fabric more compatible with the surroundings. Some authorities on interior decoration even suggest making at least two slipcovers for each piece of furniture in a room. Each set of slipcovers then provides a different "personality" for the room (e.g., cool colors in the summer and warm colors in the winter).

CLEANING SUPPLIES

Commercially prepared spot removers are sold as pastes, liquids, sticks, or as sprays in pressurized cans. Many of these items are dangerously flammable and must at all times be kept away from any flame or heat source. They should also be stored away from the reach of small children, because they contain toxic elements. You should never use a spray or liquid spot remover anywhere except in a well-ventilated room. If at all possible, work with these cleaning materials on the patio or in the yard.

Commercially prepared spot removers should not be regarded as possessing some sort of magical powers for solving all cleaning problems. If this is your belief, then you are due to be frequently disappointed. The effectiveness of a commercial spot remover depends upon the type of stain and the type of fabric. Some spot removers will work better on certain types of stains than others.

Soaps or detergents and water are commonly-used cleaning agents for many types of stains. The water should be clean. The temperature of the water depends upon the type of stain and the results desired. Cool or cold water is best with nongreasy stains since most stains are set with heat. Warm or hot water is more effective with greasy stains. If you need to wring out the cloth, do so in a second container of water. Reapply only the clean water to the stained surface. Water is also used as a rinse after other types of cleaners have been applied to a stain.

One method of using a soap or detergent for cleaning upholstery is to rub it into the stain, and then thoroughly rinse it out. Sometimes the soap or detergent is allowed to stand for several hours before rinsing.

Hydrogen peroxide is used in a three percent solution to produce a rather strong spot remover that can be used on either washable fabrics or those that must be dry cleaned. Dampen the stain with the solution and expose it to direct sunlight until it dries. If the stain has not disappeared, dampen it again with more of the same solution. Repeat this procedure until the stain is gone. Rinse the area with clean water, and allow it to dry. Hydrogen peroxide should not be used on white cottons or linens.

Chlorine bleach is a cleaning agent that can be effectively used on linens and white cottons. It may be necessary to dilute the chlorine bleach with water before using it.

Household ammonia is used in a ten percent solution and can be applied to most fabrics using the same procedure described for the hydrogen peroxide solution. However, if the fabric contains any wool or silk, dilute the ammonia on a one-to-one basis with water. A solution of ammonia and water can be used to neutralize acid.

Vinegar may also be used as a spot remover. Like ammonia, it is combined with water in a ten percent solution. The procedure for applying a vinegar solution is the same as that described for ammonia.

Oxalic acid is a strong bleach that is diluted with water for use as a cleaning agent. About one tablespoon of oxalic acid crystals in a cup of warm water will produce the proper ratio for a satisfactory solution. Do not allow the solution to dry until the stain has disappeared. After you are through using the oxalic acid solution, rinse the area with clean water. Do not allow any of the oxalic acid solution to remain in the fabric, because it can cause damage to the fabric fibers. Use caution when working with oxalic acid. It is poisonous and can cause damage to the lungs and eyes.

SOME WORDS OF CAUTION ABOUT CLEANING

Like anything else, cleaning upholstery can be done well or poorly. If you feel that this is a task beyond your abilities to do well, then I would suggest obtaining the services of a professional. The remainder of this section contains guidelines for individuals who wish to do their own upholstery cleaning. This is followed by suggestions for specific types of stains.

Those who wish to do their own upholstery cleaning should keep in mind the following cautionary advice:

1. Always try to remove a spot or stain as soon as possible. Do not allow it time to set.
2. Test the fabric for color fastness and possible reactions to the spot remover or cleaner you are using. Use a matching sample of the fabric or test a portion tacked under the frame or in some other inconspicuous section.
3. Do not allow foam padding to become too wet when applying a stain remover to a fabric. The padding will be damaged as a result.
4. Do not wipe stains—it spreads them. Blot the stain with a rag or something else absorbent. Some people use sawdust, talcum powder, or similar types of absorbents for soaking up the excess liquids.

COMMON FABRIC STAINS

ACID. Not only will acids stain fabric, the stronger types will destroy the fibers. It is necessary, then, to remove the acid from the fabric as quickly as possible. This can be done simply by rinsing it thoroughly with water. In order to neutralize any traces of acid that might remain on the fibers, dampen the area with ammonia.

ALCOHOL. Same as chocolate stains. If the treatment described under "chocolate" will not remove the stain, try rubbing the area with rubbing alcohol. Never apply full strength rubbing alcohol to an acetate. Dilute it with water first. Alcohol will cause some dyes to bleed, so it might be advisable to test a piece of the fabric before applying the alcohol.

BLOOD. Do *not* use hot water on blood stains. The heat will set the stain, and make it almost impossible to get out. Use cold water to dampen the stain. If the blood is still fresh, the cold water treatment may be sufficient to remove the entire stain. If not, rub a soap or detergent into it, and rinse it clean with cold water. A variation of the preceding method is to dampen the stain with ammonia before rubbing in the soap or detergent. A stronger treatment for blood stains is the use of small amounts of either chlorine bleach or hydrogen peroxide on a damp cloth.

BUTTER. Rub a detergent or soap into the stain and rinse it clean with hot water. If this is not successful in removing the stain, try using a commercially-prepared cleaner. Allow the material to dry. Some cleaners leave a yellow stain. This can be removed with a chlorine bleach.

CATSUP. Same as chocolate stains.

CHLORINE. Using a chlorine bleach will sometimes leave a yellow stain on the fabric. If the fabric is wool or silk, you will not be able to remove the stain. If it is another type fabric and an item that can be removed, such as a slipcover, it should be rinsed thoroughly with water and soaked 30 minutes in a solution of sodium thiosulfate (1 teaspoon) and warm water (1 quart).

CHOCOLATE. Sponge the stain with cold water or allow the material to soak in cold water for at least thirty minutes (if it is a removable slipcover). If there is still some stain remaining, rub a detergent or soap into the material and rinse clean with cold water. If a greasy stain remains, sponge with a commercial spot remover. Permit the material to dry and repeat the treatment should you feel it necessary to do so. If a colored stain remains after the material is dry, use a chlorine bleach or hydrogen peroxide. Rinse well with cold water and allow the material to dry.

The directions for removing chocolate stains also apply to cocoa, cream, gravy, mayonnaise, salad dressing, ice cream, milk, and related types.

COCOA. Same as chocolate stains.

COFFEE. Same as chocolate stains. In addition to the stain removal treatment discussed under "chocolate," there are several special treatments suitable for this type of stain. If it is a stained slipcover, pour boiling water through the stain. Be certain before you do this that the fabric will not be damaged by water at this temperature. Follow this with an application of chlorine bleach if necessary.

COSMETICS. Rub a detergent or soap into the stain and rinse thoroughly with water. Allow it to dry. If the stain still remains, repeat the procedure until you are satisfied with the results.

CRAYON. Same as cosmetic stains.

CREAM. Same as chocolate stains.

EGG. Rub soap or detergent into the stain. Allow it to set for a couple of hours. Rinse the stain thoroughly with cold water. Either chlorine bleach or hydrogen peroxide may be used if the stain has not been removed by the treatment with soap (or a detergent) and water.

FINGERNAIL POLISH. Use nail polish remover on the stain. If the stain does not disappear, apply some rubbing alcohol to it. Rinse thoroughly with warm water.

FRUIT AND FRUIT JUICES. Sponge the stain with cold water or allow the material to soak in cold water for at least thirty minutes (if it is a removable slipcover). If not all the stain has disappeared, rub detergent or soap into the stain. Rinse thoroughly with cold water. Chlorine and hydrogen peroxide may be used as a stronger stain remover for this type of stain.

GLUE. The stain remover procedure for this type of stain depends largely upon the type of glue. Most glues can be loosened by sponging the stain with hot water or allowing the material to soak in hot water for about thirty minutes (if it is a removable slipcover). If some stain remains, rub detergent or soap into the material and rinse with warm water. There are some glues that demand a different type of treatment. Airplane glues, for example, are best removed by an application of nail polish remover (acetone). Casein glue follows the same procedure except that cold water is used instead of hot for the final rinsing.

GRASS, FLOWERS, AND FOLIAGE. Work soap or detergent into the material and rinse thoroughly with cold water. Alcohol can be used instead of water for rinsing if it is safe for dye (dilute the alcohol with water for use on fabrics containing acetate fibers).

GRAVY AND MEAT JUICES. Same as chocolate.

GREASE AND OIL STAINS. If this is a fresh stain and excess grease or oil still remains on the surface of the material, try removing it by spreading an absorbent (such as starch, talcum powder, or sawdust) over the stain. Paper towels gently applied to the stain (do *not* wipe or rub the stain) will also absorb excess grease or oil. Rub a detergent into the stain, and rinse thoroughly with hot water. Allow the material to dry. If some stain still re-

385

mains, try using a commercial spot remover suitable for this type of stain. Yellow rings can be eliminated by applying chlorine bleach. Rinse thoroughly with hot water after using the bleach.

ICE CREAM. Same as chocolate stains.

INK. Work as fast as you can with ink stains. If you allow the ink to dry, it becomes very difficult to remove. Sponge the stain with nail polish remover, and rinse thoroughly with cold water. The best results are obtained by forcing water through the stain. However, this is only possible with slipcovers that can be removed from the furniture. That is why nail polish remover is recommended. You must not allow the padding beneath the fabric to become water soaked.

IODINE. Sponge the stain with cold water, and allow it to dry. If some stain remains, rub in a soap or detergent and rinse thoroughly with warm water. An alternative method is to sponge the stain with alcohol. Be certain that the dye is safe for alcohol before using it.

KEROSENE. Rub soap or detergent into the stain, and rinse thoroughly with warm water.

MARGARINE. Same as butter stains.

MAYONNAISE. Same as chocolate stains.

MEDICINE. There are so many different types of medicines that it is difficult to suggest anything other than general guidelines. For example, stains resulting from medicine dissolved in a syrup or water should be treated by sponging them with cold water. This can be followed by rubbing soap or detergent into the stain, and rinsing thoroughly with water. Medicines dissolved in alcohol should be treated with alcohol. If the fabric contains acetate fibers, dilute the alcohol with water.

MILDEW. Fresh mildew stains can be removed by sponging with cold water. Mildew mold growth weakens the fibers of a material over a period of time so it is best to remove any traces of mildew as soon as they are discovered. Chlorine bleach is used to treat the more stubborn mildew stains.

MILK. Same as chocolate stains.

MUSTARD. Rub soap or detergent into the stain, and rinse thoroughly with warm water. Use a chlorine bleach if the stain proves stubborn.

PAINT. Like medicine stains, paint stains are of many different types. Without knowing the composition of the paint, it is difficult to recommend an effective stain removal procedure. However, it is possible to suggest general guidelines for removing paint stains. As is the case with ink stains, paint stains should be treated immediately without being permitted to dry. Rub a soap or detergent into the stain, and rinse thoroughly with warm water. Turpentine is also effective as a paint remover. The fabric should be thoroughly rinsed afterwards. An alternative is to use the thinner recommended for the particular paint. This, too, should be followed by a thorough rinsing.

PERFUME. Same as alcohol stains.

PERSPIRATION. Like mildew, perspiration stains also have a weakening effect on fibers. Rub soap or detergent into the stain, and rinse thoroughly with warm water. Color fading due to perspiration stains can be treated with ammonia or vinegar. Use ammonia on a fresh stain; vinegar on an old one. Thoroughly rinse with water.

RUST. There are a number of effective rust removers available for purchase. Choose one that contains oxalic acid. Apply the rust remover to the stain, and rinse thoroughly. Remember: oxalic acid is poisonous and should be handled with extreme caution.

SALAD DRESSING. Same as chocolate stains.

SCORCH. Direct sunlight sometimes bleaches out scorch marks. A stronger bleaching method is to apply a three-percent solution of hydrogen peroxide to the scorch. Strong scorching cannot be removed.

SHOE POLISH. Follow the directions for removing cosmetic stains. If further treatment is required, treat the stain with a chlorine bleach solution. Rinse thoroughly afterwards.

SHORTENING. Same as butter stains.

SYRUP. Same as chocolate stains.

TEA. Same as coffee and chocolate stains.

UNKNOWN STAINS. Many stains will be of unknown origin. Therefore, you will have to approach them with extreme caution. Because heat tends to set certain kinds of stains, you should begin by sponging the stain with cold water. If the stain still remains, rub soap or detergent into the fabric and rinse thoroughly with cold water. Further treatment now begins to be somewhat of a gamble. Grease-based stains are most effectively handled by rubbing soap or detergent into the fabric and rinsing thoroughly with warm water. However, the use of warm or hot water will affect the fibers of some materials (wool, silk, and fabrics that are not colorfast). Some commercially prepared spot removers claim to be effective against a wide number of stains. Usually, however, one spot remover will perform well against certain classes or types of stains (e.g. cream, ice cream, milk stains), but not so well against others (e.g. lipstick, mascara, rouge, eye shadow). If you do not wish to gamble on guessing the type of stain and an appropriate removal procedure, I would suggest obtaining the services of a professional cleaner.

URINE. Same as alcohol stains. A urine stain sometimes results in the color of the fabric fading. This can be restored to a certain extent by sponging the material with ammonia or vinegar.

VARNISH. Same as paint stains.

VASELINE. Remove any excess vaseline, and sponge the stain with turpentine. Rinse thoroughly with water.

VOMIT. Sponge the stain with a solution of borax and water (about ¼ teaspoon of borax to 1 cup of water). The borax will neutralize any acid in the vomit. Rinse thoroughly with cold water.

WAX. Scrape off any excess wax before treating the stain. Rub a soap or detergent into the stain, and rinse thoroughly with warm water. A chlorine bleach solution may be used if the stain proves stubborn.

CLEANING AND REPAIRING WOOD SURFACES

Wood surfaces and the many different types of finishes that can be applied to them represent a vast and complex subject. To do this subject justice would require a book in itself. The following paragraphs represent a few guidelines for the layman to follow with special emphasis placed on the more common features of wood surface cleaning and repairing.

Furniture polishes (both oil and wax) are available in liquid creams, and as aerosol sprays. Both the liquid and cream polishes produce a longer lasting and more durable polish than the spray type. A good furniture polish will clean, dust, and polish the wood surface. The degree of protection the polish gives and the length of time it will last depends upon so many variables (e.g., the age and condition of the polish, the type of wood, etc.) that it is impossible to predict with any certainty.

Polishes should be applied in the direction of the wood grain. Apply a little at a time with a clean, soft cloth. Be sure to follow the manufacturer's suggestions.

Wood surfaces should be frequently dusted with a clean, dry cloth. A hemmed cloth is preferable to an unhemmed one. The latter leaves more lint.

Wood surfaces can and should be cleaned with soap and water occasionally. Use a pure white soap and lukewarm water. Work on small areas at a time. Do not allow water to stand on the surface for any length of time. Should the water cause white spots on the surface, a touch of alcohol on a damp cloth will help eliminate them.

COMMON WOOD SURFACE STAINS AND DEFECTS

BLOOM. Cloudy patches sometimes appear on finishes. These patches appear to be produced by dampness. They can be treated by rubbing the surface with a soft cloth dampened with a warm water and vinegar solution.

BURN MARKS. Scrape away the burned wood. Fill the cavity with a stick shellac that matches the wood.

CHIPPING, FLAKING, AND CRACKING. If the chipping is small enough and fairly localized, stick shellac (or plastic wood) may be used to build up the surface. Flaking and cracking usually indicates a deterioration of the finish. This requires stripping and refinishing.

DENTS. Dents cover a wider area than scratches do, and are usually deeper. There are a number of fillers that can be purchased for repairing large dents. The stick shellacs are probably the most popular, because they are sold in a variety of colors to match different finishes. Heat the stick and allow it to drip into the dent. Allow the stick shellac to build up slightly above the surface. When it has cooled, sand it level to the surface with rottenstone or some other equally fine abrasive.

Dents or chips along edges present a different problem. The edge will have to be built up to its former contour. To do this, you will need something with more substantial body to it than a stick shellac. Plastic wood is probably the best material to use here so long as a natural or stained finish is not being applied (the plastic wood will not absorb stain). Apply it with a knife. Use more plastic wood than is necessary to fill the dent, because it will dry and shrink. After it has dried, sand the plastic wood to fit the contour of the edge. Use rottenstone or an abrasive of similar fineness.

Small dents can be repaired by raising the wood grain. This is done by placing a damp rag against the dent and pressing down on the rag with a hot iron. The combination of moisture and heat causes the grain of the wood to rise. Sand the grain level to the surface.

WHITE SPOTS. White spots are found on varnished surfaces, and are usually caused by something wet or hot. Rub the surface with a damp cloth containing several drops of ammonia. Wipe the surface dry.

SCRATCHES. Polishing will frequently eliminate light scratches. A touch of turpentine applied with a fine brush will often restore the original color. Commercially prepared scratch removers are available for purchase. Their effectiveness varies with the brand. Deep scratches should be filled with stick shellac or plastic wood and sanded. Regardless of the method, use a polish afterwards to revive the wood finish.

SLIPCOVERS

Slipcovers were mentioned briefly at the beginning of this chapter. It is not the purpose of this chapter to describe the construction of slipcovers. This is accomplished in excellent detail in a number of good sewing books currently in print. It should be pointed out, however, that slipcovers represent a cheap and attractive method of covering upholstery that cannot be restored by cleaning.

Index

**Over a Century of Excellence
for the Professional
and
Vocational Trades and the Crafts**

**Order now from your local bookstore
or use the convenient order form at
the back of this book.**

AUDEL

These fully illustrated, up-to-date guides and manuals mean a better job done for mechanics, engineers, electricians, plumbers, carpenters, and all skilled workers.

Contents

Electrical

House Wiring sixth edition
Roland E. Palmquist
5½ x 8 ¼   Hardcover   256 pp.   150 illus.
ISBN: 0-672-23404-1 $13.95

Rules and regulations of the current National Electrical Code® for residential wiring, fully explained and illustrated: • basis for load calculations • calculations for dwellings • services • nonmetallic-sheathed cable • underground feeder and branch-circuit cable • metal-clad cable • circuits required for dwellings • boxes and fittings • receptacle spacing • mobile homes • wiring for electric house heating.

Practical Electricity fourth edition
Robert G. Middleton; revised by L. Donald Meyers
5½ x 8¼   Hardcover   504 pp.   335 illus.
ISBN: 0-672-23375-4 $14.95

Complete, concise handbook on the principles of electricity and their practical application: • magnetism and electricity • conductors and insulators • circuits • electromagnetic induction • alternating current • electric lighting and lighting calculations • basic house wiring • electric heating • generating stations and substations.

II

Guide to the 1984 Electrical Code®
Roland E. Palmquist
5½ × 8¼   Hardcover   664 pp.   225 illus.
ISBN: 0-672-23398-3 $19.95

Authoritative guide to the National Electrical Code® for all electricians, contractors, inspectors, and homeowners: • terms and regulations for wiring design and protection • wiring methods and materials • equipment for general use • special occupancies • special equipment and conditions • and communication systems. Guide to the 1987 NEC® will be available in mid-1987.

Mathematics for Electricians and Electronics Technicians
Rex Miller
5½ × 8¼   Hardcover   312 pp.   115 illus.
ISBN: 0-8161-1700-4 $14.95

Mathematical concepts, formulas, and problem solving in electricity and electronics: • resistors and resistance • circuits • meters • alternating current and inductance • alternating current and capacitance • impedance and phase angles • resonance in circuits • special-purpose circuits. Includes mathematical problems and solutions.

Fractional Horsepower Electric Motors
Rex Miller and Mark Richard Miller
5½ x 8¼   Hardcover   436 pp.   285 illus.
ISBN: 0-672-23410-6 $15.95

Fully illustrated guide to small-to-moderate-size electric motors in home appliances and industrial equipment: • terminology • repair tools and supplies • small DC and universal motors • split-phase, capacitor-start, shaded pole, and special motors • commutators and brushes • shafts and bearings • switches and relays • armatures • stators • modification and replacement of motors.

Electric Motors
Edwin P. Anderson; revised by Rex Miller
5½ x 8¼   Hardcover   656 pp.   405 illus.
ISBN: 0-672-23376-2 $14.95

Complete guide to installation, maintenance, and repair of all types of electric motors: • AC generators • synchronous motors • squirrel-cage motors • wound rotor motors • DC motors • fractional-horsepower motors • magnetic contractors • motor testing and maintenance • motor calculations • meters • wiring diagrams • armature windings • DC armature rewinding procedure • and stator and coil winding.

Home Appliance Servicing fourth edition
Edwin P. Anderson; revised by Rex Miller
5½ x 8¼   Hardcover   640 pp.   345 illus.
ISBN: 0-672-23379-7 $15.95

Step-by-step illustrated instruction on all types of household appliances: • irons • toasters • roasters and broilers • electric coffee makers • space heaters • water heaters • electric ranges and microwave ovens • mixers and blenders • fans and blowers • vacuum cleaners and floor polishers • washers and dryers • dishwashers and garbage disposals • refrigerators • air conditioners and dehumidifiers.

Television Service Manual

fifth edition
Robert G. Middleton; revised by Joseph G. Barrile
5½ x 8¼   Hardcover   512 pp.   395 illus.
ISBN: 0-672-23395-9 $15.95

Practical up-to-date guide to all aspects of television transmission and reception, for both black and white and color receivers: • step-by-step maintenance and repair • broadcasting • transmission • receivers • antennas and transmission lines • interference • RF tuners • the video channel • circuits • power supplies • alignment • test equipment.

Electrical Course for Apprentices and Journeymen

second edition
Roland E. Palmquist
5½ x 8¼   Hardcover   478 pp.   290 illus.
ISBN:0-672-23393-2 $14.95

Practical course on operational theory and applications for training and re-training in school or on the job: • electricity and matter • units and definitions • electrical symbols • magnets and magnetic fields • capacitors • resistance • electromagnetism • instruments and measurements • alternating currents • DC generators • circuits • transformers • motors • grounding and ground testing.

Questions and Answers for Electricians Examinations eighth edition

Roland E. Palmquist
5½ x 8¼   Hardcover   320 pp.   110 illus.
ISBN: 0-672-23399-1 $12.95

Based on the current National Electrical Code®, a review of exams for apprentice, journeyman, and master, with explanations of principles underlying each test subject: • Ohm's Law and other formulas • power and power factors • lighting • branch circuits and feeders • transformer principles and connections • wiring • batteries and rectification • voltage generation • motors • ground and ground testing.

Machine Shop and Mechanical Trades

Machinists Library

fourth edition   3 vols
Rex Miller
5½ x 8¼   Hardcover   1,352 pp.   1,120 illus.
ISBN: 0-672-23380-0 $38.95

Indispensable three-volume reference for machinists, tool and die makers, machine operators, metal workers, and those with home workshops.

Volume I, Basic Machine Shop
5½ x 8¼   Hardcover 392 pp.   375 illus.
ISBN: 0-672-23381-9 $14.95

• Blueprint reading • benchwork • layout and measurement • sheet-metal hand tools and machines • cutting tools • drills • reamers • taps • threading dies • milling machine cutters, arbors, collets, and adapters.

Volume II, Machine Shop
5½ x 8¼   Hardcover 528 pp.   445 illus
ISBN: 0-672-23382-7 $14.95

• Power saws • machine tool operations • drilling machines • boring • lathes • automatic screw machine • milling • metal spinning.

Volume III, Toolmakers Handy Book
5½ x 8¼   Hardcover   432 pp.   300 illus.
ISBN: 0-672-23383-5 $14.95

• Layout work • jigs and fixtures • gears and gear cutting • dies and diemaking • toolmaking operations • heat-treating furnaces • induction heating • furnace brazing • cold-treating process.

Mathematics for Mechanical Technicians and Technologists

John D. Bies
5½ x 8¼   Hardcover   392 pp.   190 illus.
ISBN: 0-02-510620-1 $17.95

Practical sourcebook of concepts, formulas, and problem solving in industrial and mechanical technology: • basic and complex mechanics • strength of materials • fluidics • cams and gears • machine elements • machining operations • management controls • economics in machining • facility and human resources management.

Millwrights and Mechanics Guide

third edition
Carl A. Nelson
5½ x 8¼   Hardcover   1,040 pp.   880 illus.
ISBN: 0-672-23373-8 $22.95

Most comprehensive and authoritative guide available for millwrights and mechanics at all levels of work or supervision: • drawing and sketching

---

• machinery and equipment installation • principles of mechanical power transmission • V-belt drives • flat belts • gears • chain drives • couplings • bearings • structural steel • screw threads • mechanical fasteners • pipe fittings and valves • carpentry • sheet-metal work • blacksmithing • rigging • electricity • welding • pumps • portable power tools • mensuration and mechanical calculations.

Welders Guide third edition

James E. Brumbaugh
5½ x 8 ¼   Hardcover   960 pp.   615 illus.
ISBN: 0-672-23374-6 $23.95

Practical, concise manual on theory, operation, and maintenance of all welding machines: • gas welding equipment, supplies, and process • arc welding equipment, supplies, and process • TIG and MIG welding • submerged-arc and other shielded-arc welding processes • resistance, thermit, and stud welding • solders and soldering • brazing and braze welding • welding plastics • safety and health measures • symbols and definitions • testing and inspecting welds. Terminology and definitions as standardized by American Welding Society.

Welder/Fitters Guide

John P. Stewart
8½ x 11   Paperback   160 pp.   195 illus.
ISBN: 0-672-23325-8 $7.95

Step-by-step instruction for welder/ fitters during training or on the job: • basic assembly tools and aids • improving blueprint reading skills • marking and alignment techniques • using basic tools • simple work practices • guide to fabricating weldments • avoiding mistakes • exercises in blueprint reading • clamping devices • introduction to using hydraulic jacks • safety in weld fabrication plants • common welding shop terms.

Sheet Metal Work

John D. Bies
5½ x 8¼   Hardcover   456 pp.   215 illus.
ISBN: 0-8161-1706-3 $17.95

On-the-job sheet metal guide for manufacturing, construction, and home workshops: • mathematics for sheet metal work • principles of drafting • concepts of sheet metal drawing • sheet metal standards, specifications, and materials • safety practices • layout • shear cutting • holes • bending and folding • forming operations • notching and clipping • metal spinning • mechanical fastening • soldering and brazing • welding • surface preparation and finishes • production processes.

III

Power Plant Engineers Guide
third edition
Frank D. Graham; revised by Charlie Buffington
5¹/₂ x 8¹/₄ Hardcover 960 pp. 530 illus.
ISBN: 0-672-23329-0 $16.95

All-inclusive question-and-answer guide to steam and diesel-power engines: • fuels • heat • combustion • types of boilers • shell or fire-tube boiler construction • strength of boiler materials • boiler calculations • boiler fixtures, fittings, and attachments • boiler feed pumps • condensers • cooling ponds and cooling towers • boiler installation, startup, operation, maintenance and repair • oil, gas, and waste-fuel burners • steam turbines • air compressors • plant safety.

Mechanical Trades Pocket Manual
second edition
Carl A. Nelson
4 × 6 Paperback 364 pp. 255 illus.
ISBN: 0-672-23378-9 $10.95

Comprehensive handbook of essentials, pocket-sized to fit in the tool box: • mechanical and isometric drawing • machinery installation and assembly • belts • drives • gears • couplings • screw threads • mechanical fasteners • packing and seals • bearings • portable power tools • welding • rigging • piping • automatic sprinkler systems • carpentry • stair layout • electricity • shop geometry and trigonometry.

Plumbing

Plumbers and Pipe Fitters Library third edition 3 vols
Charles N. McConnell; revised by Tom Philbin
5¹/₂x8¹/₄ Hardcover 952 pp. 560 illus.
ISBN: 0-672-23384-3 $34.95

Comprehensive three-volume set with up-to-date information for master plumbers, journeymen, apprentices, engineers, and those in building trades.

Volume 1, Materials, Tools, Roughing-In
5¹/₂ x 8¹/₄ Hardcover 304 pp. 240 illus.
ISBN: 0-672-23385-1 $12.95

• Materials • tools • pipe fitting • pipe joints • blueprints • fixtures • valves and faucets.

Volume 2, Welding, Heating, Air Conditioning
5¹/₂ x 8¹/₄ Hardcover 384 pp. 220 illus.
ISBN: 0-672-23386-x $13.95

• Brazing and welding • planning a heating system • steam heating systems • hot water heating systems • boiler fittings • fuel-oil tank installation • gas piping • air conditioning.

Volume 3, Water Supply, Drainage, Calculations
5¹/₂ x 8¹/₄ Hardcover 264 pp. 100 illus.
ISBN: 0-672-23387-8 $12.95

• Drainage and venting • sewage disposal • soldering • lead work • mathematics and physics for plumbers and pipe fitters.

Home Plumbing Handbook third edition
Charles N. McConnell
8¹/₂ x 11 Paperback 200 pp. 100 illus.
ISBN: 0-672-23413-0 $10.95

Clear, concise, up-to-date fully illustrated guide to home plumbing installation and repair: • repairing and replacing faucets • repairing toilet tanks • repairing a trip-lever bath drain • dealing with stopped-up drains • working with copper tubing • measuring and cutting pipe • PVC and CPVC pipe and fittings • installing a garbage disposals • replacing dishwashers • repairing and replacing water heaters • installing or resetting toilets • caulking around plumbing fixtures and tile • water conditioning • working with cast-iron soil pipe • septic tanks and disposal fields • private water systems.

The Plumbers Handbook seventh edition
Joseph P. Almond, Sr.
4 × 6 Paperback 352 pp. 170 illus.
ISBN: 0-672-23419-x $10.95

Comprehensive, handy guide for plumbers, pipe fitters, and apprentices that fits in the tool box or pocket: • plumbing tools • how to read blueprints • heating systems • water supply • fixtures, valves, and fittings • working drawings • roughing and repair • outside sewage lift station • pipes and pipelines • vents, drain lines, and septic systems • lead work • silver brazing and soft soldering • plumbing systems • abbreviations, definitions, symbols, and formulas.

Questions and Answers for Plumbers Examinations second edition
Jules Oravetz
5¹/₂ x 8¹/₄ Paperback 256 pp. 145 illus.
ISBN: 0-8161-1703-9 $9.95

Practical, fully illustrated study guide to licensing exams for apprentice, journeyman, or master plumber: • definitions, specifications, and regulations set by National Bureau of Standards and by various state codes • basic plumbing installation • drawings and typical plumbing system layout • mathematics • materials and fittings • joints and connections • traps, cleanouts, and backwater valves • fixtures • drainage, vents, and vent piping • water supply and distribution • plastic pipe and fittings • steam and hot water heating.

HVAC

Air Conditioning: Home and Commercial second edition
Edwin P. Anderson; revised by Rex Miller
5¹/₂ x 8¹/₄ Hardcover 528 pp. 180 illus.
ISBN: 0-672-23397-5 $15.95

Complete guide to construction, installation, operation, maintenance, and repair of home, commercial, and industrial air conditioning systems, with troubleshooting charts: • heat leakage • ventilation requirements • room air conditioners • refrigerants • compressors • condensing equipment • evaporators • water-cooling systems • central air conditioning • automobile air conditioning • motors and motor control.

Heating, Ventilating and Air Conditioning Library second edition 3 vols
James E. Brumbaugh
5¹/₂ x 8¹/₄ Hardcover 1,840 pp. 1,275 illus.
ISBN: 0-672-23388-6 $42.95

Authoritative three-volume reference for those who install, operate, maintain, and repair HVAC equipment commercially, industrially, or at home. Each volume fully illustrated with photographs, drawings, tables and charts.

Volume I, Heating Fundamentals, Furnaces, Boilers, Boiler Conversions
5¹/₂ x 8¹/₄ Hardcover 656 pp. 405 illus.
ISBN: 0-672-23389-4 $16.95

• Insulation principles • heating calculations • fuels • warm-air, hot water, steam, and electrical heating systems • gas-fired, oil-fired, coal-fired, and electric-fired furnaces • boilers and boiler fittings • boiler and furnace conversion.

Volume II, Oil, Gas and Coal Burners, Controls, Ducts, Piping, Valves
5¹/₂ x 8¹/₄ Hardcover 592 pp. 455 illus.
ISBN: 0-672-23390-8 $15.95

• Coal firing methods • thermostats and humidistats • gas and oil controls and other automatic controls •

ducts and duct systems • pipes, pipe fittings, and piping details • valves and valve installation • steam and hot-water line controls.

Volume III, Radiant Heating, Water Heaters, Ventilation, Air Conditioning, Heat Pumps, Air Cleaners
5 1/2 x 8 1/4 Hardcover 592 pp. 415 illus.
ISBN: 0-672-23391-6 $14.95

• Radiators, convectors, and unit heaters • fireplaces, stoves, and chimneys • ventilation principles • fan selection and operation • air conditioning equipment • humidifiers and dehumidifiers • air cleaners and filters.

Oil Burners fourth edition
Edwin M. Field
5 1/2 x 8 1/4 Hardcover 360 pp. 170 illus.
ISBN: 0-672-23394-0 $15.95

Up-to-date sourcebook on the construction, installation, operation, testing, servicing, and repair of all types of oil burners, both industrial and domestic: • general electrical hookup and wiring diagrams of automatic control systems • ignition system • high-voltage transportation • operational sequence of limit controls, thermostats, and various relays • combustion chambers • drafts • chimneys • drive couplings • fans or blowers • burner nozzles • fuel pumps.

Refrigeration: Home and Commercial second edition
Edwin P. Anderson; revised by Rex Miller
5 1/2 x 8 1/4 Hardcover 768 pp. 285 illus.
ISBN: 0-672-23396-7 $17.95

Practical, comprehensive reference for technicians, plant engineers, and homeowners on the installation, operation, servicing, and repair of everything from single refrigeration units to commercial and industrial systems: • refrigerants • compressors • thermoelectric cooling • service equipment and tools • cabinet maintenance and repairs • compressor lubrication systems • brine systems • supermarket and grocery refrigeration • locker plants • fans and blowers • piping • heat leakage • refrigeration-load calculations.

Pneumatics and Hydraulics

Hydraulics for Off-the-Road Equipment second edition
Harry L. Stewart; revised by Tom Philbin
5 1/2 x 8 1/4 Hardcover 256 pp. 175 illus.
ISBN: 0-8161-1701-2 $13.95

Complete reference manual for those who own and operate heavy equipment and for engineers, designers, installation and maintenance technicians, and shop mechanics: • hydraulic pumps, accumulators, and motors • force components • hydraulic control components • filters and filtration, lines and fittings, and fluids • hydrostatic transmissions • maintenance • troubleshooting.

Pneumatics and Hydraulics fourth edition
Harry L. Stewart; revised by Tom Philbin
5 1/2 x 8 1/4 Hardcover 512 pp. 315 illus.
ISBN: 0-672-23412-2 $15.95

Practical guide to the principles and applications of fluid power for engineers, designers, process planners, tool men, shop foremen, and mechanics: • pressure, work and power • general features of machines • hydraulic and pneumatic symbols • pressure boosters • air compressors and accessories • hydraulic power devices • hydraulic fluids • piping • air filters, pressure regulators, and lubricators • flow and pressure controls • pneumatic motors and tools • rotary hydraulic motors and hydraulic transmissions • pneumatic circuits • hydraulic circuits • servo systems.

Pumps fourth edition
Harry L. Stewart; revised by Tom Philbin
5 1/2 x 8 1/4 Hardcover 508 pp. 360 illus.
ISBN: 0-672-23400-9 $15.95

Comprehensive guide for operators, engineers, maintenance workers, inspectors, superintendents, and mechanics on principles and day-to-day operations of pumps: • centrifugal, rotary, reciprocating, and special service pumps • hydraulic accumulators • power transmission • hydraulic power tools • hydraulic cylinders • control valves • hydraulic fluids • fluid lines and fittings.

Carpentry and Construction

Carpenters and Builders Library
fifth edition 4 vols
John E. Ball; revised by Tom Philbin
5 1/2 x 8 1/4 Hardcover 1,224 pp. 1,010 illus.
ISBN: 0-672-23369-x $39.95
Also available in a new boxed set at no extra cost:
ISBN: 0-02-506450-9 $39.95

These profusely illustrated volumes, available in a handsome boxed edition, have set the professional standard for carpenters, joiners, and woodworkers.

Volume 1, Tools, Steel Square, Joinery
5 1/2 x 8 1/4 Hardcover 384 pp. 345 illus.
ISBN: 0-672-23365-7 $10.95

• Woods • nails • screws • bolts • the workbench • tools • using the steel square • joints and joinery • cabinetmaking joints • wood patternmaking • and kitchen cabinet construction.

Volume 2, Builders Math, Plans, Specifications
5 1/2 x 8 1/4 Hardcover 304 pp. 205 illus.
ISBN: 0-672-23366-5 $10.95

• Surveying • strength of timbers • practical drawing • architectural drawing • barn construction • small house construction • and home workshop layout.

Volume 3, Layouts, Foundations, Framing
5 1/2 x 8 1/4 Hardcover 272 pp. 215 illus.
ISBN: 0-672-23367-3 $10.95

• Foundations • concrete forms • concrete block construction • framing, girders and sills • skylights • porches and patios • chimneys, fireplaces, and stoves • insulation • solar energy and paneling.

Volume 4, Millwork, Power Tools, Painting
5 1/2 x 8 1/4 Hardcover 344 pp. 245 illus.
ISBN: 0-672-23368-1 $10.95

• Roofing, miter work • doors • windows, sheathing and siding • stairs • flooring • table saws, band saws, and jigsaws • wood lathes • sanders and combination tools • portable power tools • painting.

Complete Building Construction
second edition
John Phelps; revised by Tom Philbin
5 1/2 x 8 1/4 Hardcover 744 pp. 645 illus.
ISBN: 0-672-23377-0 $19.95

Comprehensive guide to constructing a frame or brick building from the

V

footings to the ridge: • laying out building and excavation lines • making concrete forms and pouring fittings and foundation • making concrete slabs, walks, and driveways • laying concrete block, brick, and tile • building chimneys and fireplaces • framing, siding, and roofing • insulating • finishing the inside • building stairs • installing windows • hanging doors.

Complete Roofing Handbook
James E. Brumbaugh
5½ x 8¼   Hardcover   536 pp.   510 illus.
ISBN: 0-02-517850-4 $29.95

Authoritative text and highly detailed drawings and photographs,on all aspects of roofing: • types of roofs • roofing and reroofing • roof and attic insulation and ventilation • skylights and roof openings • dormer construction • roof flashing details • shingles • roll roofing • built-up roofing • roofing with wood shingles and shakes • slate and tile roofing • installing gutters and downspouts • listings of professional and trade associations and roofing manufacturers.

Complete Siding Handbook
James E. Brumbaugh
5½ x 8¼   Hardcover   512 pp.   450 illus.
ISBN: 0-02-517880-6 $23.95

Companion to *Complete Roofing Handbook*, with step-by-step instructions and drawings on every aspect of siding: • sidewalls and siding • wall preparation • wood board siding • plywood panel and lap siding • hardboard panel and lap siding • wood shingle and shake siding • aluminum and steel siding • vinyl siding • exterior paints and stains • refinishing of siding, gutter and downspout systems • listings of professional and trade associations and siding manufacturers.

Masons and Builders Library
second edition   2 vols
Louis M. Dezettel; revised by Tom Philbin
5½ x 8¼   Hardcover   688 pp.   500 illus.
ISBN: 0-672-23401-7 $23.95

Two-volume set on practical instruction in all aspects of materials and methods of bricklaying and masonry: • brick • mortar • tools • bonding • corners, openings, and arches • chimneys and fireplaces • structural clay tile and glass block • brick walks, floors, and terraces • repair and maintenance • plasterboard and plaster • stone and rock masonry • reading blueprints.

Volume 1, Concrete, Block, Tile, Terrazzo
5½ x 8¼   Hardcover   304 pp.   190 illus.
ISBN: 0-672-23402-5 $13.95

Volume 2, Bricklaying, Plastering, Rock Masonry, Clay Tile
5½ x 8¼   Hardcover   384 pp.   310 illus.
ISBN: 0-672-23403-3 $12.95

Woodworking

Woodworking and Cabinetmaking
F. Richard Boller
5½ x 8¼   Hardcover   360 pp.   455 illus.
ISBN: 0-02-512800-0 $16.95

Compact one-volume guide to the essentials of all aspects of woodworking: • properties of softwoods, hardwoods, plywood, and composition wood • design, function, appearance, and structure • project planning • hand tools • machines • portable electric tools • construction • the home workshop • and the projects themselves – stereo cabinet, speaker cabinets, bookcase, desk, platform bed, kitchen cabinets, bathroom vanity.

Wood Furniture: Finishing, Refinishing, Repairing second edition
James E. Brumbaugh
5½ x 8¼   Hardcover   352 pp.   185 illus.
ISBN: 0-672-23409-2 $12.95

Complete, fully illustrated guide to repairing furniture and to finishing and refinishing wood surfaces for professional woodworkers and do-it-yourselfers: • tools and supplies • types of wood • veneering • inlaying • repairing, restoring, and stripping • wood preparation • staining • shellac, varnish, lacquer, paint and enamel, and oil and wax finishes • antiquing • gilding and bronzing • decorating furniture.

Maintenance and Repair

Building Maintenance second edition
Jules Oravetz
5½ x 8¼   Hardcover   384 pp.   210 illus.
ISBN: 0-672-23278-2 $9.95

Complete information on professional maintenance procedures used in office, educational, and commercial buildings: • painting and decorating • plumbing and pipe fitting

• concrete and masonry • carpentry • roofing • glazing and caulking • sheet metal • electricity • air conditioning and refrigeration • insect and rodent control • heating • maintenance management • custodial practices.

Gardening, Landscaping and Grounds Maintenance
third edition
Jules Oravetz
5½ x 8¼   Hardcover   424 pp.   340 illus.
ISBN: 0-672-23417-3 $15.95

Practical information for those who maintain lawns, gardens, and industrial, municipal, and estate grounds: • flowers, vegetables, berries, and house plants • greenhouses • lawns • hedges and vines • flowering shrubs and trees • shade, fruit and nut trees • evergreens • bird sanctuaries • fences • insect and rodent control • weed and brush control • roads, walks, and pavements • drainage • maintenance equipment • golf course planning and maintenance.

Home Maintenance and Repair: Walls, Ceilings and Floors
Gary D. Branson
8½ x 11   Paperback   80 pp.   80 illus.
ISBN: 0-672-23281-2 $6.95

Do-it-yourselfer's step-by-step guide to interior remodeling with professional results: • general maintenance • wallboard installation and repair • wallboard taping • plaster repair • texture paints • wallpaper techniques • paneling • sound control • ceiling tile • bath tile • energy conservation.

Painting and Decorating
Rex Miller and Glenn E. Baker
5½ x 8¼   Hardcover   325 pp.   illus.
ISBN: 0-672-23405-x $18.95

Practical guide for painters, decorators, and homeowners to the most up-to-date materials and techniques: • job planning • tools and equipment needed • finishing materials • surface preparation • applying paint and stains · decorating with coverings • repairs and maintenance • color and decorating principles.

VI

Tree Care ^{second edition}
John M. Haller
8½ x 11 Paperback 224 pp. 305 illus.
ISBN: 0-02-062870-6 $9.95

New edition of a standard in the field, for growers, nursery owners, foresters, landscapers, and homeowners: • planting • pruning • fertilizing • bracing and cabling • wound repair • grafting • spraying • disease and insect management • coping with environmental damage • removal • structure and physiology • recreational use.

Upholstering
updated
James E. Brumbaugh
5½ x 8¼ Hardcover 400 pp. 380 illus.
ISBN: 0-672-23372-x $12.95

Essentials of upholstering for professional, apprentice, and hobbyist: • furniture styles • tools and equipment • stripping • frame construction and repairs • finishing and refinishing wood surfaces • webbing • springs • burlap, stuffing, and muslin • pattern layout • cushions • foam padding • covers • channels and tufts • padded seats and slip seats • fabrics • plastics • furniture care.

Automotive and Engines

Diesel Engine Manual ^{fourth edition}
Perry O. Black; revised by William E. Scahill
5½ x 8¼ Hardcover 512 pp. 255 illus.
ISBN: 0-672-23371-1 $15.95

Detailed guide for mechanics, students, and others to all aspects of typical two- and four-cycle engines: • operating principles • fuel oil • diesel injection pumps • basic Mercedes diesels • diesel engine cylinders • lubrication • cooling systems • horsepower • engine-room procedures • diesel engine installation • automotive diesel engine • marine diesel engine • diesel electrical power plant • diesel engine service.

Gas Engine Manual ^{third edition}
Edwin P. Anderson; revised by Charles G. Facklam
5½ x 8¼ Hardcover 424 pp. 225 illus.
ISBN: 0-8161-1707-1 $12.95

Indispensable sourcebook for those who operate, maintain, and repair gas engines of all types and sizes: • fundamentals and classifications of engines · engine parts • pistons • crankshafts • valves • lubrication, cooling, fuel, ignition, emission

control and electrical systems • engine tune-up • servicing of pistons and piston rings, cylinder blocks, connecting rods and crankshafts, valves and valve gears, carburetors, and electrical systems.

Small Gasoline Engines
Rex Miller and Mark Richard Miller
5½ x 8¼ Hardcover 640 pp. 525 illus.
ISBN: 0-672-23414-9 $16.95

Practical information for those who repair, maintain, and overhaul two- and four-cycle engines – with emphasis on one-cylinder motors – including lawn mowers, edgers, grass sweepers, snowblowers, emergency electrical generators, outboard motors, and other equipment up to ten horsepower: • carburetors, emission controls, and ignition systems • starting systems • hand tools • safety • power generation • engine operations • lubrication systems • power drivers • preventive maintenance • step-by-step overhauling procedures • troubleshooting • testing and inspection • cylinder block servicing.

Truck Guide Library ^{3 vols}
James E. Brumbaugh
5½ x 8¼ Hardcover 2,144 pp. 1,715 illus.
ISBN: 0-672-23392-4 $45.95

Three-volume comprehensive and profusely illustrated reference on truck operation and maintenance.

Volume 1, Engines
5½ x 8¼ Hardcover 416 pp. 290 illus.
ISBN: 0-672-23356-8 $16.95

• Basic components · engine operating principles • troubleshooting • cylinder blocks • connecting rods, pistons, and rings • crankshafts, main bearings, and flywheels • camshafts and valve trains • engine valves.

Volume 2, Engine Auxiliary Systems
5½ x 8¼ Hardcover 704 pp. 520 illus.
ISBN: 0-672-23357-6 $16.95

• Battery and electrical systems • spark plugs • ignition systems, charging and starting systems • lubricating, cooling, and fuel systems • carburetors and governors • diesel systems • exhaust and emission-control systems.

Volume 3, Transmissions, Steering, and Brakes
5½ x 8¼ Hardcover 1,024 pp. 905 illus.
ISBN: 0-672-23406-8 $16.95

• Clutches • manual, auxiliary, and automatic transmissions • frame and suspension systems • differentials and axles, manual and power steering • front-end alignment • hydraulic, power, and air brakes • wheels and tires • trailers.

Drafting

Answers on Blueprint Reading
fourth edition
Roland E. Palmquist; revised by Thomas J. Morrisey
5½ x 8¼ Hardcover 320 pp. 275 illus.
ISBN: 0-8161-1704-7 $12.95

Complete question-and-answer instruction manual on blueprints of machines and tools, electrical systems, and architecture: • drafting scale • drafting instruments • conventional lines and representations • pictorial drawings • geometry of drafting • orthographic and working drawings • surfaces • detail drawing • sketching • map and topographical drawings • graphic symbols • architectural drawings • electrical blueprints • computer-aided design and drafting. Also included is an appendix of measurements • metric conversions • screw threads and tap drill sizes • number and letter sizes of drills with decimal equivalents • double depth of threads • tapers and angles.

Hobbies

Complete Course in Stained Glass
Pepe Mendez
8½ x 11 Paperback 80 pp. 50 illus.
ISBN: 0-672-23287-1 $8.95

Guide to the tools, materials, and techniques of the art of stained glass, with ten fully illustrated lessons: • how to cut glass • cartoon and pattern drawing • assembling and cementing • making lamps using various techniques • electrical components for completing lamps • sources of materials • glossary of terminology and techniques of stained glasswork.

Macmillan Practical Arts Library
Books for and by the Craftsman

World Woods in Color
W.A. Lincoln
7 × 10   Hardcover   300 pages
300 photos
ISBN: 0-02-572350-2 $39.95

Large full-color photographs show the natural grain and features of nearly 300 woods: • commercial and botanical names • physical characteristics, mechanical properties, seasoning, working properties, durability, and uses • the height, diameter, bark, and places of distribution of each tree • indexing of botanical, trade, commercial, local, and family names • a full bibliography of publications on timber study and identification.

The Woodturner's Art: Fundamentals and Projects
Ron Roszkiewicz
8 × 10   Hardcover   256 pages   300 illus.
ISBN: 0-02-605250-4 $24.95

A master woodturner shows how to design and create increasingly difficult projects step-by-step in this book suitable for the beginner and the more advanced student: • spindle and faceplate turning • tools • techniques • classic turnings from various historical periods • more than 30 types of projects including boxes, furniture, vases, and candlesticks • making duplicates • projects using combinations of techniques and more than one kind of wood. Author has also written *The Woodturner's Companion.*

The Woodworker's Bible
Alf Martensson
8 × 10   Paperback   288 pages   900 illus.
ISBN: 0-02-011940-2 $12.95

For the craftsperson familiar with basic carpentry skills, a guide to creating professional-quality furniture, cabinetry, and objects d'art in the home workshop: • techniques and expert advice on fine craftsmanship whether tooled by hand or machine • joint-making • assembling to ensure fit • finishes. Author, who lives in London and runs a workshop called Woodstock, has also written *The Book of Furnituremaking.*

Cabinetmaking and Millwork
John L. Feirer
7⅛ × 9½   Hardcover   992 pages
2,350 illus. (32 pp. in color)
ISBN: 0-02-537350-1 $47.50

The classic on cabinetmaking that covers in detail all of the materials, tools, machines, and processes used in building cabinets and interiors, the production of furniture, and other work of the finish carpenter and millwright: • fixed installations such as paneling, built-ins, and cabinets • movable wood products such as furniture and fixtures • which woods to use, and why and how to use them in the interiors of homes and commercial buildings • metrics and plastics in furniture construction.

Cabinetmaking: The Professional Approach
Alan Peters
8½ × 11   Hardcover   208 pages   175 illus.
(8 pp. color)
ISBN: 0-02-596200-0 $29.95

A unique guide to all aspects of professional furniture making, from an English master craftsman: • the Cotswold School and the birth of the furniture movement • setting up a professional shop • equipment • finance and business efficiency • furniture design • working to commission • batch production, training, and techniques • plans for nine projects.

Carpentry and Building Construction
John L. Feirer and Gilbert R. Hutchings
7½ × 9½   hardcover   1,120 pages
2,000 photos (8 pp. in color)
ISBN: 0-02-537360-9 $50.00

A classic by Feirer on each detail of modern construction: • the various machines, tools, and equipment from which the builder can choose • laying of a foundation • building frames for each part of a building • details of interior and exterior work • painting and finishing • reading plans • chimneys and fireplaces • ventilation • assembling prefabricated houses.